Boundaries of Religious Freedom: Regulating Religion in Diverse Societies

Series Editors

Lori G. Beaman
University of Ottawa
Ottawa, ON, Canada

Lene Kühle
Aarhus Universitet
Aarhus, Denmark

Alexander K. Nagel
Institut für Soziologie
Georg-August-Universität Göttingen
Göttingen, Niedersachsen, Germany

Processes of globalization have resulted in increasingly culturally and religiously diverse societies. In addition, religion is occupying a more prominent place in the public sphere at the turn of the 21st Century, despite predictions of religious decline. The rise in religious diversity, and in the salience of religious identity, is posing both challenges and opportunities pertaining to issues of governance. Indeed, a series of tensions have arisen between state and religious actors regarding a variety of matters including burial rites, religious education and gender equality. Many of these debates have focused on the need for, and limits of, religious freedom especially in situations where certain religious practices risk impinging upon the freedom of others. Moreover, different responses to religious pluralism are often informed by the relationship between religion and state in each society. Due to the changing nature of societies, most have needed to define, or redefine, the boundaries of religious freedom reflected in laws, policies and the design and use of public spaces. These boundaries, however, continue to be contested, debated and reviewed, at local, national and global levels of governance. All books published in this Series have been fully peer-reviewed before final acceptance.

More information about this series at http://www.springer.com/series/11839

Giorgia Baldi

Un-Veiling Dichotomies

European Secularism and Women's Veiling

Springer

Giorgia Baldi
School of Law, Politics and Sociology
University of Sussex
Falmer, Brighton, UK

ISSN 2214-5281 ISSN 2214-529X (electronic)
Boundaries of Religious Freedom: Regulating Religion in Diverse Societies
ISBN 978-3-030-79296-1 ISBN 978-3-030-79297-8 (eBook)
https://doi.org/10.1007/978-3-030-79297-8

This Springer imprint is published by the registered company Springer Nature Switzerland AG
The registered company address is: Gewerbestrasse 11, 6330 Cham, Switzerland

To Sandra

Acknowledgements

As with every research work, this book is the result of years of investigation, study and examinations. In this long journey, I was accompanied by friends, family and colleagues who sustained and inspired me, deeply contributing to shape this work. I am profoundly indebted to Prof Marinos Diamantides and Prof Peter Goodrich who provided invaluable insights during the first years of my journey. Our thought-provoking conversations and their feedback on my work have deeply influenced this book. I thank as well my colleagues and friends at the University of Sussex – Prof Nuno Ferreira, Dr Bal Sokhi-Bulley, Dr Maria Moscati, Dr Marie Hutton and Dr Liljana Cvetanoska, to mention only some – for providing comments, feedback and fruitful critiques of this work as well as for our refreshing and stimulating conversations. I must extend my thanks to Prof Donald Mcgillivray, Head of the School of Law, for giving me the space and the necessary support to complete this book, as well as all the staff at the School of Law at the University of Sussex, for constant professional and emotional support. A special acknowledgement goes to my father, Giorgio Baldi, who has always stimulated my mind through our political conversations, and to my mother and sister, for the emotional support. I am also indebted to my friends, Manuel, Shirin and Cecilia – to mention only some – for being beside me during my difficult times, and to Cecilia, Anna, Patrizia and Teresa, for giving me a sense of what feminism is. Finally, I dedicate this book to my friend, Sandra Schiassi, who passed away before the delivery of this work. She was a teacher, a mother, a sister and a friend.

Contents

Chapter 1
Introduction

In 2013, the *Victoria and Albert Museum* in London launched an exhibition named 'Light from the Middle East' which exposed the work of diverse artists across the region and from the diaspora. One of the sections, 'Reframing', showed part of Shadi Ghadirian's *Qajar* series. The artist employs painted backdrops and dresses her models in typical clothing worn during the Qajar period in Iran (1794–1925). Veiled women in traditional clothing appear with modern items such as a Pepsi can, vacuum cleaners, modern radio and Tehran contemporary newspapers. Viewing these sepia-toned images, the spectator immediately feels the contrast, the contraposition, between tradition and modernity, between capitalist and the traditional Iranian lifestyle (as most of the items exposed in the pictures are banned in Iran). The author herself declared that "my pictures became a mirror reflecting how I felt: we are stuck between tradition and modernity" (Shadi Ghadirian: Untitled (Qajar Series*)* |, n.d.). This dichotomy made me think about the work of another famous Iranian artist, Majeed Beenteha, who used the symbology of the veil to pose another dichotomy played out on women's body: that between the covered and un-covered female body. In his series, *National Riddle* (2010), the artist shows a woman wearing a white headscarf (in contrast to the black headscarf worn by Shi'a, the majoritarian religion in the country) covering only the upper torso, and leaving her naked from the waist down (Karen Mathews, 2018). While I believe that the artists have tried to show and, at times, unmask the role of women's body within the nationalist Iranian regime, what triggered my attention was the dichotomy through which the veil was portrayed, as if the only way to think about the practice passes through certain historically constructed and defined dichotomies. Ghadirian's *Qajar* series shows a clear contrast, a contraposition, between tradition and modernity, past and present; while Beeneha portrays a dichotomous opposition between the naked and the covered body, the public and the private sphere.

These binary oppositions are mirrored in contemporary western and non-western comment concerning the wearing of the female veil, which has tended to frame the issue with binary (culturalist/religious) dichotomies between women's freedom and

G. Baldi, *Un-Veiling Dichotomies*, Boundaries of Religious Freedom: Regulating Religion in Diverse Societies,
https://doi.org/10.1007/978-3-030-79297-8_1

oppression, traditional and liberal values, religious and secular norms, 'us' and 'them'. In 2019, for instance, just before Quebec passed a law forbidding public servants to wear religious symbols, the new Minister of Women's Affairs, Mrs. Isabelle Charest, declared that the Muslim headscarf "is not something women should be wearing [because] it does have, at some point, some significance about oppression of women, and the fact that they have to cover themselves, and for me it's not in my values" (Plante & Bergeron, 2019). The proposed law was pushed by a new movement in the country named *Collectif citoyen pour l'égalité et la laïcité*. In a call to ban the headscarf in public institutions, its spokesman, Mr. Mailloux, reiterated that "we shouldn't send the message to young people that women should cover their hair, ears and neck and be more modest than men [...]. Forty years ago, we took out all references to sexism in school textbooks. And now, we should have to accept a sexist symbol for teachers?" (Peritz, 2019). Likewise, for the Somalian born activist, Ayaan Hirsi Ali, "[t]he veil deliberately marks women as private and restricted property, [as] non-persons [... and] sets women apart from men and apart from the world; it restrains them, confines them, grooms them for docility [...] It is the mark of a kind of apartheid, not the domination of a race but of a sex"(Panahi, 2015). Similarly, Frank Henkel, Berlin's Interior Minister, pointed out that the full-face veil "does not fit in with our view of women", followed by the French Ambassador to the United States, Gerard Araud, who declared that the *burqa* creates women as an "object of lust, a subject and not an agent of history" (Britton, 2019). The female headscarf is not only seen as a symbol of women's oppression, but also as an item able to endanger western democracy and secularism. In 2019, after Julien Odoul, a member of Mrs. Marine Le Pen's National Rally (RN) party in France, posted a video on Twitter in which he confronted a veiled woman who was accompanying her child on a school trip, the Economy Minister Mr. Bruno Le Maire immediately highlighted that France should defend "a culture in which religion remains in the intimate, private sphere and does not have a place in (the) public sphere" ('School trip hijab clash sparks new secularism row in France', 2019). At the same time, Jeanine Pirro, a famous American TV host, commenting on the veil worn by Mrs. Omar, a first-term Democratic representative from Minnesota, observed that the veil was "indicative of her adherence to Sharia law, which is in itself antithetical to the US Constitution" (Barnes, 2019).

These polarisations (women's freedom v women's oppression, secular v religious, public v private, democracy v Islam etc.), intrinsic in the discourse concerning the wearing of the veil in the west, are mirrored also in the many European juridical decisions that have banned the headscarf, which rely on dichotomous contrapositions between a tolerant and secular west and an intolerant and religious east: in the case *Sahin v Turkey* (2005), for instance, decided at the European Court of Human Rights (ECtHR), which involved the wearing of the headscarf in Turkish universities, the veil was seen as a religious symbol in contrast with Turkey's secular values; in the *Begum* case (2006), decided in the multicultural United Kingdom (UK), the *jilbab* worn by the claimant was understood as a symbol of radical Islam, in contrast with the *Shalwar Kameez*, considered the 'sign of' a 'tolerant' Islam; while in the case of *Dahlab v Switzerland* (2001), decided at the ECtHR, concerning the possibility of teaching in a primary school veiled, the 'illiberal values' of the claimant's *hijab* were seen to be in contraposition with gender equality and women's freedom. In the legal discourse concerning the headscarf in Europe, veiled women have been placed in opposition to un-veiled 'modern' women where the covered body is associated with women's refusal to perform a normal interaction with the other sex, violating western gender hierarchies (Scott, 2017). Those legal decisions show that the accommodation of different religious gendered sensitivities automatically involves separating acceptable and unacceptable, good and bad religions which, in the discourse concerning the veil, goes hand in hand with other dichotomies such as public/private, secular/religious, individual/communal, universal/particular, women's freedom/oppression, etc. Those dichotomies are played around the definition of the headscarf, which emerges as a strict, backward religious symbol that constrains women's body and, at the same time, as an element able to endanger western culture and identity: in fact, in the European juridical decisions that have banned the veil, Muslim women are seen, on the one hand, as victims of an oppressive and intolerant religion and so in need of saving, while on the other, they are portrayed as dangerous religious fundamentalists who seek to overthrow western secular values.

The 'headscarf controversy' has attracted the attention of many scholars who have analysed the matter focusing on issues of gender equality (Gökarıksel, 2007; Sauer, 2009; Vakulenko, 2007), multiculturalism (Parekh, 2000; Wiles, 2007), and the accommodation of religion in the secular European public sphere (Elver, 2014; McGoldrick, 2006). While this literature provides important insights, little attention has been paid to the way in which the oppositional categories through which the headscarf has been framed work in the legal discourse that has banned the veil in secular Europe. The fixity of the juridical discourse about the headscarf made me think that, rather than being a truth about Muslim women or a crusade to save western/secular values, the construction of veiling through oppositional categories discloses something about the secular/liberal system that is actually hidden by the narrative constructed and fabricated over the headscarf. What do these dichotomous representations in the headscarf debate disclose about secularism and the secular legal and religious subject? Which form of public space is delimited by the juridical regulation of Muslim women's attire? And what does this entail?

This book was born out of the attempt to answer these questions. Its aim is not to offer a strict legal analysis, nor to exhaust the complexity of the issue; rather, by deliberately choosing to explore a specific angle of the debate, it presents a critique of secular juridical decisions that have banned the female headscarf by offering a perspective and line of enquiry which has not yet fully been taken into consideration. The book complicates and problematises previous work on the headscarf, engaging with the very parameters of the debate by unwrapping the way in which the tension between oppositional categories (secular v religious, women's freedom v women's oppression, public v private, etc.) is understood as absolute polarisation. Through the employment of a wide range of disciplines in the reading of the recent European debate and the legal decisions concerning the wearing of the Muslim headscarf, the book challenges the western/secular dichotomous categories through which the practice of veiling has been thought, focusing on an analysis of the implications for Muslim women of applying such dichotomies in western and Human Rights law. My argument is that the western dichotomous categories through which the veil has been historically and discursively defined are reproduced in western and Human Rights law and are productive of a series of other dichotomies. These, in turn, disclose the creation, through the force of the law, of a fixed religious and legal subject, along with a specific notion of womanhood to which Muslim women in Europe are blindly asked to conform. This imposition reveals a new relation between the individual and the sovereign power, along with the emergence of a specific form of sovereignty, which comes out as a force productive of (secular) forms of gender inequality, reframing in this way the liberal notion of autonomy and women's emancipation. I hope that the book will be an original contribution to the wider discourse concerning the banning of the veil by offering an innovative reading of the tension between the religious and secular spheres in contemporary Europe and its implications in terms of gender equality and the accommodation of different religious sensitivities.

1.1 The Centrality of Women's Body in the Secular Discourse on the Veil

In 2018, turmoil was sparked on French television when Maryam Pougetoux, a 19-year-old student union president at the Paris-Sorbonne University's Faculty of Letters, appeared on national television to speak about student protest over university choice (McAuley, 2018). However, few people listened to her, seeming only to be interested in her headscarf. After her appearance, a cabinet official accused her of proselytism for the Islamic State and of promoting political Islam, while the satirical newspaper *Charlie Hebdo* "depicted her on its cover as a doddering monkey" (McAuley, 2018). Although she broke no law as in France the headscarf is forbidden in public schools but not in universities or public spaces, many accused her of breaking secular norms. In France, as well as in many other European countries, it seems that the simple image of a veiled woman creates concerns about the principle of secularism, showing the emergence of the link between clothes, secularism and the control of women's body.

Scott's seminal work (2017) wonderfully shows the centrality of women's body in secular discourse highlighting how, in the process of secularisation in the west, the privatisation of religion has been accompanied by the privatisation of gender and sexuality: women, family life, and religion have been relegated to the private sphere in contraposition to a public sphere dominated by men and rationality. She discloses that even in key moments of western secularism's development, such as the French Revolution, women were banned from political life, not on the ground of religion, but on the ground of sex: as secularism posed nature in the place of God, women were kept in the private sphere based on biological differences (Winnifred

Fallers et al., 2015). The secular public/private divide was translated, in the nineteenth century, into the male/female opposition (from which follows the definition of proper femininity and masculinity, along with the definition of 'proper sexuality'). This is evident from the insistence of nineteenth century nature's mandate that established the opposition between religion and science (which resulted in an overemphasis on the superiority of rationality over beliefs),[1] and on the institution of marriage (defined as the private locus of love and the side of the society's reproduction) (Scott, 2017). Due to the biological role assigned to women's body, the conjugal family was placed at the centre of the division of labour in society and private marital life started to be regulated by state intervention (Scott, 2017). For Scott (2017), "in the discourse and practice of modern western secular nations, the justification for denying women citizenship rested on the marriage relationship, the ultimate embodiment of the private/public distinction, which in turn rested on, and confirmed, the naturalness of the difference of sex" (p. 95).

Floyd (2009) highlights that in liberal secular western modernity, "capital's enforcement of a strong differentiation of public from private [....] is based on its naturalization of private property, but is also ultimately inseparable from an ongoing differentiation of social labour including a gendered division of labour, a division between manual and intellectual labour, and atomizing, disciplinary specialization of knowledge itself"(p. 6). Since secular/liberalism "relies on a binary model of sex and gender,[...] [it] creates and sustains a rigidified opposition between male and female bodies and subjectivities"(Dillon, 2004, p. 3). Hence, while the secular/western nation state claimed equality for all its citizens (at least 'equality before the law'), it nonetheless maintained inequality on the ground of biological differences between men and women; "the presumed natural difference between sexes was the social foundation of modern western nation states: sexual difference secured the racial superiority of western nations to their 'others'"(Scott, 2017, p. 18).

In fact, it is exactly in the colonial encounter with the Muslim other that, in the process of secularisation, the status of women started to be linked to the notion of 'modernity' and 'civilisation' in order to justify missionary and imperialist colonial western adventures. This excessive attention towards 'other' women was strengthened by the rise of nationalism, in which women's body emerges as the symbol of the nation, the biological and cultural reproducer (Kandiyoti, 1991; Yuval-Davis, 1993, 2006) of an 'imagined community' (Anderson, 1991), marking the difference between different cultures (Anthias & Yuval-Davis, 1989; Yuval-Davis, 1993), as well as by the emergence of the nineteenth century's new notion of freedom (from 'freedom for' to 'freedom from') (Melman, 2016), which posed the female veil as the main focus of colonial and missionary movements as well as of liberal feminism (Najmabadi, 2006).

The 'struggle over the veil' has historically been framed as a battle over the appropriate meaning attached to the practice, which discloses the link between

[1] As Esposito (2015) argues, "the prevailing of reason over the body runs parallel to that of the proper over the common, the private over the public, and individual profit over collective interest" (p. 115).

veiling and specific forms of sovereign power. In fact, although anthropological, legal and cultural studies of the uses of the female veil in Muslim-majority societies disclose a multiplicity of meanings and interpretations related to gender, geographical provenience, tribal affiliations, etc., revealing that veiling is an immanent and ever-changing practice which acquires different meanings based on the wearer's personal intentions within pluralist non-liberal discursive traditions (Abu-lughod, 2000; Ahmed, 1992; Mernissi, 1991; Stowasser, 1994), it was from the colonial period that the veil started to acquire a fixed meaning and to be legally regulated. Goodrich (1998, 2008) highlights how clothing has been historically constructed through its symbolic meaning as image, metaphor, of a *specific* order of things because it has the potential to include and exclude and to delineate gendered territorial borders of an 'imagined community' (Anderson, 1991) as it expresses uniformity, hierarchy and regularity (Watt, 2013). Since clothes have been regarded as a 'symbol', a 'visible image' of a different 'other', because they operate a visible differentiation, a boundary, a dividing line, between citizens and foreigners and between the different classes of citizens, they have often been normatively regulated by the law through a sovereign act (Hunt, 1996).[2] However, unlike in the west, where clothing (including the female veil) has always been regulated by a supreme authority (be it the church or the state) (Hunt, 1996), in Muslim-majority societies, such top-down regulation of clothing did not start until the nineteenth century, with colonisation and the birth of nationalism (Fanon, 2004) and Islamism.

This is particularly evident in France's effort to place the un-veiling of Algerian Muslim women at the centre of its colonial project of assimilation (Fanon, 2004), as well as in the British colonial intervention to un-veil Muslim women in order to 'humanise them' (Esmeir, 2012). From the colonial period and the formation of western-style nation states in many Muslim-majority societies, the Muslim female veil emerges as the symbol, the visible difference, between the east and the west, where the colonised constructed the veil as the symbol of their anti-colonial struggle, while colonial powers saw in un-veiling the metaphor for a western 'civilising' mission whose rhetoric was based on the contraposition between (veiled) Muslim women, sexually oppressed by their men and their backward culture and religion, and (un-veiled) white Christian women who, despite promoting a relation of "asymmetrical complementarity" (Scott, 2017, p. 21), were (supposedly) free and liberated, rendering the western notion of womanhood the standard of civilisation against colonial subjects. In other words, from the colonial period, "the human of secular liberalism has been historically constructed and is being disseminated through international institutions and practices so that it is, to some extent, everywhere -translated, resisted, vernacularized, invoked in political struggles, and made the standard language enforced by power"(Abu Lughod, 2010, p. 85).

---

[2]As Goodrich (1995) points out, "legal concern with dress was a concern both with the indigenous, with a vernacular civility free of the stranger and with all other cults that were suggestive of traditions and forces extrinsic to the native soil. It was also and more specifically a concern with the internal ordering of the realm and specifically the coding of status in dress" (pp. 87–8).

The twentieth century narrative constructed and fabricated over the veil strategically placed women's sexuality and their freedom of choice at the centre of Christian/secular civilisational difference against the Muslim 'other' (Scott, 2017) while secular discourse started to equate secular/Christian civilisation with universal values, creating a division between civilisational status (that is, a separation between women who, thanks to secularism, were emancipated, and women who had yet to enter into the western secular civilised world) (Cady & Fessenden, 2013). This division was reinforced by liberal/feminist rhetoric which often served to highlight the difference between western modern/enlightened women and Muslim women, subjugated by their patriarchal culture and in need of being saved (Razack, 2007). It was through the twentieth century project of women's emancipation that the contraposition between western and Muslim women, 'us' and 'them', started to acquire a pivotal place (Abu-Lughod, 2004; Kandiyoti, 1991; Moghadam, 1992) in 'modernisation' national projects (Kandiyoti, 1991). In fact, while "few writers appear to notice that the dominant stories about modernity and modernization have necessary but repressed or split-off gendered components"(Flax, 1993, p. 75), it is through the juridical regulation of women's attire that modernity is pursued.[3]

This is evident in Tunisia where, after independence from colonial forces, the state portrayed the veil as a symbol that contrasted with the nation's desire for modernity: as Cotton (2006) points out, the anti-*hijab* measures taken by Tunisia after independence was "to show the West that Tunisia was committed to secularism and democracy" (p. 3) where unveiled women become the "emblem of an era of new hopes and desires, and of aspirations for modernity and the hijab became a rare sight, even in rural areas" (Ahmed, 2011, p. 39). The association between secularism, modernity and veiling is also exemplified in Ataturk's effort to re-fashion Turkey by un-veiling women (Kasaba, 2010). His project to create a 'visibly modern' woman, along with a 'privatised' Muslim one, was linked to "a project of modernization à la West that was defined primarily by its secularizing measures" (Arat, 2012, p. 3): in light of this, the new woman emerged as the symbol of a Muslim westernised secularity (Göle, 1996), establishing in this way the opposition between modern/religious and posing gender at the centre of this dichotomy. As Göle (1996) observes, although "traditionalism, Islamism, reformism and Westernism all changed and acquired new meanings through the course of time, the 'question of women' as the main point of divergence between them remained unchanged"(p. 65). Hence, "women became the 'ground' upon which notions of being modern became articulated" (Parla, 2001, p. 70) where modernity, in this book, is understood as a series of linked projects aimed at institutionalising specific liberal/secular

[3] The association between veiling, secularism, and modernity is linked also to a specific western understanding of Islam whereas the struggle over the veil in the Middle East is seen as the symbol of the tension between modern and traditional view of Islam. The assumption is that all modernists consider thc un-veiling of Muslim women a progress towards modernity. While this is an overstatement, as not all Islamic modernist call for the removal of the female veil, it supposes that modernism means a disaffiliation from the Islamic past, rather than a re-configuration (Najmabadi, 2006).

principles through the employment of technologies that create new experiences, behaviours, and forms of knowledge (Asad, 2003).

Literature on gender and modernity (Najmabadi, 2006; Razack, 2007) provides important insights into understanding why women's body, and in particular the veiled female body, continues to be at the core of the discourse of social and political transformation. Scott (2017) observes that gender and race operate differently in the narrative of European national identities: while race and religion work to establish the outsider, women are men's other, but still necessary for the future of the nation, given their role in reproducing biological and cultural boundaries. Since women are internal to the national body and deeply influence the conceptualisation of 'us' and 'them', gender is at the heart of the articulation of communal identity and for this reason it occupies an important place in today's discourse concerning the accommodation of different religious sensitivities, showing how women's reproduction of space is a key element of the articulation of the secular itself (Gökarıksel, 2007; Knott, 2010): in fact,

> "[j]ust like any other political ideology, secularism operates through the construction, organization and encoding of spaces that represent, embody and sometimes enforce 'secular' values, norms and practices […] Women's bodies, dress and practices are key to the construction of each space as secular, modern, or religious" (Gökarıksel, 2007, p. 62).

This book interrogates which secular and religious sensitivities are produced in today's legal discourse concerning the veil in Europe and what kind of religious and secular sphere is delimited by this discourse. As women's body re-produces the boundary between religion and the secular, it is through it that is possible to understand what is hidden by secular constructions of dichotomous categories in the discourse concerning the veil. In fact, the relation between the self and representation of the other is of fundamental importance for understanding something about ourselves, as it is through representations that knowledge of the self and the other is produced (Asad, 1993). In the case of the headscarf ban, the representation of Muslim veiled women through oppositional categories, at the heart of European decisions to ban the veil, discloses something about the secular system that is actually hidden behind secular rhetoric on the visibility of the veil in the European public sphere. What, then, do those dichotomies disclose about secularism?

1.2 Secular Dichotomies and Beyond

Secularism is an historically produced idea (Milbank, 1990) based on the notion that the religious and political spheres are separate. The secular articulation of the Enlightenment view of morality and universal rights was a response to the violent religious conflicts in Europe from the sixteenth to the beginning of the eighteenth century. The division of power between church and state served to establish a neutral and non-sectarian public sphere which ensured a common identity by transcending particular allegiances and beliefs (Laborde, 2005). Taylor (2007) highlights that the aim of the secular state, which he considers the only neutral force able to negotiate conflicts, is to create citizens and to shape a common identity that could transcend rivalry between different groups. For this reason, secularism was seen as the *conditio sine qua non* for the existence of a democratic, modern and tolerant system where different religions could coexist peacefully and share a common secular space (Taylor, 2007; Davis, 2008); a "triumphalist narrative" that "came(s) to mark the conditions of possibility for the emergence of the political qualities designated 'modern', particularly the nation-state and its self-conscious citizen" (Davis, 2008, p. 11).

In recent years, a wide body of scholarly work (Asad, 2003; Hurd, 2008; Mahmood, 2005; Scott, 2013) has started to analyse secular historical paradigms. The analysis operated by those scholars discloses the intertwining of secularism and religion in western historical development, showing that secularism is not a neutral category, but a distinctive feature of the modern western/liberal state. I have chosen to draw on this literature as I have found it a useful starting point to analyse how secularism operates in the legal discourse about the veil. For this reason, in this book I understand 'political secularism' as the "state's relationship to, and regulation of, religion" (Mahmood, 2015, p. 3) and secularism/secularity as "a concept that articulates a constellation of institutions, ideas, and affective orientations that constitute an important dimension of what we call modernity and its defining forms of knowledge and practice—both religious and nonreligious"(Hirschkind, 2011, p. 633), shaping in this way a specific notion of personhood, ethics and community. It is important to highlight that the 'religious' and the 'secular' "are not essentially fixed categories" (Asad, 2003, p. 25); rather, secularism is an indeterminate category that shapes the individual and continuously re-draws the line between public and private on which it is based (Agrama, 2010). For this reason, my focus does not reside in what exactly secularism is, but in what it does through its normative categories.

For Asad (2003), "the secular is neither singular in origin nor stable in its historical identity, although it works through a series of *particular oppositions*"(p. 25)[4] which form a specific dynamic (Hirschkind, 2011). These oppositions, I argue, have important implications for Muslim as well as western women in Europe. Scott's analysis (2017) of the relation between secularism and gender equality shows that secular oppositions (public/private, east/west, religion/state, free/un-free, women/men, beliefs/rationality, etc.) have historically worked to exclude both religion and women from the public sphere where the definition of 'proper religion' went hand in hand with the definition of 'proper sexuality'(Fernando, 2017, p. 689). For Scott (2013, 2017), rather than providing equal rights for women, secular/binary dichotomies established in the process of secularisation in the west have signified the privatisation of religion and familial/sexual life in opposition to the realm of the public and political, legitimising the exclusion of women from the public sphere.

[4] *Italics added.*

This book analyses how secular/dichotomous oppositions, which historically had important implications for western women, work in today's discourse on the veil through their embeddedness in western and Human Rights law. In fact, as my analysis discloses, the dichotomies through which the veil has been narratively constructed (public v private, women's freedom v women's oppression, secular v religious, etc.), are embedded and reproduced in the juridical discourse concerning the veil. In the fourth chapter, I analyse and problematise those dichotomies by taking into consideration the juridical opposition between *forum internum* and *forum externum* encoded in article 9 of the European Convention on Human Rights (ECHR) ('Freedom of thought, conscience and religion'), which leads to a specific definition of religion and the female legal/religious subject. This is linked to another dichotomy: that between public and private embedded in the right of religious freedom, which reveals not only the emergence of secular paradoxes, but also a new relation between the individual and the sovereign power. In fact, the historical genealogy of the western notion of religious liberty, which is based on the division between an inviolable private and a regulated public sphere, presupposes the (paradoxical) active intervention of the state into the private life of its citizens through the notion of public order, a concept deriving from the European Christian and colonial past which is linked to occidental early preoccupation with religious plurality (Danchin & Mahmood, 2014). Human Rights law, with its claim to free the whole of humanity, does not solve those dichotomies and paradoxes. Rather, it poses a further dichotomy: that between humanisation and de-humanisation (Esmeir, 2006), revealing its exclusionary power and its inability to include the whole of humanity within the protective wings of the law. Those dichotomies, in the juridical discourse concerning the banning of the veil in Europe, are translated into the dichotomy veiling/un-veiling, inclusion/exclusion from the protective wing of the law, where Muslim veiled women have been excluded from the secular public sphere because their way of dressing does not mirror the secular/liberal imaginary. This leads us to question which representation of the human and the female subject is recognised and therefore protected by secular/liberal and Human Rights law, as well as to problematise the form of humanity that is promoted through secular legal instruments that have banned the use of the veil.

Drawing on Mahmood (2015), who argues that "to critique a particular normative regime is not to reject or condemn it: rather, by analysing its regulatory and productive dimensions, one only deprives it of innocence and neutrality so as to craft, perhaps, a different future"(p. 21), I problematise western dichotomous categories on which the legal discourse on the veil is based. In particular, I try to understand the implications of conceiving the practice through western/secular oppositional categories and whether it is possible to think about veiling beyond them. This analysis allows me to unmask the limits of the secular system which, contrary to its prerogative to be the best system to deal with different religious subjectivities and to defend the principle of toleration, plurality and gender equality, produces a certain violence towards other religious creeds while creating new (secular) forms of gender inequality.

In order to challenge the secular binary dichotomies on which European decisions to ban the veil are based, I analyse a wide body of literature on religious techniques of the body (Agamben, 2013; Asad, 2009; Mahmood, 2005) because the body escapes the western binary logic as "it falls neither under the category of person nor under that of things, the body has long oscillated between one and the other without finding a permanent place"(Esposito, 2015, pp. 4–5). The body, which, historically, many powers (such as the church, the state, and the individual) have claimed ownership of, is neither the subject nor the object, but part of the human and yet different from it. For Esposito (2015), since the body connects persons to things, it acquires a special place because it can fill the gap between entities (subject and object, internal and external, etc.) that western philosophical and legal traditions have divided into dichotomous categories: in fact,

> "while the body has always been the ground where persons pass into things, it is also the point of resistance that opposes this passage- not in the sense of a return from thing to person, but as a rejection of the dichotomous order that has always organized the relationship between the two"(Esposito, 2015, p. 144).

Hence, while the body is able to reject western/secular binary oppositions, it restores, at the same time, both categories to a non-dichotomous relationship (Serafini, 2017). Given that "veiling is an embodied spatial practice that transforms the self through bodily performance, as well as through the multiple experiences of the mobile body/self-moving across different normative regimes governed by different sets of formal or informal rules, norms and expectations" (Gökarıksel, 2009, p. 658), it emerges as the key element for thinking about the legal and religious subject beyond western/secular dichotomous categories.

In fact, as I will argue in chapter five, it is through the analysis of Muslims' performative practices that it is possible to understand a relation between norms, the body and forms of authority different from the secular/western one. This understanding, in turn, allows us to challenge the secular/western divide between *forum internum* and *forum externum*, faith and manifestation, signifier and signified, women's freedom and oppression, on which European decisions to ban the veil are based, revealing the possibility of thinking about different notions of religion and the religious female subject and thus a different understanding of the relation between life, norms and bodily practices. While, on the one hand, my analysis shows the existence of different gendered religious subjectivities, then on the other, the universalisation of western/secular categories in western and Human Rights law emerges as constitutive of the exclusion of the actual plurality of European society. This exclusion, operated *by* and *through* law, entails the delimitation of a specific public and private sphere and the creation and imposition of a monolithic female law and religious subjectivity which is drawn through the regulation of Muslim women's bodies: through the force of the law, secularism objectifies Muslim women's body and introduces a new understanding of women's empowerment and emancipation (Scott, 2017), producing and re-producing new forms of secular gender inequalities. This imposition, I argue, has been rendered necessary in order to save an imagined, yet fractured, European identity and to assimilate different subjectivities to an abstract, fixed and monolithic religious/secular/modern subject. Far from protecting Muslim women's rights, the struggle over the veil, played over women's body, reveals something new about the secular system, the law and women's body: something that I will try to sketch in this book.

1.3 Structure of the Book

The book is composed of introduction, conclusion and four chapters which can be conceived as divided into two main parts: the first offers an analysis of the dichotomies around the practice of veiling, while the second challenges those dichotomies in order to understand what they disclose about secularism and what they entail for Muslim women in Europe. In this chapter, I have tried to sketch the main argument and the aim of this book, providing the reader with background information and key points essential for understanding the research problem and its significance in the analysis of the operation of today's form of secularism.

In the second chapter I analyse the first dichotomy that emerges from the history of the veil; that between plurality and singularity. In fact, while my analysis shows that veiling is an immanent, ever-changing practice which acquires different meanings, it is from the colonial period and the birth of western-style nation states in many Muslim-majority societies that the female veil started to acquire a fixed and singular meaning linked to a 'clash of civilisation' between a tolerant west and a backward east and to be legally regulated. I draw on anthropological and political literature on the juridical regulation of clothes in order to unmask the so called 'clash of civilizations' symbolised in the veil as being associated with a specific form of sovereign power, disclosing the link between veiling, women's body and a specific form of sovereignty.

The third chapter takes into consideration the dichotomies on which some ECtHR (European Court of Human Rights) and national European juridical decisions to ban the practice of veiling are based (public v private, women's freedom v women's oppression, secular v religious, faith v manifestation etc.). I offer an analysis of how different European countries (France, Germany, and the United Kingdom), with different understandings of state-church relations, have dealt with the regulation of the Muslim female veil in the public sphere, along with an examination of outstanding legal cases decided at the ECtHR, disclosing similarities and differences between different forms of secularism. I show how, despite differences, those juridical decisions[5] that have banned the veil disclose remarkable similarities: firstly, they reveal a specific notion of religion as located in the private sphere of the individual. Secondly, in all the legal decisions, secularism is understood as a synonym of 'neutrality', 'modernity', 'democracy', 'nationhood', and 'gender equality',

[5] In this book I will refer to the legal cases that I take into consideration in chapter three as 'European juridical decisions'.

considered essential categories in the formation of the modern western nation states. Thirdly, those legal decisions are based on dichotomous oppositions (such as public v private, secular v religious, women's freedom v women's oppression, etc.) which have operated a differentiation between 'proper' and 'improper' religious symbols. I investigate the paradoxes of the secular/liberal system when defining the veil as an 'improper' religious symbol, showing that it is through the juridical regulation of the headscarf that secularism re-draws the line between public and private on which is based.

By employing theoretical elements of different disciplines, the fourth chapter focuses on the analysis and problematisation of western/secular/liberal dichotomies embedded in western and Human Rights law and on the examination of the notion of religion and the religious subject that emerges from European decisions to ban the veil, something often neglected, as secularism has come to denote a neutral and normal way of being. The chapter analyses three main dichotomies that emerge from the legal decision to ban the veil: that between faith and manifestation enclosed in art. 9 of the European Convention on Human Rights; that between public and private embedded in the notion of religious liberty; and that between humanisation and de-humanisation encoded in Human Rights law. My analysis discloses the emergence of a specific female/religious/secular subject that is protected by western and Human Rights law, revealing that the exclusion of many veiled Muslim women from the European public sphere has been rendered possible exactly through the employment and universalisation of liberal/secular dichotomies in western and Human Rights law. In light of this, the twentieth century liberal/secular project of universal emancipation, through the combination of legal positivism and human rights, in reality works to assimilate differences into Christian/secular understandings of law and politics and to control and forge private sentiments in the public sphere; failing to be re-born in the image of modern law's subject can literally result in the removal of the individual from the public sphere.

The fifth chapter explores whether it is possible to conceive of the religious and legal subject beyond secular/western categories. Through an exploration of Christian and Muslim techniques of the body, I challenge the internal/external division embedded in western and Human Rights law. This, in turn, challenges the semiotic understanding given to the practice of veiling by western judges as well as the assumption that veiling is a limit to women's freedom and their possibility of agency. This analysis allows us to understand the implications of legally applying universalist secular values in today's heterogeneous Europe and to unmask the paradoxes and limits of a western/secular/liberal system which, while claiming to save the principle of gender equality, creates new secular forms of gender inequality through the creation of a specific relation between the individual and the sovereign power, aimed at maintaining an imagined unity and homogeneity in a still fractured Europe. I conclude with a summary of my argument which, I hope, will open new lines of enquiry and fruitful critiques on the operation of secular/western law and new forms of control of women's body.

References

Abu Lughod, L. (2010). Against universals: The dialects of (Women's) human rights and human capabilities. In J. M. Molina & D. K. Swearer (Eds.), *Rethinking the human* (pp. 69–94). Harvard University Press.

Abu-lughod, L. (2000). *Veiled sentiments: Updated with a new preface: Honor and Poetry in a Bedouin Society* (2nd Revised ed.). University of California Press.

Abu-Lughod, L. (2004). *Dramas of nationhood: The politics of Television in Egypt*. American University Press in Cairo.

Agamben, G. (2013). *The highest poverty: Monastic rules and form-of-life*. Stanford University Press.

Agrama, H. A. (2010). Secularism, sovereignty, indeterminacy: Is Egypt a secular or a religious state? *Comparative Studies in Society and History, 52*(3), 495–523.

Ahmed, L. (1992). *Women and gender in Islam: Historical roots of a modern debate /*. Yale University Press.

Ahmed, L. (2011). *A quiet revolution: The Veil's resurgence, from the Middle East to America*. Yale University Press.

Anderson, B. (1991). *Imagined communities: Reflections on the origin and spread of nationalism*. Verso.

Anthias, F., & Yuval-Davis, N. (1989). *Woman-nation-state*. Macmillan.

Arat, Y. (2012). *Rethinking Islam and liberal democracy: Islamist women in Turkish politics*. SUNY Press.

Asad, T. (1993). The construction of religion as an anthropological category. In T. Asad (Ed.), *Genealogies of Religion: Discipline and Reasons of Power in Christianity and Islam*. Johns Hopkins University Press.

Asad, T. (2003). *Formations of the secular: Christianity, Islam, modernity*. Stanford University Press.

Asad, T. (2009). *Genealogies of religion: Discipline and reasons of power in Christianity and Islam*. JHU Press.

Barnes, T. (2019). Trump defends 'judge' Jeanine Pirro after fox news host taken off air over Islamophobic hijab comments. *The Independent*. https://www.independent.co.uk/news/world/americas/us-politics/trump-judge-jeanine-pirro-ilhan-omar-hijab-tweet-fox-news-a8827771.html

Britton, B. (2019, August). *What makes the burqa and burkini so controversial? - CNN*. CNN. https://edition.cnn.com/2016/08/19/europe/burqa-burkini-bans/index.html

Cady, L. E., & Fessenden, T. (2013). Gendering the divide: Religion, the secular, and the politics of sexual difference. In L. E. Cady & T. Fessenden (Eds.), *Religion, the secular, and the politics of sexual difference* (pp. 3–24). Columbia University Press.

Cotton, J. (2006). *Forced Feminism: Women, Hijab, and the One-Party State in Post-Colonial Tunisia*. Thesis, Georgia State University, 2006. https://scholarworks.gsu.edu/rs_hontheses/2

Danchin, P. G., & Mahmood, S. (2014). Politics of religious freedom: Contested genealogies. *South Atlantic Quarterly, 113*(1). https://doi.org/10.1215/00382876-2390401

Davis, K. (2008). *Periodization and sovereignty: How ideas of feudalism and secularization govern the politics of time*. University of Pennsylvania Press.

Dillon, E. M. (2004). *The gender of freedom: Fictions of liberalism and the literary public sphere*. Stanford University Press.

Elver, H. (2014). *The headscarf controversy: Secularism and freedom of religion* (Reprint ed.). Oxford University Press.

Esmeir, S. (2006). On making dehumanization possible. *PMLA*, 1544–1551.

Esmeir, S. (2012). *Juridical humanity: A colonial history*. Stanford University Press.

Esposito, R. (2015). *Persons and things: From the body's point of view*. John Wiley & Sons.

Fanon, F. (2004). Algeria unveiled. *Decolonization: Perspectives from Now and Then*, 5.

Fernando, M. L. (2017). Intimacy surveilled: Religion, sex, and secular cunning. In D. L. Boisvert & C. Daniel-Hughes (Eds.), *The Bloomsbury Reader in Religion, sexuality, and gender*. Bloomsbury Academic.

Flax, J. (1993). Is enlightenment emancipatory? In J. Flax (Ed.), *Disputed subjects: Essays on psychoanalysis, politics and philosophy*. Routledge.

Floyd, K. (2009). *The reification of desire: Toward a queer Marxism*. University of Minnesota Press.

Gökarıksel, B. (2007). A feminist geography of veiling: Gender, class and religion in the making of modern spaces and subjects in Istanbul. *Women, Religion, and Space*, 61–80.

Gökarıksel, B. (2009). Beyond the officially sacred: Religion, secularism, and the body in the production of subjectivity. *Social & Cultural Geography, 10*(6), 657–674. https://doi.org/10.1080/14649360903068993

Göle, N. (1996). *The forbidden modern: Civilization and veiling*. University of Michigan Press.

Goodrich, P. (1995). *Oedipus lex: Psychoanalysis, history, law*. University of California Press.

Goodrich, P. (1998). Signs taken for wonders: Community, identity, and a history of sumptuary law. *Law & Social Inquiry, 23*(3), 707–728.

Goodrich, P. (2008). Visive powers: Colours, trees and genres of jurisdiction. *Law and Humanities, 2*(2), 213–231.

Hirschkind, C. (2011). Is there a secular body? *Cultural Anthropology, 26*(4), 633–647.

Hunt, A. (1996). *Governance of the consuming passions: A history of sumptuary law*. Macmillan Press.

Hurd, E. S. (2008). *The politics of secularism in international relations*. Princeton University Press.

Kandiyoti, D. (1991). Identity and its discontents: Women and the nation. *Millennium, 20*(3), 429–443.

Kasaba, R. (2010). Turkey from the rise of Atatürk. In *The New Cambridge History of Islam: Volume 5: The Islamic World in the Age of Western Dominance* (Vol. 5, pp. 299–335). Cambridge University Press.

Knott, K. (2010). Theoretical and methodological reources for breaking open the secular and exploring the boundary between religion and non-religion. *Theoretical and Methodological Reources for Breaking Open the Secular and Exploring the Boundary between Religion and Non-Religion*, 1000–1019.

Laborde, C. (2005). Secular philosophy and Muslim headscarves in schools. *Journal of Political Philosophy, 13*(3), 305–329.

Mahmood, S. (2005). *Politics of piety: The Islamic revival and the feminist subject /*. Princeton University Press.

Mahmood, S. (2015). *Religious difference in a secular age*. Princeton University Press.

Mathews, K. (2018, April 25). Shirin Neshat: Fervor and Turbulent. *The Miami Rail*. https://miamirail.org/reviews/shirin-neshat-fervor-and-turbulent/

McAuley, J. (2018, May 30). Maryam Pougetoux*: France's headscarf debate focuses on a Muslim student leader*. The Washington Post. https://www.washingtonpost.com/world/europe/frances-headscarf-debate-focuses-on-a-muslim-student-leader/2018/05/30/9f190ed6-6347-11e8-81ca-bb14593acaa6_story.html

McGoldrick, D. (2006). *Human rights and religion: The Islamic headscarf debate in Europe*. Hart Publishing.

Melman, B. (2016). *Women's orients: English women and the Middle East, 1718–1918: Sexuality, Religion and work*. Springer.

Mernissi, F. (1991). *The veil and the male elite: A feminist interpretation of women's rights in Islam /*. Perseus.

Milbank, J. (1990). *Theology and social theory: Beyond secular reason*. Blackwell.

Moghadam, V. M. (1992). Revolution, Islam and women: Sexual politics in Iran and Afghanistan. *Nationalisms and Sexualities*, 424–446.

Najmabadi, A. (2006). Gender and secularism of modernity: How can a Muslim woman be French? *Feminist Studies, 32*(2), 239–255. JSTOR. https://doi.org/10.2307/20459085.

Panahi, R. (2015). *This is a symbol of oppression. Please don't celebrate it | Daily Telegraph*. The Daily Telegraph. https://www.dailytelegraph.com.au/rendezview/this-is-a-symbol-of-oppression-please-dont-celebrate-it/news-story/45843572e31a0cda3b2218d63f419fd8
Parekh, B. C. (2000). *Rethinking multiculturalism: Cultural diversity and political theory*. Macmillan.
Parla, A. (2001). The "honor" of the state: Virginity examinations in Turkey. *Feminist Studies, 27*(1), 65–88.
Peritz, I. (2019, May 7). *Quebec launches hearings on controversial secularism bill*. The Globe and Mail. https://www.theglobeandmail.com/canada/article-quebec-launches-hearings-on-controversial-secularism-bill/
Plante, C., & Bergeron, P. (2019, February 6). *Quebec status of women minister calls Muslim head scarf a symbol of oppression*. The Canadian Press. https://globalnews.ca/news/4931098/quebec-status-of-women-minister-calls-muslim-head-scarf-a-symbol-of-oppression/
Razack, S. H. (2007). The 'sharia law debate' in Ontario: The modernity/Premodernity distinction in legal efforts to protect women from culture. *Feminist Legal Studies, 15*(1), 3–32. https://doi.org/10.1007/s10691-006-9050-x
Sauer, B. (2009). Headscarf regimes in Europe: Diversity policies at the intersection of gender, culture and religion. *Comparative European Politics, 7*(1), 75–94.
SchooltriphijabclashsparksnewsecularismrowinFrance.(2019,October15).France24.https://www.france24.com/en/20191015-school-trip-hijab-clash-sparks-new-secularism-row-in-france
Scott, J. W. (2013). Secularism and gender equality. In L. E. Cady & T. Fessenden (Eds.), *Religion, the secular, and the politics of sexual difference* (pp. 25–46). Columbia University Press.
Scott, J. W. (2017). *Sex and secularism*. Princeton University Press.
Serafini, L. (2017). Beyond the Person: Roberto Esposito and the Body as 'Common Good'. *Theory, Culture & Society, 34*(7–8), 215–228.
Shadi Ghadirian: Untitled (Qajar Series). (n.d.). LACMA Collections. Retrieved February 25, 2020, from https://collections.lacma.org/node/580927
Stowasser, B. F. (1994). *Women in the Qur'an, traditions, and interpretation /*. Oxford University Press.
Taylor, C. (2007). *A secular age*. Belknap Press of Harvard University Press.
Vakulenko, A. (2007). Islamic headscarves' and the European convention on human rights: An intersectional perspective. *Social & Legal Studies, 16*(2), 183–199.
Watt, G. (2013). *Dress, law and naked truth: A cultural study of fashion and form*. Bloomsbury Publishing Plc.
Wiles, E. (2007). Headscarves, human rights, and harmonious multicultural society: Implications of the French ban for interpretations of equality. *Law & Society Review, 41*(3), 699–736.
Winnifred Fallers, S., Hurd, E. S., Mahmood, S., & Danchin, P. G. (2015). Introduction. In W. F. Sullivan, E. S. Hurd, S. Mahmood, & P. G. Danchin (Eds.), *Politics of Religious Freedom* (pp. 1–12). The University of Chicago Press.
Yuval-Davis, N. (1993). Gender and nation. *Ethnic and Racial Studies, 16*(4), 621–632.
Yuval-Davis, N. (2006). Belonging and the politics of belonging. *Patterns of Prejudice, 40*(3), 197–214.

Chapter 2
On Plurality and Singularity: Law, Power and the Muslim Female Dressed Body

In recent years, the Muslim female headscarf has been in the spotlight of discourses related to east/west relations: the 9/11 attacks on the twin towers, the bombs in London and Paris and the various western 'wars for democracy and civilization' have intensified civilizational differences and located the veil as the symbol, the metaphor, of an intrinsic incompatibility between the east and the west. While in the 'east' the veil has been elevated as an identitarian Islamic symbol by emerging Islamist groups, in the west Muslim women's veil has started to be understood as something endangering society (MacMaster & Lewis, 1998). Representing Muslim veiled women as threatening the peace of a society goes hand in hand with the idea that veiled women are inherently oppressed by a backward and patriarchal religion. In March 2016, for instance, the French minister for women's rights, Ms. Laurence Rossignol, compared women who wear the veil to 'Negroes who supported slavery' (Allen, 2016). She criticized western fashion companies for selling items such as the *burqini* and new, fashionable and 'modern' *hijabs*. For Ms. Rossignol, a legal regulation over the practice of veiling was necessary to 'save' Muslim women from a backward anti-secular religion that oppressed them. Similarly, the British Conservative MP Sarah Wollaston declared that "[it] should be clear that the burka is a symbol of oppression and segregation," while the Telegraph journalist Allison Pearson declared that "'bin-bags' prevent women from playing a full part in society" (Pearson, 2014). The idea that the veil is a threat to secular values and gender equality, expressed by politicians, columnists and journalists, contributes to the visual construction of the Muslim woman as oppressed and needing to be saved by tolerant and liberal western values. This notion has been strengthened by western mass media which have repeatedly portrayed veiling as the symbol of violent (Islamic) political/religious values and un-veiling as the symbol of women's liberation. During the Iraqi war, for instance, western mass media widely reported how the American/European occupation of Iraq and its (weak) political institutions improved the life of Iraqi women by releasing them from the normative burden to

G. Baldi, *Un-Veiling Dichotomies*, Boundaries of Religious Freedom: Regulating Religion in Diverse Societies,
https://doi.org/10.1007/978-3-030-79297-8_2

veil imposed by religious/rebel groups in the country after the fall of the Saddam regime (Mclaughlin, 2017). Similarly, in 2017, when part of Syria was liberated by the Kurdish People's Protection Unit (YPG) and the Syrian Democratic Forces (SDF), western media showed repeated images of Syrian women removing and burning their veils (Pasha-Robinson, 2017) as the symbol of the liberation from Islamic State's rules (IS) and violent occupation. While the symbolic juxtaposition of veiling and un-veiling echoes Said's (1994) understanding of the western construction of the 'other' as backward, it also reveals the fundamental dichotomies through which the practice is constructed. In fact, most of the discourses related to the practice of veiling focus on 'us' v 'them', modernity v tradition, public v private, religion v secularism, veiling v un-veiling.

While analysis of the dichotomies through which the practice of veiling has been constructed is the main focus of this book, I want to begin with the first important dichotomy: plurality and singularity. In this chapter, I juxtapose the plurality of the meanings given to the practice of veiling by women who wear the veil, with the singular meaning attached to veiling for political goals. This contraposition, embedded in the history of the meanings given to the practice – a history of plurality and singularity- discloses the link between women's body, clothes and forms of sovereignty and authority. Hence, while on the one hand the veil hides women's body, on the other it reveals something that is intrinsically related to a specific form of sovereignty and to the sovereign prerogative to intervene in the private life of the individual in order to forge its internal and external world. Not the veil itself, then, but the meaning attached to veiling reveals a link between clothes, women's body, and power that is unique to the practice. This may be why the veil, a simple piece of cloth worn for centuries by women and men, has acquired, in the past as well as today, so central a place in the narratives of many societies, especially those of the west.

The history of veiling starts long before Islam. Veiling, a non-compulsory practice in Islam, was a pre-Islamic custom in use in many societies – the Mesopotamian, Hellenic, Byzantine, Sassanian, Persian and Greek as well as in the Christian Middle East and Mediterranean regions (Ahmed, 1992). Veiling, then, emerges as the visible symbol of the historical accommodation operated by Islam with heterogenous cultures of the area, and has historically assumed different meanings (Ahmed, 1992; Mernissi, 1991b): the practice has been a useful tool to define and express not only class, gender, caste, marital status and kinship/community belonging, but also political agency and national identity. The particularity, plurality, and situationality of the practice is mirrored in the different shapes, colours, and uses of the headscarf: in Yemen, women wear the *lithma*, in Iran they wear the *chador*, in East Africa women wear traditional fabric wrapped around their head, while in Morocco both women and men are accustomed to wearing a head-cover (El Guindi, 1999).

It may be the elusiveness and unintelligibility of the practice that has attracted the attention of the legal and political authorities that have particularly focused on the female veil. While veiling in western history has always been an obsession for different forms of sovereign powers, for whom it is linked to social control, in the east legal regulation of the practice began in the colonial period and with the born of western-style nation-states in Muslim majority societies. The spread of nationalist ideals during the colonial period saturated the veil with a new (monolithic) meaning related to 'civilizational missions' on the one hand and resistance narratives on the other. It is from this period that the veil, a simple piece of cloth worn for many reasons and to many effects, started to acquire a central place in the representation of east/west relations. The centrality of the discourse over the veil in the colonial and post-colonial periods indicates that the practice (whether banned or imposed), has been a useful tool to strengthen national unity and identity and to create a homogeneous law's subject through the fashioning of women's body in the public sphere: regulation of the veil is therefore related to the establishment and strengthening of a form of sovereignty which creates and makes possible a specific relation between clothes, power, statecraft and women's body.

The regulation of clothes is not a new phenomenon. Historically, clothes have been intended as images, symbols and metaphors of a specific internal self and for this reason they have the power to operate a visible differentiation, a boundary, a clear-cut dividing line, between citizens and foreigners and between the different classes of citizens: through clothes, symbols and metaphors it is thus possible to conceptualize nationality, geography and gender, as it is through the visible that the public sphere comes to be shaped. Since clothes have been conceived as images, and images have the power to rhetorically construct (visible) forms of knowledge, the definition attached to a particular article of clothing emerges as an act of sovereign power aimed at maintaining the unity and homogeneity of a people. As Goodrich (1998) argues, "understood as a crucial part of the law of images, and equally as a dimension of the legal construction of the symbolic order, the regulation of appearance can be reinterpreted as a key component in the identity of those 'imagined communities'"(p. 724). The regulation of women's clothes through the force of the law emerges as a useful tool to fashion not only the public sphere but also, more importantly, the private sphere of the individual. The 'politics of clothes', then, which, as I shall argue, is an integral part of European and non-European history, not only reveals a certain anxiety in relation to clothes' regulation, but also, more importantly, it emerges as one example of the increasing intrusion of the state in the private life of its citizens. Hence, the regulation of clothes is intrinsically linked to sovereignty formation and, I argue, to a specific relation between the individual, the law and state power: a relation played over women's body.

In view of this history, today's obsession with veiling/un-veiling women, shared by western liberals and Islamist radicals, is to be understood through the lens of this unique relation between clothes, women's body, and particular forms of sovereign power. This relation is translated in the symbology attached to the practice of veiling which is based on the dichotomy between plurality (of meanings and uses of the veil) and singularity (of meaning given to the practice to bolster specific forms of sovereign power). I employ Diamantides' (2012, 2015) comparative study of sovereign formation in the east and in the west to argue that today's fixed symbology attributed to the practice of veiling has been a useful tool to create an imaginary clash between two dissimilar universal(ist) legal and political systems: the secular/liberal and the Islamist one. In fact, both Islamist and liberal-state fetishists are concerned with the legal regulation of the female headscarf and agree that the dress code of Muslim women cannot be a woman's personal choice: but while Islamists advocate compulsory veiling by referring to a westernized and secularized version of *Sharia* law, western liberals call for the un-veiling of women as a means to include them within the pale of western/Christian/secular and human rights law. Both, in contrast to the pluralism of Islamic laws and practices, aim at instituting through the force of (positivized) rules of law a fixed law subject bound to a unique, fixed, and universal(ist) law through the control and juridical regulation of women's body. Thus, more than the symbol of a profound 'incompatibility' between the east and the west, the veil emerges as the symbol, the metaphor, of the anxiety produced by the encounter between two forms of universal(ist) legal and political systems: one triumphant, and the other aspiring. Both create a link between women's body, dress and sovereignty at the expense of women's freedom and their possibility of agency. In fact, since "law demonstrates anxiety when individuals attempt to perform their own public face, through personal modes of dress and undress" (Watt, 2013, p. 123), women who choose to wear or remove a veil are seen as a threat because they appropriate their right to regulate their own relation between their private life and the civil public sphere.

2.1 The Veil and Islamic Law

The web site 'Umma–the Online Muslim Community' offers a virtual forum of discussion for the wide Muslim community scattered over the western world. Searching the word *'hijab'* directs the reader to a page in which a 'guest' asks:

> "Is the *hijab* compulsory in Islam? [...] The *Qur'an* just says to draw the clothes over the bosoms (breast/chest). This is not the hair. I just want to know what the Arabic of these words really mean. I want to know if the wives and female believers had to have the hijab on or if they were able to walk without it. I wish it was compulsory but I don't think it is" (Is the HIJAB really COMPULSORY? (n.d.)).

Another 'guest' answers: "if you want to wear it then wear it *inshallah*. Don't go confusing yourself", while another, called 'beardedbrother', explains that

> "you need to see what the *tafseer* [exegeses/interpretation of the *Qur'an*] is behind that *ayaah* [*Qur'anic* verse] and you need to understand that the English translation of the Arabic does not do justice and that the Arabic words have deeper meanings [...] you need to see what the scholars of the *sunnah* [Muslim tradition based on the study of Muhammad life and actions] say about this ayah and the *mufasireen* (scholars of *tasfeer*) [...] we cant just interpret *ayaahs* from *Qur'an* to our own understanding because this would lead to great problems within the Muslim *Umma* [Muslim community], we need to understand the ayah as the Prophet and his Companions understood the ayah" (Is the HIJAB really COMPULSORY? (n.d.)).

Uthman Ibn Affan, a member of the forum who chooses to call himself one of Muhammad's Companions, has the privilege of the 'last word' in the forum: through the reading of a few (interpretable) *Qur'anic* verses (*ayah*), and an accurate choice of specific scholars' interpretations and translations, he tries to demonstrate that the veil is compulsory for Muslim women and that it is legally required by the *Qur'an*. This debate does not mirror a general confusion among Muslims over God's commandments; rather, it highlights the plurality intrinsic to the very structure of classical Islamic law. In fact, as Asad (2009) points out, since Islam is a 'discursive tradition' based on the interpretation of the past for a reformulation of practices in the present, it should not be studied as a fixed or unchanged religion: veiling, like many other Islamic practices, is an ever-changing phenomenon which is lived, experienced, and interpreted differently by believers. The practice has assumed different meanings based on the many interpretations of the sacred Islamic texts. This multiplicity of understandings of Islam and Islamic practices has important implications for the construction of specific gender roles and implies a multiplicity of ways to practice and understand veiling.

The hierarchy of legal sources for Muslims is highly complex and is the result of a gradual historical process of accommodation of Islam within different cultures. For Muslims, the revelation is entrusted in the *Qur'an*, the holy text of Islam, which is not the outcome of a divinely-inspired human such as the Gospel for Christians, but the word of God that was received *verbatim* by the Prophet Muhammad: for this reason, it is the most important religious text and the primary religious and legal source for Muslims in every aspect of their lives.[1] The *Qur'an,* however, gives only general exhortations, mostly of an ethical nature (comprising, for instance, commandments on worship, fasting, pilgrimage, marriage and divorce);[2] hence, as a legislative book, the *Qur'an* raises several problems because it does not provide a code of law. It is for this reason that, in the course of history, Muslim scholars have spent considerable time and energy in interpreting Mohammad's words and have created diverse books of Islamic law according to different schools of thought. According to this view, *Shari'a* (Islamic law) is a comprehensive, pluralistic, juridical system that emerges as the result of the accommodation operated by Islam with the customary law of the conquered populations as well as of the authority and power relations which were continuously negotiated in the history of Islam (Geertz, 2000). *Sharia* law, a human-source, derives from the study of the *Sunna* ('the trodden path'), a pre-Islamic practice that emulates distinguished persons–including the Prophet Mohammad. The *Sunna* is documented in the *Hadith* (the verb derives from the Arabic *haddatha*, 'to recount' or 'to tell'): a collection of testimonies and stories of the Prophet gathered by his Companions or those who followed his Companions. The function of the *Hadith* is to clarify and detail how a good Muslim should behave in order to follow the path of the Prophet Muhammad, who acted completely in conformity with the demands of the *Qur'an* (Sedgwick, 2006). In other words, for devout Muslims, "the example of the Prophet Mohammad and of the community he established is to be followed as much as possible" (Sedgwick, 2006, p. 9) because his actions cannot be in conflict with what is written in the sacred book, as they

[1] Since the *Qur'an* is the most important legal source for Muslims, Koranic exegesis (*Tafsir*) has emerged as one of the most important disciplines in Islam (Ahmed, 1992).

[2] The number of 'legal' verses in the *Qur'an* (between 200 and 500) represents a small portion of the 6300 verses of the holy book (Saeed, 2006).

derive from the same source. Generations of Muslim scholars have collected *Hadith* from direct or indirect testimonies: to evaluate the validity of each, *Hadith* scholars have to establish the legitimacy of *Isnad*, the chain of people who transmitted the source (Siddiqi, 1996; Mernissi, 1991b). Once the *Isnad* is established, scholars can accept (*maqbul*) the *Hadith* as authentic (*sahih*), 'agreeable' (*hasan*), or they can simply reject it (*mardud*). Islamic legal analysis is based on two main principles: *Ijma* (consensus) and *Qyas* (analogy). The *Ijma* is the unanimous agreement of the congregation of Muslims about a precise matter: it is a pre-Islamic customary practice of the Arabian Peninsula, where it was common to legislate based on the consensus of the whole community.[3] Islamic law is based on five main categories: 'forbidden' (*haram*), 'allowed' (*mubaha*), 'recommended' (*mustahabb* or *Sunna*), 'discouraged' (*makruh*), and 'obligatory' (*Wajib*). The establishment of these categories has given a certain flexibility of interpretation to what is considered right or wrong and has facilitated the accommodation of Islam with different cultures (Sedgwick, 2006).

Thus, *Sharia* law is not a fixed legal system; rather, it is a 'pluralistic' legal system, a 'polyglot discourse', based on the consensus of the *Umma* (the 'Islamic community'). There was no single Islamic law in the past, nor is there today; on the contrary, there exist many books of Islamic law which allow a certain flexibility in the regulation of Muslims' daily lives. The Islamic principle of *Ijma*, the unanimous agreement of the congregation of Muslims about a precise matter, provides an umbrella for the accommodation of various and different interpretations of Islamic law. In order to reduce the tension between different schools of thought, Muslim scholars have set up the principle that each Muslim is free to follow the school of his/her choice and to change his/her school of law on particular legal issues (Coulson, 1969). Hence, it is possible to say that when Muslim jurists don't agree, 'they agree to disagree'. This notion is clarified by a famous saying of the Prophet that "difference of opinion within my community is a sign of the bounty of Allah".[4] This notion also seems to resonate in an old Arab proverb which assumes that "the person who does not understand divergence in doctrine [...] has not caught the true scent of jurisprudence (*Man la ya'raf al-ikhtilaf lam yashumma ra-ihata 'l-fiqh*)" (Coulson, 1969, p. 20–1).

This pluralistic concept of law emerges from the lack of authoritative hierarchical structure among scholars and Islamic schools of thought and it is based on the idea that no human interpretation can be the unique and final legal authority. It is exactly the *Ulama*'s lack of a hierarchical structure that makes it "possible for every Muslim to have a voice in religious debates on issues about which they are knowledgeable" (Winter, 2009, p. 21). This is an important feature of the analysis of Islamic law because it allows a myriad of interpretations by local religious clerics that vary from place to place based on specific socio/political/economic contexts.

[3] Nowadays, there is a consensus only about the fundamentals of Islam, such as the five daily prayers, the *Qur'an* as the word of God, the unity of God, Mohammad's prophethood, fasting and pilgrimage to Mecca (Saeed, 2006).

[4] The supporting Koranic verse states "Let there be no compulsion in religion" (2:257).

Hence, there is no obvious singular response to the question: 'how should a Muslim behave? Or what interpretation(s) of Islam is normative and applicable?' Or 'is the veil compulsory?' The veil, like many other Islamic practices, should be understood within the wide plurality of Islamic sources and legal interpretations.

In Arabic, the veil is known as the *hijab*: the verb indicates the act of covering or hiding something (*yahjib* or *hajaba*) for the purpose of protection. The word is found seven times in the *Qur'an*[5] and it has different meanings such as 'barrier', 'separation', 'messenger', 'veil' and 'darkness' (Mernissi, 1991a). Hence, the term does not always indicate women's dress code.

In the *Surah* 24, 'An Nur' verse 30 and 31, the *Qur'an* introduces the concept of *hijab* with a commandment to lower the gaze in order to protect chastity:

> "30: Tell the believing men to lower their gaze and be modest. That is purer for them. Allah is aware of what they do. 31: And tell the believing women to lower their gaze and be modest, and to display of their adornment only that which is apparent, and to draw their veils over their chests, and not to reveal their adornment except to their own husbands or fathers or husbands' fathers, or their brothers or their brothers' sons or sisters' sons, or their women, or their slaves, or male attendants who lack vigor, or children who know nothing of women's nakedness. And let them not stamp their feet so as to reveal what they hide of their adornment. And turn to Allah together. Oh believers, in that you may succeed."

The verse, which concerns both men and women, is an exhortation to lower the gaze and to cover the *awra* (private parts) as well as 'beauty and ornaments' (in relation to women). This *ayah* is understood differently by Muslim scholars: in fact, the word *zinah* (adornments, ornaments) can signify either *zahirah* (apparent adornment) or *batinah* (hidden adornment). Based on Imam Tabari's[6] interpretation, for instance, this verse means that a woman must cover herself in public, apart from her face and hands. Women are permitted to use make-up and jewellery since they constitute the *zinah zahirah* (apparent adornment) which are ordinarily visible in public. Furthermore, as he points out, the command, 'they should draw their veils over their bosoms', means that women should cover the rest of their bodies and their hair, necks and earrings. To this interpretation, Qurtubi[7] adds that it is unlawful to reveal women's hidden adornments to any man except for the husband, father, sons, or to those with specific conditions, such as men who have no sexual appetite (the impotent, the insane, the slaves etc.) (Hasan, 2011).

But it is in the *Surah* 33, *Al-Ahzab, ayah 53* that many Islamic scholars found the command of the *hijab* intended as the headscarf worn by Muslim women:

[5] *Surah* 7, *Al–A'raf*, verse 46; *Surah* 17, verse 45–46; *Surah* 24, verse 30 and 31; *Surah* 38, *Sad*, verse 32; *Surah* 41, *Fussilat*, verse 5 (in this *Surah* the word *hijab* indicates a cover in the heart of the unbelievers towards Muhammad's call from Islam), *Surah* 42, *Ash-Shura*, verse 51; *Surah* 19, *Maryam*, verse 1; *Surah* 33, *Al-Ahzab*, verse 53–59. See (The Holy Qur'an, 2000).

[6] Abu Ja'far Muhammad ibn Jarir al-Tabari (224–310 AH; 838–923 CE) was a prominent and influential Kharji scholar, historian and exegete of the *Qur'an* from Persia (Iran).

[7] Imam Abu 'Abdullah Al-Qurtubi was a famous *muhaddith* and *faqih* scholar from Cordoba of Maliki origin. He is most famous for his commentary of the *Qur'an*, *Tafsir* al-Qurtubi.

"53: Oh You who believe! Enter not the dwellings of the Prophet for a meal without waiting for the proper time, unless permission be granted you. But if you are invited, enter, and, when your meal is ended, then disperse. Linger not for conversation. That would cause annoyance to the Prophet, and he would be shy of (asking) you (to go); but Allah is not shy of the truth. And when you ask of them (the wives of the Prophet) anything, ask it of them from behind a curtain *(hijab)*. That is purer for your hearts and for their hearts. And it is not for you to cause annoyance to the messenger of Allah nor that you should ever marry his wives after him. That in Allah's sight would be an enormity".

This verse was pronounced by Mohammad during his wedding with Zainab bint Jahsh. After the wedding ceremony, three discourteous guests remained in the house: this annoyed the Prophet who, according to the disciple Anas, recited the verse when the guests departed from his house. As the *ayah* was pronounced during a special occasion, scholars and jurists disagree whether the verse relates just to the Prophet's wives, conferring them a special status, or to all Muslim women. For al-Tabari, the true meaning of the verse has to be found in the division of the space between two men: the Prophet and Anas, the witness of the event. The interpretation of the word *hijab* as a delimitation of space (a 'curtain' that separates the space) (Stowasser, 1994) is supported by many other scholars (Mernissi, 1991b) as "the Prophet loosened while standing on the threshold to Zainab's chamber, with one foot in the room and the other outside, in order to bar his servant Anas Ibn Malik […] from entering" (cited in Stowasser, 1994, p. 90). However for Ibn Sa'ad,[8] the *hijab* command was issued after Muhammad saw some men outside Zainab's house the day after the wedding, while other traditions attributed to Umar Ibn al-Khattab[9] the advice to seclude Muhammad's wives as "both the righteous and the wicked enter into your house" (Stowasser, 1994, p. 90).

Although, at the time of the Prophet, only his wives used to veil, the *ayah* 59–60 (*Surah* 33) seems to extend the command to all Muslim women:

"59: Oh Prophet! Tell your wives and your daughters and the women of the believers to draw their cloaks close around them (when they go out). That will be better, so that they may be recognized and not annoyed. Allah is ever Forgiving, Merciful. 60: If the hypocrites, and those in whose hearts is a disease, and the alarmists in the city do not cease, We verily shall urge you on against them, then they will be your neighbours in it but a little while".

This *ayah* clearly refers to women's appearance when outside the home: it is not, therefore, related to seclusion *within* the household. The verse is divided into two parts: the first is an exhortation for women to cover themselves, while the second highlights the reasons for the commandment. Traditional commentators such as al-Tabari, Qurtubi and Ibn Abbas[10] agree that this *ayah* was pronounced in order to protect Muslim women of Medina from sexual harassment. In fact, at that time, the men of Medina used to harass women walking in the street, thinking they were

[8] Ibn Sa'ad (784 CE–845 CE) was a prominent Sunni scholar of the Arabian Peninsula.

[9] Umar Al-Khattab (583–644 CE) was an influential Muslim scholar and one of the most important and powerful Muslim caliphs in history.

[10] Abd Allah ibn Abbas was a paternal cousin of the Prophet: expert in *Tafsir*, he is revered by Muslims for his knowledge.

slaves or prostitutes: women, then, used to wear a veil in order to distinguish themselves from the slaves and as a means of protection from male harassment. As Ibn al-Arabi argues,[11] the *ayah* does not require excessive covering, but clothing that can be a visible sign of the difference between the 'free' and the 'slave'. It can be argued, though, as some modern interpreters do (Ahmed, 1992), that the question of being distinguished as a free woman becomes inconsistent after the abolition of slavery throughout the world (Ghamidi, 2013). As Ahmed (1992) points out, the veil was a practice in use before the advent of Islam by Greeks, Roman, Jews and Assyrian women who wore it to indicate high social status: based on this interpretation, it seems that Muhammad was trying to create "in non-architectural terms the forms of segregation –the gynoecium, the harem quarters – already firmly established in such neighbouring patriarchal societies as Byzantium and Iran, and perhaps he was even borrowing from those architectural and social practices" (Ahmed, 1992, p. 55). Thus, it can be argued that the matter of identity formation could have a particular significance in a world where Islam was an emerging religion and needed to be distinguished and recognized by the whole society. In the same vein, Ibn Kathir[12] notes that one of the purposes of the verse was to distinguish the free woman from women of the era of ignorance (*jihiliyyah*)[13] and thus to show her Muslim identity: as, at the time of the pronouncement of the *ayah*, living conditions in Mecca were particularly harsh due to repeated military defeats, the command seems to indicate the privileged, elite *status* of Muslim women, as confirmed in medieval *Hadith* (Hasan, 2011). It remains, though, unclear whether the veil was prescribed only for the Prophet's wives or for all Muslim women (Ahmed, 1992). Qurtubi, for instance, suggests that the command to cover should be extended to all women, whether free or slaves, because all their body is *awra,* private. However, he admits that some Prophet's Companions recount that the *jilbab* covered just the upper body and not a woman's whole body (Hasan, 2011).

While many contemporary scholars such as Maududi (1903–79) identify veiling with women's seclusion (Maududi & Sloan, 2011), others such as Sultan Muhammad Shah (also called Aga Khan III),[14] argue that because the veil was not in use in Mohammad's time it is not compulsory (Al-Azmeh, 2006; Calderini, 2013). Other contemporary scholars analyse the *Qur'an* precepts by taking into consideration social, political and historical factors of Muhammad's age (Ahmed, 1992; Mernissi, 1991a). Fatima Mernissi (1991b), for instance, argues that the definition given to the word *hijab* is three-dimensional, and these three dimensions often blend into one another:

---

[11] Ibn al-Arabī (1165–1240 AD) was an Arab Andalusian Sufi mystic and philosopher.

[12] Ismail ibn Kathir (1301–1373) was a Muslim *muhaddith, faqīh, mufassir,* historian, and commentator of *Shaaf'I* school.

[13] Muslims refer to *Jahiliyyah* as the period before the advent of Islam.

[14] Aga Khan was the 48th *imam* of the Imami Shi'I Nizari Isma'ilis, a Muslim community settled in India, Pakistan, Syria, Lebanon and East Africa.

> "The first dimension is a visual one: to hide something from sight. In fact, the root of the verb hajaba means 'to hide'. The second dimension is spatial: to separate, to mark a border, to establish a threshold while the third dimension is ethical because it belongs to the realm of the forbidden. So we have not just tangible categories that exist in the reality of the sense–the visual, the spatial–but also an abstract reality in the realm of ideas; a space hidden by a hijab is a forbidden space" (p. 93).

Mernissi's analysis (1991b) in relation to the veil takes into consideration not only various interpretations of *Quranic* verses, but also the historical period when the Prophet pronounced them. At that time, year five of the *Hejira*, the Islamic calendar, the Prophet's armies suffered numerous military defeats; it was a particularly disastrous year from a military point of view and, consequently, a year of political stagnation. In fact, the *Surah* describes, among other issues, the siege of Medina. This epoch of doubt and political uncertainty eroded the morality and manners of Medina's population. It seems therefore that "the Prophet, during a troubled period at the beginning of Islam, pronounced a verse that was so exceptional and determining for the Muslim religion that it introduced a breach in space that can be understood to be a separation of the public from the private, or indeed the profane from the sacred, but which was to turn into a segregation of the sexes"(Mernissi, 1991a, p. 101).

Other scholars (Ahmed, 1992; Stowasser, 1994) argue that the reasons for the *hijab* revelation was the intention to give privacy to the female elite of Islam. At that time, Medina was a crowded city, especially the Mosque, which was the centre of public affairs: the female room of the Mosque was an extension of the Prophet's wives' apartment and the verse indicates the need for privacy. Unlike in the west, the concept of privacy in the Arab/Muslim world "is based on a specific cultural construction of space and time central to the functioning of Islamic society in general [...]. Space in this construction is relational, active, charged and fluid" (El Guindi, 1999, p. 77). Hence, in Muslim/Arabic culture, space and time are fluid concepts within which people manoeuvre their agency. El Guindi (1999) observes that the western idea of privacy, which is based on a binary opposition between private and public and its corollary honour and shame, has been used to create a link between space and gender which has been universalized by western feminists and translated into the polarity domestic/public life: a notion that has been erroneously imposed over Muslim culture.

Not only the *Qur'an*, but also the *Hadith* are considered an important legal source for Muslims. The '*Hadith of Asma'* is the most commonly quoted by scholars to indicate the importance of modest clothes for Muslim women. Durayk reported that Aisha, one of the Prophet's wives, recounted that Asma, her sister, visited Muhammad wearing transparent clothes. On this occasion the Prophet lowered his gaze and pointed out that an adult woman should be covered in public. However, even Abu Dawud, the main transmitter of this fact, doubts the authenticity of this *Hadith* because Asma was known as a woman of piety and she would not introduce herself to the Prophet with transparent garments. Moreover, as Abu Dawud argues, it seems that Khalis B. Durayk, the narrator, has never met Aisha (Hasan, 2011).

Besides, there is a wide body of literature about the 'mothers of the believers', the Prophet's wives, in the *Hadith*: they are considered a model of piety and devotion for their role as protectors of Islamic norms and values. Hence, as Stowasser (1994) argues, their behaviour, their dress and their conduct in general must be read as "(para)legal texts in that their intended meaning is normative, not descriptive. [...] This process involved a dynamic spiral of mutual reinforcement of its two constituent components, that is, the principle of these women's righteousness on the one hand, and their function as categorical norm-setters on the other" (115).

This understanding that religious practices are related to a model to be followed is of great importance in my analysis, as it is exactly through the way in which many Muslims experience their religious life that is possible to challenge western secular dichotomies through which the practice of veiling has been understood. Many Muslim women recall some *Hadith* as confirmation of their understanding of Islamic religious practices. There are many *Hadith* describing how the Prophet's wives used to hide themselves in the presence of male strangers. Aisha, for instance, used to veil even in front of the Prophet's grandchildren as well as during the prayer and the circumambulation of the *Ka'ba*. Veiling, however, has never been synonymous with seclusion: there are many *Hadith* recounting how the Prophet's wives used to take care of the injured during war time, for example, or how Aisha used to pull up her garments to carry water for Muslim warriors on the battlefield (Abbott, 1941).[15]

Analysis of the main Islamic legislative texts concerning the practice of women's veiling indicates that a fixed and monolithic interpretation of Islamic legal sources on the command of *hijab* does not exist: as there is no scholarly consensus over the necessity for Muslim women to wear the veil, it is possible to state that veiling is not compulsory in Islam. However, given the different interpretations of Islam and the practice, many women understand veiling as a religious obligation. As I have briefly pointed out, the *hijab* had a precise function of identity formation, especially during the emergent phase of Islamic religion in heterogenic societies such as Medina, but it also offered a means of protection in times when women were harassed. Over the centuries, Muslim scholars developed a myriad of interpretations regarding the veil (Stowasser, 1994) although nowadays conditions for the interpretation of the *Qur'an* and *Sunna* are limited compared with the first period of Islam (Esposito, 2005). Hence Islam has historically given a pluralist meaning to the practice of veiling. This is furthered by the ability of *Ulama* to release *fatwa*. *Fatwa* represents the 'practical' aspect of Islamic law and it is promulgated in response to a precise need of a particular Muslim community (Layish, 1996): it assumes a 'legal value' not for

[15] Although it is not the topic of this book, it is worth pointing out that in the *Hadith* it is possible to find many references to men's garments, especially to the male veil. Historical ethnography reveals that men, in pre-Islamic societies, were also accustomed to wear the veil: it seems that even the Prophet wore the veil on certain occasions. For instance, in the *Hadith* Sahih al-Bukhari 5360, the Prophet introduced himself to Abu Bakr face-veiled. In the same *Hadith*, as Abu Bakr–the witness of the event–testified, Muhammad entered Aisha's room and covered his face with garments because two slaves were dancing and playing drums in front of him (El Guindi, 1999).

the whole Muslim community, but for the local community that follows a particular scholar. In 2013, for instance, an influential Saudi cleric, Sheikh Ahmed Bin Qassim al-Ghamdi, issued a *fatwa* stating that women do not need to veil and they can travel alone (Hubbard, 2016), while at the same time the Saudi scholar Sheikh Abdullah Daoud issued a *fatwa* calling for female babies to wear the *burqa* as a mean of protection from sexual harassment (Mcdermott, 2013). *Fatwa* can be issued publicly or privately: believers are accustomed to asking precise questions of scholars or *Ulama* who then release specific religious edicts (*fatwa*). This is the case for Aishah Azmi, for instance, a British teacher who refused to remove her *hijab* at school because she was obeying a *fatwa* issued personally to her by an Islamic cleric (Taher, 2006). The differences among interpretations of God's commands have rendered the matter of veiling extremely heterogeneous: not only have scholars issued very different *fatwa* concerning the veil, but also, more importantly, when locating the practice within Islamic texts and exegesis, what emerges is a plurality of different interpretations that do not find a unanimous consensus within the Muslim community. Thus, instead of giving a fixed meaning to the practice, Islam has incorporated the practice while embracing its intrinsic plurality.

2.2 Accommodating Diversity: Islam, Culture and the Veil

Lithma is a "brightly coloured thin material or muslin draped around the head in such a way as to cover the hair and the forehead, while the lower part of it can be pulled down to uncover or pulled up to cover the whole face except the eyes" (Makhlouf & Obermeyer, 1979, p. 30). In Yemen, this specific kind of veil is associated with the concept of femininity while among Bedouins and Berbers, it is considered as a 'sign of' masculinity and virility (El Guindi, 1999). This plurality of meanings in relation to veiling expresses the intrinsic variety of the practice: in fact, like any other piece of cloth, the veil has been a useful tool to communicate instances of gender, kinship/group belonging, social status etc.: as Rugh (1987) argues, clothes "provide a code which can decipher the complexities of social structure and the values on which they are based" (pp. 4–5). In Nubian society, for instance, the veil is seen as a sign of modesty and respectability, but it is also understood as a tool to communicate a woman's life's phases as well as her marital status. Here, not only does the veil, along with its different uses, emerge as a mark of gender, but it also indicates maturity and adulthood (El Guindi, 1999). For the Tuareg, however, veiling does not communicate gender difference, but it formalizes "the group status of the individual, the identity of the group and the sacredness of privacy" (El Guindi, 1999, p. 126). Notably, the veil does not conceal identity; rather it is worn by men and women (men wear a 'face veil' which reveals only the eyes while women wear a decorated scarf over their heads) as a symbol of maturity, honour and social class (Murphy, 1964). Historically, the veil has also been a useful tool to indicate an individual's social status: among the Rashayda, (female) dress serves not only to separate the individual's life into phases, but also to indicate a woman's identity, her 'reputation' and social status, which is acquired through the material, artistic achievements of both men and women (Young, 1996). Similarly, in Yemen, where the practice dates back to the pre-Islamic period and a wide range of different headscarves is worn by men and women, the use of different veils indicates a specific social status. Outdoors, women wear the *sitara,* a large red, blue and green piece of cloth that coves the whole body, accompanied by a piece of black transparent batik that covers the face, or the *sharshaf,* a three-part garment covering the head and shoulders (Makhlouf & Obermeyer, 1979). Upper-class women tend to wear the *sharshaf*, while women of lower socio-economic status wear the *sitara*, and non-Yemenis and servants do not veil: notably, this use of the headscarf as indicating a status symbol is typical of stratified urban societies of the area (El Guindi, 1999). Among Egyptian peasants, the veil is worn to indicate a specific regional, socio/economic and religious identity, while in Palestine, the headscarf is often used to indicate (pre-1948) regional/kinship belonging. Similarly, peasants of the Ghanyari, a community settled in the Himalayas, wear the veil to indicate kinship relationship and social restrictions (Sharma, 1978). As, historically and contextually, the veil has been a useful tool to communicate and demarcate matters of gender, class and territory, it also expresses power relations within a society. In fact, the veil is also used by women as a symbol of power: El Guindi (1999) reveals that among the Rashayda a prize pinned to their *milayah* is given to women who dance best at weddings. In Bahrain, peasant women attach the key of the house to their headscarves, while in the past Muslim Indian women used to beat their husbands with their headscarves as part of an ancient ritual (El Guindi, 1999). The many meanings and uses of the veil reveal the impossibility of fully understanding this pluralistic and ever-changing practice: "the absence of a single, monolithic term in the language(s) of the people who at present most visibly practice 'veiling' suggests significance to this diversity that cannot be captured in one term" (El Guindi, 1999, p. 7). Thus, the veil is more than the interpretation of *Shari'a* law; it is a complex phenomenon that embarks on a wide analysis of ethnic/cultural/local customs as well as social/political/historical and economic factors and is the most visible symbol of the accommodation operated by Islam with different and heterogeneous populations.

With the expansion of Islam, the 'Medina Community' came face to face with the conquered local population, especially the Byzantine and the Sassanian empires, where the seclusion of urban upper-middle class women was a common practice (El Guindi, 1999; Stowasser, 1994). After the death of the Prophet, Islamic jurisprudence was a still-developing apparatus, and the first caliphs kept the local traditions and cultural norms of the conquered populations: judges were appointed to administer local affairs by applying local customs based on their own understanding of the *Qur'an*. The practice of veiling, as Ahmed (1992) observes, was not introduced by Muhammad;[16] rather, it was a custom belonging to many pre-Islamic societies–the Mesopotamian, Hellenic, Byzantine, Sassanian, Persian, and Greek Empires as well

[16] It is worth remembering that pre-Islamic Arabia was essentially a matriarchal/matrilineal society which was slowly becoming a patriarchal/patrilineal society at the time of Muhammad's birth: during his life, only his wives used to veil (Ahmed, 1992).

as in the Christian Middle East and Mediterranean regions. Thus, what today is considered the 'Muslim veil' is in reality the visible symbol of the accommodation that Islam operated in its history with various heterogeneous populations. In fact, the uses, shapes and meanings of veiling have changed during the course of history and have been interconnected with several political and social factors; in pre-Islamic societies, the veil was worn by women for many reasons such as honour, protection, and to indicate a specific social status. The practice was adopted mainly by upper-class urban women who enjoyed considerable freedom, while peasant women were slow to adopt the practice because it interfered with their work in the fields (Esposito, 2005). While Assyrian law rendered the veil compulsory for upper-class women, the patriarchal structure of classical Greece interpreted the practice of veiling as being linked to women's seclusion (Ahmed, 1992). On the other hand, in ancient Egypt, where men and women enjoyed a form of legal equality, the practice of veiling was not associated with women's seclusion; rather, the veil was worn solely to communicate geographical belonging. Veiling, then, was adopted in Islam as a consequence of its encounter with other populations of the area where the practice was already in use: probably, the higher status of Arabs, the influx of wealth, and the example given by Muhammad's wives, also (but not exclusively) led to the adoption of the practice in Islam. In fact, "Islam selectively sanctioned customs already found among some Arabian tribal societies while prohibiting others" (Ahmed, 1992, p. 45). Thus, the varied uses of the veil in the area, which carried different meanings, emerged as the expression of different cultures, and not as a strict symbol of women's seclusion or Islamic religion.

During the Abbasid period, when the Muslim empire was at the apex of its expansion, women's veiling and seclusion became a common practice: their household role was important while men were abroad maintaining governmental structures of the emergent Islamic civilization. The Abbasid, which adopted the practice of women's seclusion from the Persian and Byzantine empires, operated a broad Arabization and Islamization of the conquered populations and the texts produced during that period mirror general assumptions of the chauvinist society of the time (Ahmed, 1992; Mir-Hosseini, 2007). Despite that, even during the Abbasid period, different Muslim communities maintained their own traditions, such as Sufi and Qarmatians, who were not secluded and never embraced the practice of veiling.

Nevertheless, Ahmed's analysis (1992) attests that from the fifteenth to the nineteenth century, during the Mamluk and Ottoman empires, women were quite active and present in the public sphere: they inherited property, as Islam permits it, worked in many business and textile activities, though with a modest income, and studied in different *madrasas* (schools). Moreover, most *Ulama* class women seem to have reached a high level of education. Ahmed (1992) reveals that women had a continuous interaction with other male Muslim scholars and that they were taught by both sexes.[17] It is worth noting, however, that women also experienced short periods of seclusion: in 1437, for instance, the plague was spreading in the Muslim empire. At that time, the sultan held a meeting with judges and jurists in order to find a way to

[17] Sufi women used also to be *sheik* and to perform religious chanting (Ahmed, 1992).

resolve the problem. It was decided that the plague was God's punishment for people's sin, especially 'adultery'. If, before the plague, women used to walk outside day and night, while the disease was spreading women were secluded and forbidden to leave their houses. These kinds of extreme limitations, however, lasted for very short periods (Ahmed, 1992). It is during the colonial period, to which I will return, that the veil comes to be understood (by westerners) as a fixed symbol of universal women's oppression and seclusion and (by the colonized) as a monolithic symbol of resistance. Before that period, as I have pointed out, veiling was not necessarily associated with women's seclusion and it took different meanings, shapes, and colours in the different geographical areas in which Islam took hold.

In fact, as Geertz (1971) argues, the universality of Islam comes exactly from its "ability to engage a widening set of individual, even idiosyncratic, conceptions of life and yet somehow sustain and elaborate them all" (p. 14). Some examples can be useful to understand how the expression of Islam in society has changed with time, cross-cultural interaction, gender, ethnicity and class. Local populations have adopted Islamic rules selectively in accordance with individual or group interests and the current realities of each geographic area. There are many examples of this pluralist understanding of Islam and the practice of veiling. I want to illustrate some of the most significant: Kazakhstan, the Minangkabau people in West Sumatra, and Niger/Nigeria. The first illustrates the accommodation of Islam with nomadic populations and syncretic religions; the second describes how Islam has been accommodated within a matrilineal system; while the third concerns the accommodation of Islam within African animist traditions. These varied and pluralist interpretations translate into different understandings of the practice of veiling.

The experience of women in central Asia is of particular interest considering the socio-ethnic variety and complexity of the region and the strong influence of socialist regimes over religions, which led to a different assimilation of Islamic precepts (Tohidi, 1998). The construction of gender roles in Kazakhstan is different from that of other central Asian Muslim communities due to the country's nomadic heritage. Islam gained a foothold only in the nineteenth century, when Tartar merchants and missionaries started to build Islamic schools and mosques. Prior to the arrival of Islam, Kazaks believed in one or two forms of syncretic religion and considered the *shaman* their spiritual leader. Examples of the accommodation of Islam with Kazak pre-syncretic religions can be found in many practices: when a *Mullah* (Islamic religious leader) is not present, for instance, it is the oldest men of the community who perform his tasks; the pilgrimage to Mecca, one of the five pillars of Islam, can be replaced with five visits to the grave of Hoja Akhmed Yassawi, an important poet and Islamic mystic. As their nomadic heritage is incompatible with the practice of female seclusion, Kazak women have never embraced this practice, nor the use of the veil, and they mingle freely with men: however, veiling has been adopted by sedentary Kazak women in recent years (Michaels, 1998).

Another interesting example is that of Minangkabau people, an ethnic/indigenous group situated in the highlands of West Sumatra, Indonesia, and in Malaysia (which is considered one of the most Islamized parts of the region) (Abdullah, 1966). Within Minangkabau society, magic and syncretic traditions are bound up with Islamic traditions and the *adat* local matrilineal system: the lives of the Minangkabau are thus regulated by Islamic precepts as well as by cultural norms (Sanday, 2003). This is mirrored in their ceremonials, which emerge as a mix of Islamic rituals, syncretism, animist and magic ceremonies. The complementary relation between *adat* and Islam is also mirrored in a famous aphorism, which states that "Minangkabau customary laws are based on the Holy Book, the Qur'an. For religious law, orders, *adat* applies. Nature is the teacher of humankind" (Joseph, 2005, p. 243). Although Muslim leaders in Minangkabau believe that women should be covered in Islamic dress style, except for their face and hands, to save their chastity and morality, many women simply wear modest dresses because the Minangkabau perception of morality is based on both *adat* and Islam. In contrast with Minangkabau women from Indonesia, those from Malaysia have assimilated Islam differently and Islamic law has supplanted the *adat*: most Minangkabau/Malaysian women wear the typical middle eastern *hijab* or a *jilbab* (a triangular fabric secured under the chin that covers the body from the head to below the shoulders) along with the traditional Muslim dress style, which comprises a loose tunic, called *sarogon*, and a filmy headscarf (Chadwick, 1991).

Niger/Nigeria is another interesting example of the accommodation of Islam with different cultural, historical and political contexts. In 1808, 'dan Fodio, a prominent Fulani Muslim scholar, launched a *jihad* (holy war) against the Hausa-speaking aristocracy based in Gobir,[18] which continued for almost half a century and culminated in the victory of the Fulani and the establishment of two caliphates. Before this, the region practised a wide and syncretic variety of Islam(s): although during the fourteenth and fifteenth centuries Islam was considered the most-practiced religion in the area, few people observed the five pillars of Islam, including the pilgrimage to the Mecca. During that period, people of the area drew their practices from both Islamic and animist traditions: "the two could be reconciled because much of the Islamic world recognizes the existence of spirits, or genies"(Cooper, 1998, p. 23). Thus, spirit cults, led by aristocratic urban women, continued to be performed in conjunction with Islamic practices, at least until the Fulani era. In the pre-Fulani period, then, women fully participated in the life of the community, working in the fields side by side with men, and leading religious rituals. Only upper-class women were veiled, and seclusion was not contemplated. With the victory of the Fulani, a less pluralist and more monolithic interpretation of Islam was introduced and established. However, in the Maradi Valley, where many emigrated during the Fulani's *jihad*, women continued to integrate Islamic precepts with their own way of life, whereas veiling and seclusion remained a custom of aristocratic women, as during the pre-Fulani period (Cooper, 1998). Yet, Nigerian women continue to use different kind of veils as a result of the accommodation of Islam with different cultures and traditions. Hausa wear the *Kallabi* (a one square metre of cloth tied to the forehead which covers only the head, sometimes partially),

[18] The advent of Islam within the Hausa population is dated from at least the fifteenth century, or even prior to that (Cooper, 1998).

or the *Gyale* (a two metre cloth which only partially covers the head), while Kanuri wear the *Mandil* (similar to the *Gyale*) or the *Lefaya* (similar to the Indian *Sari,* it is wrapped around the body to cover the shoulders from the back to the front). However, since the expansion of Islamic law at the end on the 1990s, the compulsory *hijab* has been introduced as a part of the school uniform (Mahdi, 2009).

Veiling, then, is lived, performed, and experienced differently, and acquires different meanings and interpretations based on historical, cultural and geographical contexts (Ahmed, 1992; El Guindi, 1999). The veil, like any other item of clothing, should be studied as a tool to understand social, cultural, and normative implications within a specific society: as Simmel (1957) observes in relation to clothes, "through their capacity to symbolize a social order, what is and what should be, [they] are related to social action and communication in a dynamic way" (p. 29). As the uses and the meaning of clothes change in different historical and cultural contexts, dressing becomes a 'situated body practice' which embodies and incorporates fluctuating power relations (Entwistle, 2000; Woodward, 2007) whereas the 'dressed body' emerges as a performance of embodied practices (O'Connor, 2005; Woodward, 2005). Likewise, veiling, like every other use of clothing, should be studied as a 'situated practice' which takes different shapes, colours and meanings based on specific cultural, historical and political contexts. Historically, the veil has emerged as an act of communication materialized by the reiteration of regulatory performative norms and it has assumed a multitude of meanings: it might indicate an individual's place within society; identity; geographical provenance; kinship; race; rank; class, territoriality, ethnicity, gender, etc. (Rubinstein, 1986; Whisner, 1982). The many meanings of, and differences over, the practice of veiling, this 'diversity within unity' (Bodman & Tohidi, 1998), indicates that, in order to understand why and how women wear the veil in Muslim majority societies, it is essential to take into consideration many factors, including, but not exclusively, Islamic precepts. In fact, thinking about Islamic law and culture as something fixed and monolithic obscures the process by which the practice of veiling is socially, politically and culturally constructed. As with many other cultures, Islam provides a general framework within which groups and individuals negotiate practices and construct different meanings of those practices based on specific historical and cultural contexts (Charrad, 1998).

2.3 From Plurality to Singularity: The Regulation of Female Clothes in the Era of Nations

Until the colonial period, in Muslim majority societies, both men and women wore the veil or other kinds of headscarf/face covering for many reasons and to many effects. The violent western economic/political/cultural imperialist colonization, along with the creation of western-style 'nation-state' in many other Muslim majority countries in the nineteenth century, has completely changed the meaning of the practice of veiling. From a plurality of meanings and performative outcomes, the (female) veil becomes a monolithic and static symbol of state/national identity/belonging: in fact, on the one hand, the veil has been elevated as a 'sign of' anti-western/anti-colonial/anti-imperialist struggles by Islamist and nationalist movements, while on the other, colonizers have seen in the practice of veiling a symbol of the backwardness of conquered populations needing to be 'saved' by colonizing forces. In other words, while my research shows that women who wear the veil understand the practice as carrying multiple meanings (Brems, 2014), the sovereign power (be it nationalist or colonial) has attached to the practice a fixed meaning for political goals. Notably, that only the female headscarf has been elevated as a symbol of cultural belonging is important as it reveals that in nationalist thought, women's body emerges as the terrain upon which territoriality, ethnicity and culture are established and reproduced. Since women within nationalist thought represent the biological and cultural reproducers of an 'imagined community', their plurality of performative practices, represented in the many uses and meanings of the veil, has been reduced to a singular, national, fixed subjectivity able to pursue a fictitious unity and homogeneity (Hasso, 1998).

For Anderson (1991), 'nation' is a socially constructed cultural 'artifact', an 'imagined community', which implies a process of imaginary individuals' identity formation, where people recognize themselves as belonging to a particular group/community: this sense of belonging is negatively constructed through differentiation and contraposition between the 'self' and the 'other', 'insider' and 'outsider' (Woodward, 2004). Women's body becomes a symbolic dividing line between different 'imagined communities', a useful tool to create unity and homogeneity through the figurative construction of an 'imagined' 'national' history, culture, and tradition. If individuals' perceptions are codified through symbols because they work at an individual's pre-symbolic level (Goodrich, 1995), then nationalism appropriates images, metaphors and symbols in the public sphere to create a specific paradigmatic and binary opposition between the self, citizen of the territorial 'nation-state', and the 'other', the 'outsider' (Landes, 2003) through women's body. In nationalism, men's and women's roles and responsibilities toward the nation became the focal point of the nation building process (Enloe, 1989). While women, according to nationalist thought symbolize the nation (the heart, the soil, the home, social customs and traditions), men assume the role of creating, building, and protecting the nation (Hogan, 2008). In nationalist thought, women's body emerges as the biological reproducer of ethnic/national group boundaries, the transmitter of ideology and culture, and as signifier of ethnic/national differences (Anthias & Yuval-Davis, 1989). This indicates that women's role within nationalist discourse lies in the symbolic meaning attributed to their bodies by nationalist thought: since they symbolize the community's biological/ethnic/cultural reproducer, they represent 'national boundaries', the signifier of ethical/cultural differences, the image of the 'Other' (Anthias, 1992).[19] One needs only to reflect on the many myths of

[19] Shachar (2001) notes that the word 'nation' derives from the Latin 'nascere' (to be born).

women's abduction, such as Helen of Troy or Ram and Sita, to understand "how gender and sexuality serve as the ground over which epic struggles about territoriality and morality have been historically waged. That women's bodies figure prominently in almost all nationalist and communitarian struggles (whether ethnic, racial, or religious) in the modern period only serves to strengthen this claim" (Mahmood, 2012, p. 56). Yet, it is not the exchange or the abduction of women, but their control which is the basis of social order and identity formation (Yuval-Davis, 1980). It is through the visual rhetorical construction of women's body that the nation-state produces a visible differentiation, a contraposition, a 'clash' between the 'self' and the 'other' which creates a homogeneous and fixed identity of the citizen of the nation-state.

With the 'politics of clothes', exemplified in the struggle over the veil, colonial power created a link between women's oppression and the culture of the 'other' to be used and abused to justify its colonization and occupation of 'Eastern' land. The 'politics of clothes', a 'politic of differentiation', has placed the veil as the most powerful symbol of the 'clash' between two dissimilar political systems: on the one hand, colonizers have seen in the veil the symbol of the backwardness of Muslim culture, while on the other, "standing in the relation of antithesis to thesis [...] [the colonized] reversed –but thereby also accepted – the terms set in the first place by the colonizers by elevating the veil as the symbol of their nationalist struggles. Thus, it is western discourse that in the first place determined the new meanings of the veil and gave rise to its emergence as a symbol of resistance" (Ahmed, 1992, p. 164).

In both cases, however, women's body emerges as an objectified symbol of the newly created nation-state: in other words, it becomes a field of struggle. Some examples can help us to understand how nationalism has appropriated and shaped women's body, specifically the (performative) practice of veiling, into a monolithic symbol of 'national difference': Palestine, Algeria, and Iran. These case studies provide interesting examples of how the meaning attached to the practice of veiling changed in the colonial period and how the female headscarf has been a useful tool to create a dividing line between 'us' and 'them'. In Palestine and Algeria, the meaning of the veil arose from the colonial context, while in Iran, invasive western influences, coupled with the creation of a 'modern' western-style nation-state by the Shah, have transformed the veil into the Iranian national symbol.

The identity of Palestinian women has been deeply shaped by the complex political context: the Israeli occupation, the strong impact on the country of foreign policies and the growth of anti-western nationalist movements have profoundly affected women's lives. In the case of Palestine, anti-colonial nationalist movements, "in adapting European nationalist thought to local conditions, [...] were faced with the task of defining not only the roles of men and women in the nationalist project, but also what a non-European nationalist masculinity would look like, and what kind of performances would guarantee it" (Charrad, 1998, p. 477). In fact, as Butler (1990) argues, nationalism, as well as sexual and gender identities, are performatively produced and reproduced by the regulatory practice of nationalist agency. Before the first intifada (1987), or 'Palestinian uprising', only peasants wore the veil as a symbol of geographical provenance or kinship belonging, while urban women were accustomed to wearing modest western-style garments. But the outbreak of the Intifada, in employing European nationalist practices, changed the pluralistic uses of the veil typical of the area: on the one hand, religious/nationalist parties, such as Hamas, started to call for a strict female 'Muslim attire' by linking Islamic faith with the national liberation struggle, while on the other, secular/nationalist parties, such as Fatah, 'abused' the character of the (veiled) peasant as a 'sign of' a past untouched by western powers and the violence of the Israeli occupation. By 1988, the streets of Gaza, where Hamas gained wide support, were filled with graffiti stating "Daughter of Islam, abide by *Shari'a* dress!" and "women who don't wear the *Hijab* are not patriotic", while 'un-veiled' women were repeatedly harassed (Hammami, 1990, p. 25). Women who did not conform with nationalist values were accused of being 'disloyal' to their community and their common national liberation struggle (Nagel, 1998).[20] In the West Bank, on the other hand, where national/secular parties were particularly strong, it was the image of the veiled peasant that distinguished Palestinian national identity from other Arab identities in the area (Swedenburg, 1990); in both cases, however, women's body became the symbol of Palestinian national, cultural and traditional values. Palestinian women became the symbol of the 'nation', the 'soil', the 'home', while men were the defenders of the 'nation'.[21] Women's body thus emerged as a matter of national honour and the defence of their bodies became the defence of the 'nation' itself. As a matter of fact, in the introduction of the Palestinian National Charter, as well as in Yasser Arafat's speech at the UN in 1974, the Israeli conquest of Palestine is pictured as a 'rape' of their land, while Palestinians are portrayed as the children of an 'abused' mother (Massad, 1995). Similarly, as Said (1985) argues, Zionists have seen Palestine both as the 'motherland' to which to return, and the 'virgin-land' ready to be fecundated by the newly created 'Jewish state'. Interestingly, during the 2014 Israeli-Gaza war, the City Council of Or Yehuda displayed a ban stating ""Israeli soldiers, the residents of Or Yehuda are with you! Pound their mother and come back home safely to your mother" (Sheen, 2014): in Hebrew, the term 'kansu' means 'beat', but it also has a colloquial connotation of 'sexual penetration'. The banner appeared after a sexualized image of an Arab woman was shared in Israeli social networks: the image portrays a woman labelled 'Gaza' who wears a black *niqab* and it is dressed from the waist up, showing her naked body from the waist down. The accompanying Hebrew text states: "Bibi, finish inside this time! Signed, citizens in favor of a ground assault" whereas, in Hebrew language, the term 'finish' has a colloquial meaning of 'ejaculate' (Sheen, 2014). Thus, as Mosse (1988) points out,

> "nationalism and respectability assigned everyone his place in life, man and woman [...] Alongside the idealization of masculinity as the foundation of the nation and society, woman [...] was at the same time idealized as the guardian of morality and of public and

---

[20] It should be noted that the emergence of the peasant as a national signifier is related to Zionism's refusal to recognize a specific Palestinian identity and 'land' (Swedenburg, 1990).

[21] As Pettman (1996) argues, in nationalism, the 'nation' is gendered female, while men, the main agent of the nation, represent the 'state'.

private order. The roles assigned to her were conceived of as passive rather than active [...] guardian, protector and mother [...] woman as a national symbol was the guardian of the continuity and immutability of the nation, the embodiment of its respectability" (p. 16).

In Algeria, the practice of veiling has situationally and historically assumed different meanings: before the colonial period, the *hijab* was worn by women to indicate tribal belonging. During the colonial period, however, the veil was portrayed by colonizers as a symbol of Algerian backwardness and at the same time elevated as a symbol of anti-colonial struggle by colonized people. In 1830, France colonized Algeria and assumed control over the country's political and economic sectors. Most importantly, French colonizers, supported by the massive Christian proselytising mission operated by the Church, imposed French law over the governing *Shari'a* law, destroying, in this way, the normative system that have governed the local population for centuries: education in the Arabic language was forbidden and even the academic curriculum was designed to mimic the French one. For the French, colonization was primarily a cultural battle aimed at transforming Algerians into 'French citizens'. Along with amending the legal and educational system, the French concentrated their efforts on changing the cultural heritage of the country. The veil became the benchmark for France's cultural and civilizing battle and emerged as the visual and symbolic form of colonization (Ahmed, 1992). By appropriating the visibility of Algerian women's body, French colonizers charged Algerian women with transforming Algerian men and the whole of Algerian society. Their political doctrine was simple: "if we want to destroy the structure of Algerian society, its capacity for resistance, we must first of all conquer the women" (Fanon, 2004, pp. 163–164). The metaphoric meaning given to the practice reveals that symbols are rhetorically constructed through competing national images and identities through which imaginary boundaries of nation, citizenship and geography are established (Vivian, 1999). In Algerian colonial discourse, the veil was "invested with a two-fold visibility of desires: a libidinal desire to pierce the veil – a desire to see beneath it – as well as an imperial desire to civilize or modernize Muslim society by removing the veil" (Vivian, 1999, p. 123). This is particularly clear in the postcard produced and sold by French colonizers at that time: images that portrayed sexualized veiled women revealing only the breast, or un-veiled/liberated Algerian upper-class women, to indicate the victory of France's 'mission of civilization'. The aim of the colonizers was to transform Algerian people into French citizens and the veil was the visible 'sign of' difference between France's 'civilization' and its colonies. The 'politics of clothes', in colonial Algeria, emerged as a marker of national homogeneity for both colonizers and colonized (Mcclintock, 1995). In fact, as a result of the passionate battle against the veil implemented by French colonizers, the *hijab* also assumed a new meaning for Algerians. The harsh conditions of colonized Algeria and the consequent feeling of injustice and dispossession had reinforced traditional behaviour and social norms and rendered the veil the symbol of Algerians' anti-colonization struggle (Fanon, 2004): in colonial Algeria, "every veil that fell, everybody that became liberated from the traditional embrace of the *haik* [the typical Algerian headscarf], every face that offered itself to the bold and impatient glance of the occupier, was a negative expression of the fact that Algeria was beginning to deny herself and was accepting the rape of the colonizer" (Fanon, 2004, pp. 167–168). The visible transformation of women's body was a key factor during de-colonization struggles in the country. In the Algeria national liberation struggle, women wore European dress in the heart of France, carrying messages or military equipment without attracting suspicion, while they wore the veil in their own country as a symbol of resistance against the occupation. Once women's role in the Algerian liberation movement had been revealed, the French launched a tremendous offensive against them. El Guindi (1999) reports French troops raping and torturing Algerian women: by violating women's body, French colonizers also violated Algerian men's honour, so support by the local population for the anti-colonial movement increased, until the withdrawal of French troops from the country in 1962 (Knauss, 1987).

In Iran, the veil has assumed different political meanings in different historical periods, revealing how women's body has been fashioned by different state ideologies (Roded, 2011): Iranian women's body has emerged as a field of struggle over identity claims (Najmabadi, 2005). In the Iranian case, women's opposition to veiling or un-veiling has emerged as an act of resistance to an assigned state/nationalist identity which passes through the juridical regulation of their bodies. Sedghi (2007) identifies three distinct economic and political phases of nineteenth century Iran: the Qajar dynasty, the Pahlavi dynasty, and the Islamic Republic of Iran. In each of these phases, Iranian policies of veiling, un-veiling and re-veiling have been a key element of the changing state national image: in every moment of political transition "the depiction of women's bodies as uncovered or masked, exposed or concealed and their designation as 'western' or 'Islamic' contribute to a specific form of national identity" (Sedghi, 2007, p. 277).

In pre-Islamic Persia, veiling was a common practice; during the Achaemenid Empire women observed seclusion and wore the traditional *chador*, a long veil that covers the body from head to toe. They were referred to as *zai'feh*, the weak sex, and *moti'eh*, obedient to men's will; their lives were strictly controlled by men and they were confined to the household (Sedghi, 2007). This situation lasted until the end of the Qajar dynasty (1925). When Reza Shah took power, the country was passing through a period of economic and political stagnation. The Shah, encouraged by the 1906 constitutional revolution, which saw a great and active participation of women claiming their constitutional and educational rights, gradually started implementing several reforms for the modernization of the country. Inspired by Ataturk, in 1936 the Shah decided to ban the veil in the name of Iranian westernization and modernization.[22] The ban was so strict that if women did not comply with it, they incurred a fine, or in some circumstances detention. The ban was enforced particularly in the country's main cities, in centres of capitalist development, while in villages women continued to wear the traditional rural *chador*. If, on the one hand, women protested

[22] In Turkey, Ataturk introduced many modernizing and westernizing reforms including the banning of the veil as a symbol of modernization (Ahmed, 1992).

against the ban, then on the other the promise of equal access to public space was underscored by the forced imposition of this law which, in the name of women's rights, denied them the freedom to choose what to wear: as Spivak (1988) argues, "it is in terms of this profound ideology of the displaced place of the female subject that the paradox of free choice comes into play" (p. 300). In essence, Iranian women at that time were placed in the position of choosing to accept the modernizing policies of the Shah or being targeted as 'obstacles' to the nation's renovation and modernization (Naghibi, 1999). As the ban attracted criticism from the clergy as well as from many women who felt uncomfortable walking in the street without the veil, in 1941 the Shah decided to repeal the ban. But the Shah's 'secular' government did not mean it to last for long; the general climate of dissatisfaction with western political and economic influence, coupled with the westernization policies operated by the Shah, created strong anti-Shah/anti-western feelings. In fact, the Shah allowed western powers to directly control the country's oil, sugar and tobacco industries in order to pay its debts to foreign powers: the population, then, started to see the newly established secular-national government as a puppet in the hands of the US. In the eyes of Iranians, the US was not only responsible for 'stealing' the country's natural resources, but also for imposing western cultures and values on the Iranian population (Davary, 2009). The rejection of western values spurred the demand for a 'return' to an authentic and 'untouched' 'imagined' past and the *hijab* became the most powerful symbol of the 1979 Iranian revolution broadcast by western media: while western women at the time gained the right to wear the 'mini-skirt', in Iran, women decided to re-veil and publicly show their support for the Islamic state by enforcing the revolutionary demands (Sedghi, 2007).

If, during the revolution, the veil acquired the symbolic meaning of public anti-western and anti-monarch feelings, after 1979, the newly established Islamic Republic of Iran adopted the veil as a symbol of national identity and passed a law to render the practice of veiling compulsory (Tohidi, 1994); in this way, the new government linked women's body with the newly established Iranian Republic where the safeguarding of women's appearance become the safeguarding of the state. From being a religious/cultural symbol, the *hijab* becomes a national symbol. In fact, the juridical regulation of women's bodies was part of a wider Islamization policy operated by Khomeini after the revolution[23] where the image of Iranian women mirrored anti-western positions and the *Shi'a* roots of Persian society. In the Iranian case, the regulation of women's body, particularly the practice of veiling, has continued to serve patriarchal powers, whether secular/nationalist or religious/nationalist, whereas the significance and visibility of the veil has been translated into concepts of nationhood, citizenship and cultural borders.

The cases I have taken into consideration reveal the gendered and misogynist practices and assumptions of nationalism. Racialized images of veiled women as victims of a chauvinist culture have justified imperialist wars and, more importantly,

[23] The Islamization policies of the Republic of Iran consisted mainly in three areas: first, the *Ulema*'s (the clergy body's) monopoly of power in the political system, second, the introduction of the penal Islamic code and third, the Islamization of social norms and morality.

they have produced a visual rhetoric of abjection toward the 'other': in the colonial period, the veil emerges as the dividing line between the 'self' and the 'other', 'citizen' and 'alien', 'friend' and 'enemy'; the visual representation of an 'imaginary' 'clash of civilizations' between good and evil (Cloud, 2004). It is during this period that the veil, a simple multi-meaning piece of cloth worn by women and men for a plurality of reasons, becomes the 'Muslim veil', a fixed symbol of the fluctuating Muslim culture. In particular, the genealogy and the history of the practice of veiling indicates that it was western discourse that created a link between the (backward) 'culture of the 'other' and women's body: this was later adopted by the colonized (Chatterjee, 1986; Said, 2003). Ultimately, "they are mirror images of each 'other'. The resistance narrative contested the colonial thesis by inverting it – thereby also, ironically, grounding itself in the premises of the colonial thesis" (Ahmed, 1992, pp. 165–166). As gender, nation and ethnicity are intertwined with nationalist and colonialist discourses, the racialized, gendered and fixed image of Muslim women's body has been a useful tool to justify imperialist struggles in the west as well as in the east (Spivak, 1988; McClintock et al., 1997; Yuval-Davis, 1997). In fact, in the colonial and post-colonial period, it is the 'image of the (female) veil', and not the veil itself, that becomes the symbol of the 'clash of civilizations' (Cloud, 2004); contrary to its intrinsic plurality, the veil has been constructed as a fixed symbol of the incompatibility between a 'backward' 'East' and a 'civilised' 'West'. Thus, in the colonial period, not only did the veil become a 'political symbol' but also, more importantly, it emerged as the example of the 'politics of clothes' in the nineteenth and twentieth centuries in the 'West' as well as in the 'East' (Charrad, 1998). In fact, it is through clothes, the most immediate and perceptible images in the public sphere, that a society constitutes its sense of uniqueness and belonging. What colonial powers did first, and then nationalist/religious/secular movements in Muslim majority societies, was to apply a secularized form of privatization of

> "religion that, in turn, helped secure the foundational distinction between the public and the private. The privatization of this aspect of social life did not mean, of course, that they feel outside the purview of the state; rather, they came to be increasingly regulated by the centralized state and its various political rationalities (no longer administrated by local muftis, qadis, customary norms, and parochial moral knowledge)" (Mahmood, 2012, p. 54).[24]

Therefore, the regulation of the veil can be seen as the regulation of private sentiments operated by a newly created centralized sovereign state, be it 'religious' or 'secular'. To the extent that veiling becomes a legal obligation, the veil, far from preserving Islamic values, hides an obsession with centralized law shared by both 'eastern' and 'western' nationalism.

---

[24] Notably, the distinction between private and public, absent in classical *sharia* law, was introduced by western colonizers and it is typical of the modern 'secularized nation-state'(Mahmood, 2012, p. 58).

2.4 Regulating Clothes, Regulating Subjectivities

The regulation of clothes, which reveals the link between clothes, forms of authority and women's body, has received considerable scholarly attention. For Hansen (2004), "because [clothing] both touches the body and faces outward toward others, dress has a dual quality [...] this two-sided quality invites us to explore both the individual and collective identities that the dressed body enables" (p. 372). In fact, since "forms of dress, as with forms of architecture, are not [only] mere metaphors for the power and authority of the political state [but] they instantiate the power and authority of the political state" (Watt, 2013, p. xv), the sovereign power has always had a particular interest in regulating clothes in the public sphere. After all, from Charles the Great until today, rulers have always tried to regulate dress in order to fashion similarity and differences in the public sphere (Brewer & Porter, 2013; Quataert, 1997): in the Roman Empire, for instance, citizens sentenced to exile were forbidden to wear the toga which was used to distinguish between the 'citizen' and the 'barbarian'. Similarly, the so called 'sumptuary laws', promulgated throughout European history to restrict luxury and extravagance, emerge as an intrinsic element in the formation of a specific 'visible' social order (Goodrich, 1998). In this sense, the regulation of clothes becomes a tool of political, social, and economic regulation, especially in periods of political and social change (Baldwin, 1923; Sponsler, 1992; Webb, 1912). In fact, since clothes are perceived as 'images', and 'images' have the power to fashion the public sphere, the legal regulation of clothes emerges as "the law's cultural commitment to the fabrication of a certain idea of the civil face and the force with which it seeks to fashion that face for itself and to enforce it on (and perform it for) society at large" (Watt, 2013, p. 144–5). In western and non-western history, the appropriation by the authorities of images and icons in the public sphere has been compounded with the implementation of rules related to clothes which, in the past and present, represent cultural boundaries, accepted or rejected images of an (imagined) community. Thus, by regulating clothes, law also regulates subjectivities; it places a mask on the real subject in the name of a fixed and monolithic law's subject.

In the course of history, rulers have spent considerable time and effort promulgating laws related to the individual's apparel in the public sphere. In teleological terms, clothes have been conceived through their symbolic meaning, as images, metaphors, of a specific order of things. Tertullian's interest in apparel, for instance, reveals how the regulation of the proper clothes to be exposed in the public sphere should mirror a divine transcendental order (Dunn, 2012). In his treatise, clothes emerge as a powerful image of an 'ordered society' through which the individual reads and interprets the external world, which, in turn, shapes her/his internal soul: in other words, for Tertullian, the external world should mirror the individual's internal 'being'. In fact, not only do clothes "make the human body visible"(De la Haye & Wilson, 1999) as they are located at the border between the internal self and the external world, but also, more importantly, their symbolic meaning is understood as a semiotic code which shapes our and others' perception of the world

(Eco, 1987).[25] Drawing from Saussure's system of language, Barthes (2006) argues that clothes are not simply a cultural phenomenon which defines a personal identity in a specific group, location and time, but they are a vehicle of meanings: they signify structures behind what is represented. As with every image, clothes have the potentiality to include and exclude and to delineate gendered territorial borders of an 'imagined community' (Anderson, 1991); as clothes express uniformity, hierarchy and regularity, they are concerned with the imaginary order of a community (Blake, 1994).

In Medieval Europe clothes were conceived as a mark of difference, a visible symbol of belonging, social status, religion and gender. In mid-to-late thirteenth century Europe, sumptuary laws aimed at restricting the wearing of certain apparel to the elites (as in Tertullian's treatise) or distinguishing Christian from non-Christian communities settled in the area. In 1215, for instance, the Fourth Lateran Council ruled that Jews and Saracens should wear different clothes in order to avoid confusion between them and the Christian majority. With the promulgation of sumptuary laws, the synod aimed at preventing the mingling of different religious groups: "it happens occasionally that through error Christians have sexual relations with the women of Jews or Saracens, and Jews or Saracens with the women of Christians" (cited in García & others, 1981, p. 107). Soon, Lateran IV shifted the legal regulation of clothes with the imposition of diverse 'signs' by introducing round badges of different colours: Jews were ordered to wear a red circular patch over their breast, Muslims and unbaptized people a yellow patch, while Christians who broke or challenged 'sumptuary laws' were forbidden to enter any church of the reign (Berend, 1997). Similarly, in thirteenth century Hungary, clothes were used to designate the 'other', the 'outsider', the 'stranger', an element of difference from the Christian majority settled in the country (Mellinkoff, 1993; Moore, 2008). However, the regulation of clothes to distinguish between different religions is not only a feature of European countries: in the near Middle East, the Umayyad Caliphs introduced diverse types of belt and headgear to distinguish Muslims from non-Muslims (Berend, 1997).

But sumptuary laws were not only aimed at distinguishing between religions: in the Ottoman empire, during the reigns of Sultan Osman III (1754–57) and Mustafa III (1757–74), both of which periods were characterized by internal conflicts and political stagnation, the regulation of clothes was used as a disciplinary tool to address order, social discipline, honour and austerity (Quataert, 1997): through the legal regulation of different headgear, clothes were used to indicate a specific individual's place within the society and to give people a sense of identity and belonging to a specific group in a 'well-ordered society'. The Ottoman empire, which at that time was facing many military defeats, needed to "assure Ottoman subjects and

[25] It is worth pointing out that, in Western history, clothes have always been understood as a 'sign of' an individual's interiority. Drawing from Saussure's system of language, Barthes (2006) argues that fashion is a form of language which is composed by signifier and signified. I will argue in the last Part of this book, clothes are not only a 'sign of', but they can also be used as 'means to' acquire specific values.

elites that the world was still an orderly place in which all retained their respective political and social positions" (Quataert, 1997, p. 407). Hence, clothing regulations were implemented to strengthen power relationships and the superiority of one group over another (men over women, Muslim over non-Muslim etc.). As Goodrich (1998) argues,

> "a person's place in the imaginary order of nation or class was also a question of the order of images [...], the regulation of dress, ornament, and food was linked to a theological and moral concern with the proper signs of identity and community. The legislation of the licit image of a person was linked indissolubly to the order of images and the role of symbols, of [...] the 'visible world' in public and private life" (p. 711-2).

The regulation of clothes served also to demarcate and secure sex and gender identities. A feature of women's clothes regulation concerned cross-dressing. In 1443 Venice, men who dressed as women were subjected to heavy fines, while in fifteenth century France, Louis XI imposed harsh punishments for prostitutes who wore male clothes. Meaningfully, in Medieval Europe, a great number of edicts and statutes relating to women's clothes were imposed: as women were excluded from the social public life, their position was related to that of men as the head of family (Hunt, 1996). If on the one hand, 'social anxieties' about dress have fluctuated in relation to women, on the other, what remains stable is the persistent obsession with women's modesty and morality through the centuries. This, in turn, has been associated with a certain anxiety in relation to the controllability of women: Hunt (1996) suggests that sumptuary laws related to gender emerge as a central part of the 'political economy of marriage' which is exemplified in the link between the dowry system and the promulgation of laws related to clothes. While for men the regulation of clothes expressed a specific social and economic class, for women sumptuary laws aimed at showing their respectability. In Siena, for instance, sumptuary laws prescribed a specific length of women's skirts (only married women could wear long trains) while in Florence, in 1464, sumptuary laws were more concerned with women's décolletage (women were allowed to wear a décolletage three centimetres below the collarbone). Tertullian's *De virginibus velandis* (Dunn, 2012) is one of the most important moral treatises of Christianity regarding the *De habitu virginum*, 'on the behaviour of virgins'. In his Treatise, he managed to justify virgins' compulsory veiling as motivated by God's will, and not local customs. His obsession for women's veiling was motivated by the desire to solve the problem of the different customs, cultures and traditions of the wide Christian community settled in diverse cultural and religious contexts. Rejecting the idea that Christianity could be an umbrella under which different customs and traditions could live together, for Tertullian the control of women's body was essential to create a strong and united Christian community. Interestingly, in trying to strengthen the unity of the Christian community, he elaborated the link between modesty and sexuality as a negative connotation: if virgins do not wear the veil in church, not only God but also other men will know about their virginity, hence their sexuality. Thus, virgins should veil in order to create a barrier between men and women who should reveal their body only to God. For Tertullian, the barrier created by the veil was a defence of the male desire for the female body, and vice versa. Notably, the link between the veil and women's sexuality drawn by Tertullian resonates in today's discourse about the Muslim veil, which understands the practice as a symbol of women's seclusion. Unlike in Muslim majority societies where the veil has assumed different meanings, in the west, from the Middle Ages, the veil has been negatively linked to sexuality, modesty and identity.

The focus on women's body in Medieval Europe, for instance, had particular emphasis during the period of the struggle between religious and secular authority. Though there was general consensus about the inferiority of women, secular and religious power constructed different discourses in relation to the 'woman question': for the Church, women's identity should be related to morality because signs of luxury were seen as a sin, while within secular discourse, women's luxury was associated with the 'economic wrong of extravagance' (Hunt, 1996). This tension is exemplified by (European) women's veiling; whereas, on the one hand, the veil was seen by the Church as a sign of religious piety and sexual modesty, on the other, the veil facilitated the concealment of identity. Thus, on the one hand, the Church favoured women's head covering while on the other, secular authorities expressed anxieties over the anonymity of women. As a matter of fact, in Siena, officials were obliged to ask veiled women the name of their father or husband: in the case, "what was at stake was the degree of freedom veils allowed for assignations that breached patriarchal control and exhibited some degree of personal and sexual licence. This is borne out by the fact that prostitutes were frequently forbidden to wear the veil" (Hunt, 1996, p. 223). Besides, there was always strict cooperation between secular and religious authorities, especially in Italy where the Church had a foothold (Hunt, 1996). All in all, what is significant about the attention paid to women's apparel is that it continues to be an obsession even nowadays: "appearance continues to be 'read' in much the same way as physiognomy was in the eighteenth century as a means of access to some underlying social essence [...] appearance is still read as a means of discerning the boundary between insiders and outsider" (Hunt, 1996, p. 397).[26]

Clothing regulations were also implemented to create unity and homogeneity: in 1337 Edward III of England forbade the exportation and the wearing of foreign clothes except by the royal family (Robson, 2013). The law stated that anyone acting or dressing as an 'Egyptian', a gypsy or a stranger was to be declared an outlaw. The fact that, in sixteenth century England, over twenty enactments on apparel were promulgated indicates the power of clothes to shape the public sphere and to create not only differentiation, but also homologation: if, on the one hand, clothes were regulated to establish class/group differentiation, then on the other the 'English man' was to be recognized exactly by his clothes. As, traditionally, external signs

[26] It is worth noticing that the veil was worn by European women until last century: in France, in the late nineteenth century, veiling was a symbol of fashion and elegance. It was worn for protection from the dust during a great architectural reordering of Paris but also to indicate a 'bourgeois respectability'. In eighteenth century London, women used to wear a full face velvet mask when walking in public parks (Watt, 2013).

were considered the mark of internal states, "legal concern with dress was a concern both with the indigenous, with a vernacular civility free of the stranger [...] and with all other cults that were suggestive of traditions and forces extrinsic to the native soil" (Goodrich, 1995, p. 88).

Therefore not only do clothes provide a sense of belonging, but also, more importantly, they delineate the border between 'citizen' and 'foreigner': the first is included within the pale of the law, while the latter comes to be excluded by the law (Goodrich, 1998). As identity is built through the negation of the 'image of the other', the rejection of 'foreign' clothes (with their specific shapes, cuts, and colours) is a precise political strategy to avoid 'foreign vices' and to create a sense of national belonging. Clothes, then, have been legally regulated not only to create the image of an 'ordered society', but also, more importantly, of a territorial unified (imagined) community. During a period of internal instability consequent upon the political challenge by Greek rebels to the centralized Ottoman empire (1821–1832), Mahmud II (1808–1839) imposed a fixed attire for different religious/cultural groups in order to shape a monolithic national identity and to create a sense of unity and identity in the fractured Ottoman empire. The law, as Quataert (1997) argues, was an anticipation of the *tanzimat* and its promises of equality before the law. The emphasis on unity is further exemplified by the 1934 Turkish Dress Act, which banned the wearing of religious symbols and attire (except in places of worship) in the attempt to create a strong and unified western-style nation-state (Elisabeth Johnson, 2008). Dis-similarly, in 1720s Turkey, where Muslim women were accused of dressing as Christians, a law enforcing modest dress was promulgated; the streets of Istanbul should have 'the face' of a Muslim country (Quataert, 1997). In both cases, the regulation and control of images in the public sphere emerges as a tool to create a specific legal subject by demarcating the boundaries of social thought and social reproduction through the regulation of women's body: since the power of images lies exactly in the opposition between orders of imagination, the legal regulation of specific clothes is a precise political strategy aimed at institutionalizing a mode of thinking based on the control of images, clothes, desires and human emotions by a centralized sovereignty, which institutes subjectivity through the control of images in the public sphere (Goodrich, 1995). In fact, as images have been instituted to transmit social power and to establish a specific political order, they have the power to constitute a specific kind of law's subject who is bound to a specific order of power and imagination represented and protected by the rules of law: thus,

> "whichever form the image took, either licit or illicit, iconic or idolatrous, its function was structural, it established the order of meaning and of law, it governed the soul by dictating what the heart could see or the mind portray of itself [...] the definition of an order of true reference, a doctrine or creed, required the designation of an order of signs through which the [...] subjects of law, could be ordered to imagine, perceive, understand, or know the invisible truth"(Goodrich, 1995, p. 42).

The aim of controlling clothes and images in the public sphere is therefore to institute a 'particular form of governance' and, along with it, a particular form of 'regulated' behaviour, where the law's subject emerges as emotionally attached to an 'imagined community'. In this sense, law allows a double movement: on the one hand, it excludes difference in the name of 'homogeneity' by excluding the 'stranger', the veneration of other gods and the possibility of other forms of rhetoric, while on the other, by imposing differentiation of clothes among different economic and social/gendered classes, it highlights differences between citizens. It is exactly in this sense that the new legal subject, with his/her new clothes, emerges as the image, the mirror, of a precise legal order, of law's appearance in the social realm. Hence, it is through a specific visibility, a form of appearance, that the identity of the sovereign and its community is formed.

In fact, as Foucault (2002) reveals, knowledge embraces both the 'visible' and the 'sayable' whereas each historical moment is the combination of these two elements: the 'visible', in contrast with the 'sayable', is a form of knowledge able to create multiple networks of power relations and subjectivities. The place assigned to the visible "demonstrate[s] that rhetoric functions epistemologically not only by virtue of the sayable [...] but also [...] through ways of seeing. The visible, as a means of knowledge-production, is rhetorical because such knowledge, rendered through complex networks of seeing and being seen that define entire fields of the visible" (Vivian, 1999, p. 132). Images, then, as well as clothes, create meanings: through their symbolic power, they 'move the mind' and they create a link between 'internal' and 'external', 'form' and 'substance'. As images are central in the construction of meanings, they function to create a link between rhetoric and ideology in the process of nation building (Edwards & Winkler, 1997). As I have pointed out, clothes are not only intended as mere 'appearance' but they should be analysed through their symbolic meaning, through which it is possible to conceptualize nationality, geography and gender as a rhetorical form of the visible which "make[s] the world known to different individuals, who thereby engage, on the basis of such knowledge, in the ongoing refashioning of life in the public spaces" (Vivian, 1999, p. 120). Thus, the visible, unlike the 'visual', which is a simple 'representation', depends upon a symbolic order that rhetorically produces forms of knowledge and behaviour. It is therefore clear that the aim of the law is not to 'cover' or 'uncover', but to 'order' and control the public sphere in order to rhetorically construct meanings and subjectivities.

The idea that clothes can cause 'disruption', or that they can be intended as 'a threat to the values of a society', as in the never-ending legal debate over the veil, shows that it is not the simple article of clothing but its symbology that can threaten the *status quo*. The power of clothes, I have argued, lies exactly in their location: since they are at the margin of the body, they symbolize the boundary between the self and the external world (Entwistle, 2001). It is therefore clear why, for centuries, rulers have promulgated laws related to clothes: the law intervenes to re-order what escapes from the control of a singular and fixed state sovereignty. Being a means of differentiation or homologation, the appropriation and control of images in the public sphere, mirrored in the laws related to clothes, becomes a useful tool to establish a collective national identity within 'nation building' processes through the visible negation of the 'other' (Robson, 2013). Hence, the juridical regulation of clothes emerges as the expression of the state's power and control over the private life of its subjects: in other words, the expansion of *regia potestas* over the subject's soul.

From now on, what is at stake in the regulation of clothes is the relation between the individual and the state: this relation, as Agamben and Murray (2008) argues, "concerns the routine inscription and registration of the most private and most incommunicable element of subjectivity –the biopolitical life of the body" (pp. 201–202). In fact, the regulation of clothes reveals that "public reason defines a private being which only has a legitimate existence within the public sphere of its representation" (Goodrich, 1995, p. 92). In fact, as I will argue in chapter four, the legal subject that emerges from the juridical decisions concerning the practice of veiling is a fixed and abstract mask, created and subjugated *by* and *through* the regulation of a specific form of visibility. As Goodrich (1998) reminds us, the subject is said to have a 'legal personality': the term derives from the Latin *persona* which indicates the actor's mask. But as the mask does not correspond with the wearer, the legal person does not correspond with the human (Esposito, 2015). *Persona*, then, is not the individual, but the representation of its legal status which varies according to power relations.[27] From now on, *persona* emerges as an appearance, an optical presence, a mask that gives visibility to the human within a public sphere which is understood as a mere place of visibility.

2.5 On Plurality and Singularity: The Symbology of the Veil as a 'Clash of Civilizations'

As I have argued, historically the regulation of clothes had the power to establish the link between specific forms of sovereignty, the (female) subject, and the visibility of her clothed body. In today's discourse the headscarf is often portrayed as the symbol of a 'clash of civilizations' between a modern/liberal west and an intolerant east. Despite the plurality of meanings in the practice of veiling, today's discourse indicates that the veil has been assigned a fixed meaning that bolsters a specific form of sovereignty through the visible regulation of women's body. I employ Diamantides' analysis (2012, 2015) of sovereignty formation in the east and in the west in order to disclose how western forms of sovereignty are intrinsically linked to the visibility of the female body. Diamantides' (2012, 2015) comparative study reveals that the so called 'clash of civilizations' is the progeny of similarities rather than differences. If anything, where Muslim female attire is concerned, those two modern and political systems–secularised Christian and fundamental Islamist–should be analysed in their similarities. In fact, both are obsessed with the regulation of women's dress and agree that the dress code of Muslim women cannot be a question of personal choice within the ordinary and changeable confines of current fashion and public decency rules; where the two sides disagree is on whether to enforce the so called religious dress code or its opposite, one that reveals more than conceals. My

[27] Esposito (2015) reminds us that *persona* in Roman legal doctrine refers to an individual's social role.

analysis reveals a symmetry between the use of western positive law, and 'positivized' *Shari'a* law – such as that proposed by Islamists – not so much to physically dress or undress Muslim women but to bind their bodies to a fixed, transparent and singular identity. More or less clothed, more or less naked, women's bodies, associated with male pleasure and social reproduction, must emit desirable information. Thus, the female body, clothed or exposed, Muslim or Christian-cum-secular, emerges as an 'objectified' field of struggle, a still quite patriarchal modernity – secular or Islamist; as women are seen as the reproducers of ideologies and transmitters of tradition and culture (Landes, 2003; Yuval-Davis, 1993), they have to be able to reproduce a specific law's subject who is bound to a fixed and universal law.

Diamantides' comparative analysis of sovereignty formation in the 'East' and in the 'West' draws on Nancy's (2003) 'monotheist model of social organization.' He argues that in all monotheistic societies religious law gradually expands to cover more 'secular' concerns, to the point where the process of production of legal meaning is secularized, with little or no connection to core religious beliefs. In this way, by authorizing a system of law that deals with the temporal, religion itself is 'demystified': this process, as Martel (2014) points out, leads to a fetishization of law as a substitute for the withdrawn God. Nancy (2003) identifies three 'auto-deconstructionist characteristics' typical of all 'monotheistic model[s] of social organization' which lead to the 'demystification of religion'. Firstly, monotheism 'is in truth atheism'. In fact, the presence of many gods in the 'pre-monotheist' societies corresponded to an effective plurality in nature which is organized by religion through myths; in this sense, "the unicity of God [...] signif[ies] the withdrawal of God from presence and thus also from the power thereby understood"(Nancy, 2003, p. 42). Secondly, 'monotheistic religion' manifests itself historically as a composition of narratives and myths and emerges as the elaboration of Greek philosophical consciousness and Roman/statist juridical legacy. The third characteristic follows the former: the 'demythologization/demystification of religion', which founds its expression in the construction of mythical narratives, was gradually substituted by narratives concerning human affairs, such as concepts of human rights and democracy in the west, and liberation/decolonization theories in the near east and elsewhere; ultimately, these 'secular' western concepts produced a legalism which is nothing more than the substitute for God's supreme power. For Diamantides (2006), the above framework allows the comparative analysis of two "structurally similar and contingently dissimilar" (p. 97) legal systems of religious origins. While the comparison reveals that in both cases the power to make law acts as a substitute for God's supreme power, only in the west was this fully articulated with the development of the doctrine of sovereignty. By contrast, Islamic law's precise relationship with political power has developed in a much less linear way and the different periods of its cross-fertilization with Greek philosophy and Roman law, before and after colonialism, should be analysed.

The history of Islam is marked by three important periods: the first is characterized by a clear separation between political and legal power in which local judges enjoyed great freedom in their legal adjudications; the second is marked by a partially successful assimilation of Graeco-Roman-Christian elements, which was fundamental for the creation of an 'expansionist nation-state'; while the third is signed by the 'westernization' and 'secularization' of Islamic law, which founds its expression in concepts such as nationalism, liberation/decolonization and self-determination theology, typical of the 'new modern secular ideology'.

After the death of the Prophet (632 CE), the early caliphs (632–661 CE) ruled the conquered provinces far from the capital, and left legal and administrative matters to local *qadis* (early judges), wise people respected by the conquered population (Hallaq, 2005). They were accustomed to adjudicating legal cases based on the principle of *ra'y*, discretionary opinion, which was based on *Sunna Madiya* (past exemplary actions including the life of the Prophet and the earlier caliphs) and common sense, while "rules of law as the *Qur'an* and the *Sunna* established were regarded simply as ad hoc modifications of the existing customary law" (Coulson, 1978, p. 4). The first period of Islam was marked by lack of centralization policies where *qadis* enjoyed interpretative freedom while the production of jurisprudence was case driven and sensitive to local customs. One immediate result of this was the safeguarding of the conquered population's customary law and pre-Islamic practices (Hallaq, 2005), including the practice of veiling which, as I have argued, was used to indicate class, gender, geographical provenance, kinship belonging, etc.

The seventh century marked a profound change in the function of the *qadis*: they were no longer wise people recognized by the local population but experts in law, appointed solely for judicial functions. Hence, the domain of legal procedures was in the hands of the new 'specialized' class while the study of legal discipline was in the hands of the *mufti*, or *Ulama*, who served as legal consultants for the *qadi* and on the issue of *fatwa* when it was needed. This historical moment of Islamic law's evolution marked not only the professionalization of the *qadis* and the development of specialized legal scholars (*Ulama*), but also the pluralistic textualization of the law and the development of many Islamic juridical schools.[28] Jurists generated *fiqh*, the body of legal knowledge, in the main Islamic centres scattered throughout the vast Muslim empire and elaborated a heterogeneous system of law, differing from place to place and from school to school (or *madhhab*). The scholars of each *madhhab* followed the legal doctrine of a particular *Ulama* who, in turn, followed the positive doctrine of his predecessors (Hallaq, 2005). The first period of Islam was therefore characterized by a pluralist interpretation of Islamic law and by the gradual development of a professional, but not hierarchically organized, judiciary body. The established law included all the subjectivity of the heterogeneous society of the time (including Christians and Jews, considered part of the *Umma*, the Muslim community, in the *Qur'an*).

This "version of law-bound-universality" (Diamantides, 2006, p. 100) represented a challenge for a new generation of caliphs, the Umayyad (661–750 CE), who attempted to create a centralized and expansionist state. It was during the Umayyad period that Islam witnessed the first attempt at law's appropriation by

---

[28] It is worth nothing that despite the proliferation of *Hadith*, legal jurisprudence continued to be based also on the *ra'y*, discretionary opinion, until the eighth century (Hallaq, 2005).

political power, the gradual separation of the ruling elite from the people and the egalitarian form of governance of the firsts caliphs. Scholars and *qadis* started to identify political power with dishonesty, corruption and depravity in contraposition to the pious jurists. By the eighth century, anti-Umayyad sentiments spread and tension between political and legal powers increased when many jurists began to defend the population in preference to the ruling class. As a tool to struggle against the central political power, the *Ulama* started to use the hermeneutic system of interpretation of the *Hadith*. The development by the *Ulama* of a sharpened technique for authenticating the prophetic *Hadith* "*was* precisely a means to control the process of legitimation of state power by association with (invented) good practice"(Diamantides, 2012, p. 58). This phase of Islamic law's evolution is marked by a clash between local and centralized concepts of power, where the *Ulama* played a radical 'political role' in defending their legal authority from the appropriation of legal affairs by the central political power. Clearly, the ruling elite needed control of the law in order to govern the population, and jurists represented the link between the ruling political elite and the masses; in other words, they were the only ones that could give legitimacy to the political authority. This had diverse political implications in the history of Islamic law:

> "a ruler who has no say at all in the definition of the law by which his subjects have chosen to live cannot rule those subjects in any but a purely military sense [...]. Rulers were obeyed as outsiders to the community, not as representatives of it [...] The state was thus something which sat on top of society, not something which was rooted in it" (Crone, 1986, p. 109).

The struggle between legal and political power came to an end in the middle of the fourteenth century, when the political power, lacking the support of the local population, recognized that only the *Ulama* could interpret the law of God and accepted the existence of different books of Islamic law. Although the Umayyad dynasty never succeeded in creating a unique law valid for all its citizens, they marked the 'Arabization' and 'Islamization' of the Muslim empire through a process of conversion and assimilation of 'non-Muslims'. Notably, the regulation of clothes started with the Umayyad, when Islam witnessed the first (unsuccessful) attempt at 'secularization' in the name of a new (fixed) 'Islamic identity'; in order to fashion the new centralised Islamic empire and to create an 'Islamic identity', the Umayyad introduced different coloured belts to distinguish between Muslims and non-Muslims and they instituted the *ghiyār*, a term used to indicate a specific item of cloth, behaviour and hairstyle (Yarbrough, 2014).

An attempt at western-style centralization and sovereignty under a self-proclaimed 'God's Caliph' was further pursued by the Abbasid dynasty. The new 'centralized Islamic theocracy' (750–1258 CE) tried to concentrate political and legal power in the figure of the caliph to gain absolute power over the vast Muslim empire (Esposito, 2005). The Abbasid caliphs financed the translation of classical Greek work into Arabic in an attempt to promote a singular canon law to be interpreted and applied using Aristotelian logic and dialectic disputation. For the first time in the history of Islam, legal scholars employed by and loyal to the caliphs started to use dialectic concepts in the hermeneutic interpretation of the *Sunna*.

Scholars were asked to compose books based on logic and dialectic argumentation to oppose the 'heretics': they imposed the *Mihna*, or inquisition, on those who refused to obey the sovereign and its law and, for the first time in the history of Islam, the veil started to be legally regulated (Hallaq, 2005). The Abbasid interpreted the term *hijab* as 'confinement', and women's body as *awra*: since women's body was a source of *fitna* (chaos), the Abbasid imposed women's seclusion and the use of the face veil for all women, except for female slaves (Mir-Hosseini, 2007). The Abbasid period witnessed the closing of the door of legal interpretation and the formation of the four main Sunni Islamic schools of thought as well as the production of the book of *fiqh* (Islamic jurisprudence): Islamic law started to cover systematic legal principles. Caliph Mansur (754–775 CE) tried to create a comprehensive body of law valid for all the conquered population. He sought to create a monolithic, united and universal Muslim juridical community and offered the founder of the Maliki school of thought an endorsement of his book of law as the unique law valid in the whole empire: surprisingly, however, Maliki refused, alleging his respect for the other schools of thought by referring to a famous dictum of the Prophet; 'my community will never err' (as cited in Schimmel, 1992, p. 61).

The Abbasid's attempt to create a fixed, unique and positivised Islamic law mirrors the operation of western Christian scholars, who reinterpreted Roman law to found the canon law. Returning to Nancy's thesis of 'monotheist model of social organization' (2003), law becomes central in the sense that all monotheistic religions seek to be materialized in a collective conscience. In the west, the operation of medieval theologians, who re-elaborated the Roman law of heritage and translated it in favour of a unique sovereign with an *infinite* and absolute authority, be it the king or the pope, represented a 'political' re-elaboration of Christian mythologies in the name of a common identity. Western medieval theologians managed to create the concept of absolute 'sacred sovereignty' (absent in the Muslim world) through the sacralisation of the institutional body, in which the royal power emerged as the 'rightful power' to rule both the relationship between humans and that between God and humankind (Bloch, 1973). The codification of Roman law in the name of the 'public good guided by God' had developed a power that expressed itself through legislation whereas, on the one hand, law acquired a universal value supposedly suitable outside European borders, while on the other, tribunals acted in the place of God.

Differently, in the Islamic world the struggle between legal and political powers, between *Ulama* and caliphs, prevented the process of law codification, and the law's textualization was constantly in need of negotiation with the local legal authority. Although both, the west and the east, passed through the assimilation of a Roman/statist/juridical legacy and Greek dialectic concepts, only in Islam did this assimilation signify a shift from a relative freedom of judges and jurists to a more structured legal system. Hence, prior to the Ottoman empire and the colonization period, the problem of creating a united people represented by a sovereign did not exist in the Muslim world, as collective representation was never totally embodied by a (unique) sovereign authority. In fact, unlike Christian ecclesiastical law and positive law, in Islamic law the concept of *Umma* is central. The *Umma*, which includes a plurality of heterogeneous religions, suggests that not all human associations need an absolute sovereign that separates 'us' from 'them': importantly, "the *Umma* retains its integrity despite lacking in a corresponding theory of doctrinal and political unity–be it of the Kelsian (normative) or the Schmittian (substantive) sort" (Diamantides, 2012, p. 60). In fact, in the Muslim world, the clergy body has developed a rational and coherent jurisprudence without relying on Hartian theories. This is related to the fact that Islam does not have a hierarchical structure and jurists and scholars did not have any interest in gaining power from their local *Umma*.

The situation did not change until the nineteenth century, when the Ottoman sultans (1299–1922)[29] modelled their new 'Muslim empire' on the European sovereign 'nation-state' (similar to the 'western model of state organization' but unfamiliar with the heterogeneous local cultures of the area) by rendering the Hanafi book of law the only one valid in the empire in the hands of the sultans, and by introducing elements of the French legal system. Ottomans set up a new form of centralized administration in which *Ulama* and jurists were appointed directly by the central power and incorporated within the state's bureaucracy (Hallaq, 2002). By absorbing Islamic institutions within the state, sultans tried to fashion a comprehensive 'Muslim identity' where "Islam becomes an identity defined by external differences from 'others' and law frames the points of distinction"(Diamantides, 2006, p. 116): the world started to be divided into 'the house of Islam' (*dar al Islam*) and 'the house of war' (*dar al harb*) and the sultan became the guardian of a new Islamic order. With the Ottomans the process of 'secularization of Islam' began to be westernized. In order to create a 'well-ordered' society and to halt internal political conflicts, the sultans used the regulation of clothes as a disciplinary tool: they imposed the wearing of different headgear based on socio-economic class and imposed different attire to distinguish between different religious affiliation.

The subsequent colonization period (from the sixteenth to the mid-twentieth century) marked even more profound changes with a 'modernizing' and 'westernizing' process; the imposition of law codification; the adoption of legal positivism by newly created law faculties; and the parallel decline of the *Ulama* system of education which corresponded to the loss of communication of ideas among different Muslim schools of thought, now confined to 'family law'. The codification of Islamic law signified a reduction of legal and cultural plurality typical of the Muslim world: consequently, the individual was gradually bound to a singular, monolithic, and positivised law emanating from a 'sovereign' of the 'new nation-state' (Hallaq, 2002). As Hallaq (2002) points out, "codification is not an inherently neutral form of law-making, nor is it an innocent tool of legal practice, devoid of political or other goals. It is in fact a deliberate choice in the exercise of political and legal power, a means by which a conscious restriction is placed upon the interpretative freedom of jurists, judges and lawyers" (p. 1712).

[29] After the Abbasid's defeat, three main Muslim empires arose: the Ottoman empire (which included North Africa, the Arab world and Eastern Europe), the Persian Safavid empire, and the Mogul empire (which included modern Pakistan, India and Bangladesh) (Esposito, 2005).

A fixed, monolithic and positivized Islamic law in the hands of a unique sovereign is nowadays re-claimed by Islamists. In fact, what Islamists are seeking is not the 'true', 'pure' Islam, typical of Medina, where the law was made locally and reflected the plurality of cultures of the *Umma*, but the legal edifice sought in the Abbasid period which reinforces central political power by binding the community to a singular all-encompassing legal code as well as a 'national' 'Muslim identity'. Like the Abbasid, Islamists advocate the use of the veil as a fixed symbol of compliance with Islamic precepts (Ahmed, 1992; Guthrie, 2013; Mir-Hosseini, 2007) and call for the establishment of a 'positivized' (*Sharia*) law able to bind subjects to a fixed unique national identity: in this sense, Islamists try to finish what previous expansionist Muslim empires tried, unsuccessfully, to achieve and, using Nancy's terms, to operate a 'secularization of Islam'. In fact, Islamist fundamentalists rely more on the body of *fiqh*, which they invest with an absolute political power, than on the Islamic legal primary sources (*Qur'an* and *Sunna*).

Returning to Nancy (2003), if the 'demystification/secularization process' operated by monotheistic religions ultimately means the creation of a legalism as substitute for God's supreme power, then in the west, the 'secularization of religion' founds its political expression in principles such as democracy and human rights, while in the Islamic world it founds its political expression in ideas such as nationalism, liberation theology and self-determination; hence, the 'post-colonial instrumentalization' of Islamic law operated by Islamists corresponds to an unconscious return of western elements where law is uniform and centrally produced (Diamantides, 2006). Thus, while the west conceives a universal, abstract identity valid for everyone which is historically tied to Christianity and was exported to Muslim majority societies during the colonial period, Islamists respond by trying to change the content but maintain the same Christian/liberal/secular western structure of one universal law imposed by the appropriate authority. In other words, the Islamist political system emerges as a secularized form of Islamic religion, exactly as secular contemporary western governments are a secularized form of the Christian religion in the name of an absolute, binding, power. As in the west, the political transformations in which Islamists believe are to happen through law's enforcement and the regulation of images in the public sphere: "in both cases law produces the subject and that is why it carries an absolute value" (Diamantides, 2006, p. 113).

Diamantides' (2006, 2012, 2015) comparative analysis indicates that the difficulties between the Islamic and western worlds are not related to a 'clash of civilizations', as much of the media echoes: rather they express the tensions between the encounter of two universalist forms of monotheism. In light of this, the so called 'clash of civilizations', symbolised in the practice of veiling, is nothing more than the anxiety produced by two dogmatic legal systems over the condition of their own incompleteness and internal shortcomings (Diamantides, 2006): on both sides a mechanism of defence and attachment to their respective laws develops. Both western liberals and Islamists aim at instituting through the force of the rules of law a fixed law's subject bound to a positive unique and universal(ist) law. Both are concerned with the legal regulation of the female body, in particular the headscarf: but while Islamists advocate compulsory veiling, referring to a westernized and secularized version of *Sharia* law, western liberals call for the un-veiling of women as a means to include them within the pale of western/Christian/secular law. Both (patriarchal) regimes aim at legally regulating and controlling women's attire by inscribing women's bodies as a monolithic symbol of cultural belonging, and not as subjects of history. In fact, as I have argued, the female figure and/or dress code are common collective group and nationalist symbols which disclose the link between the dressed female body and forms of sovereignty.

Today's obsession over the *hijab* hides a fundamental similarity, namely, the desire of authority to bind the subject to fixed rules of law through the juridical regulation of women's body. Therefore, what the history of the meaning(s) attached to the practice of veiling reveals is the increasing intrusion of the state's authority into the individual's private sphere, where the regulation of the visibility of women's body emerges as a useful tool to change both the internal and the external world of the subject, thereby creating an emotional attachment to an imagined community.

References

Abbott, N. (1941). Women and the State on the Eve of Islam. *The American Journal of Semitic Languages and Literatures, 58*(3), 259–284.

Abdullah, T. (1966). Adat and Islam: An examination of conflict in Minangkabau. *Indonesia, 2*, 1–24.

Agamben, G., & Murray, S. J. (2008). No to biopolitical tattooing. *Communication and Critical/Cultural Studies, 5*(2), 201–202.

Ahmed, L. (1992). *Women and gender in Islam: Historical roots of a modern debate*. Yale University Press.

Al-Azmeh, A. (2006). *Making governance work against radicalisation*. DIIS working paper. https://www.econstor.eu/handle/10419/84517

Ali, A. Y. (2000). *The holy Qur'an*. Wordsworth Editions.

Allen, P. (2016, March 30). *Minister compares veiled women to "negroes who supported slavery."* Mail Online. http://www.dailymail.co.uk/news/article-3516233/French-minister-compares-veiled-women-negroes-supported-slavery-Politician-sparks-outrage-questioning-rise-fashion-lines-cater-Muslims.html

Anderson, B. (1991). *Imagined communities: Reflections on the origin and spread of nationalism*. Verso.

Anthias, F. (1992). *Racialized boundaries: Race, nation, gender, colour and class and the anti-racist struggle*. Routledge.

Anthias, F., & Yuval-Davis, N. (1989). *Woman-nation-state*. Macmillan.

Asad, T. (2009). The idea of an anthropology of Islam. *Qui Parle, 17*, 1–30.

Baldwin, F. E. (1923). *Sumptuary legislation and personal regulation in England* (Vol. 44). The Johns Hopkins Press.

Barthes, R. (2006). *The language of fashion* (English ed.). Berg.

Berend, N. (1997). Medieval patterns of social exclusion and integration: The regulation of non-christian clothing in thirteenth-century Hungary. *Revue Mabillon, 8*, 155–176.

Blake, C. F. (1994). Foot-binding in neo-Confucian China and the appropriation of female labor. *Signs, 19*, 676–712.

Bloch, M. L. B. (1973). *The Royal Touch: Sacred monarchy and scrofula in England and France*. McGill-Queen's University Press.

Bodman, H. L., & Tohidi, N. E. (1998). *Women in Muslim societies: Diversity within Unity*. Lynne Rienner Publishers.

Brems, E. (2014). *The experiences of face veil wearers in Europe and the law*. Cambridge University Press.

Brewer, J., & Porter, R. (2013). *Consumption and the world of goods*. Routledge.

Butler, J. (1990). *Gender trouble: Feminism and the subversion of identity*. Routledge.

Calderini, S. (2013). Female seclusion and the veil. two issues in political and social discourse. In T. Gabriel & T. Hannan (Eds.), *Islam and the veil. theoretical and regional context*. Bloomsbury Academic.

Chadwick, R. J. (1991). Matrilineal inheritance and migration in a Minangkabau community. In *Indonesia* (pp. 47–81). Cornell University Press.

Charrad, M. (1998). Cultural diversity within Islam: Veils and Laws in Tunisia. In H. L. Bodman & N. Tawhīdī (Eds.), *Women in Muslim societies: Diversity within unity*. Lynne Rienner Publishers.

Chatterjee, P. (1986). *Nationalist thought and the colonial world: A derivative discourse?* Zed for the United Nations University.

Cloud, D. L. (2004). "To veil the threat of terror": Afghan women and the< clash of civilizations> in the imagery of the US war on terrorism. *Quarterly Journal of Speech, 90*(3), 285–306.

Cooper, B. M. (1998). Gender and religion in Hausaland: Variations in Islamic practice in Niger and Nigeria. In H. L. Bodman & N. Tawhīdī (Eds.), *Women in Muslim societies: Diversity within unity*. Lynne Rienner Publishers.

Coulson, N. J. (1969). *Conflicts and tensions in Islamic jurisprudence*. University of Chicago Press.

Coulson, N. J. (1978). *A history of Islamic law* (Pbk. ed.). University Press.

Crone, P. (1986). *God's Caliph: Religious authority in the first centuries of Islam*. Cambridge University Press.

Davary, B. (2009). Miss Elsa and the veil: Honor, shame, and identity negotiations. *Journal of Feminist Studies in Religion, 25*(2), 47–66.

De la Haye, A., & Wilson, E. (1999). *Defining dress: Dress as object, meaning, and identity*. Manchester University Press.

Diamantides, M. (2006). Toward a Western-Islamic conception of legalism. In P. Goodrich, L. Barshack, & A. Schutz (Eds.), *Law, text, terror: Essays for Pierre Legendre*. Glass House Press.

Diamantides, M. (2012). Shari'a, faith and critical legal theory. In M. Diamantides & A. Geary (Eds.), *Islam, law and identity*. Routledge.

Diamantides, M. (2015). Constitutional theory and its limits – Reflections on comparative political theologies. *Law, Culture and the Humanities, 11*(1), 109–146. https://doi.org/10.1177/1743872112437683

Dunn, G. D. (2012). Tertullian. In R. S. Bagnall, K. Brodersen, C. B. Champion, A. Erskine, & S. R. Huebner (Eds.), *The encyclopedia of ancient history*. Wiley.

Eco, U. (1987). *Travels in hyperreality* (W. Weaver, Trans.). Picador.

Edwards, J. L., & Winkler, C. K. (1997). Representative form and the visual ideograph: The Iwo Jima image in editorial cartoons. *Quarterly Journal of Speech, 83*(3), 289–310.

El Guindi, F. (1999). *Veil: Modesty, privacy, and resistance*. Berg.

Enloe, C. (1989). *Bananas, beaches and bases*. Pandora Press.

Entwistle, J. (2000). *The fashioned body: Fashion, dress, and modern social theory*. Polity Press.

Entwistle, J. (2001). The dressed body. In J. Entwistle & E. Wilson (Eds.), *Body dressing*. Berg.

Esposito, J. L. (2005). *Islam: The straight path* (Rev. 3rd ed., updated with new epilogue.). Oxford University Press.

Esposito, R. (2015). *Persons and things: From the body's point of view*. Wiley.

Fanon, F. (2004). Algeria unveiled. In *Decolonization: Perspectives from now and then* (p. 5). Routledge.

Foucault, M. (2002). *The order of things: An archaeology of the human sciences*. Psychology Press.

García, A., & others. (1981). *Constitutiones concilii quarti Lateranensis una cum commentariis glossatorum* (Vol. 2). Biblioteca Apostolica Vaticano.
Geertz, C. (1971). *Islam observed: Religious development in Morocco and Indonesia* (Phoenix ed.). University of Chicago Press.
Geertz, C. (2000). *Local knowledge: Further essays in interpretive anthropology*/(3rd ed.). BasicBooks.
Ghamidi, J. A. (2013). Norms of gender interaction. In T. Gabriel & R. Hannan (Eds.), *Islam and the Veil. Theoretical and Regional context*. Bloomsbury Academic.
Goodrich, P. (1995). *Oedipus lex: Psychoanalysis, history, law*. University of California Press.
Goodrich, P. (1998). Signs taken for wonders: Community, identity, and a history of sumptuary law. *Law & Social Inquiry, 23*(3), 707–728.
Guthrie, S. (2013). *Arab women in the middle ages: Private lives and public roles*. Saqi.
Hallaq, W. B. (2002). Muslim rage and Islamic law. *Hastings Law Journal, 54*, 1705.
Hallaq, W. B. (2005). *The origins and evolution of Islamic law* (Vol. 1). Cambridge University Press.
Hammami, R. (1990). Women, the hijab and the intifada. *Middle East Report, 20*(3 & 4), 24–28.
Hansen, K. T. (2004). The world in dress: Anthropological perspectives on clothing, fashion, and culture. *Annual Review of Anthropology, 33*, 369–392.
Hasan, U. (2011). The veil: Between tradition and reason, culture and context. In T. Gabriel & R. Hannan (Eds.), *Islam and the veil. theoretical and regional context*. Continuum International Publishing Group.
Hasso, F. S. (1998). THE "WOMEN'S FRONT" nationalism, feminism, and modernity in Palestine. *Gender & Society, 12*(4), 441–465.
Hogan, J. (2008). *Gender, race and National Identity: Nations of flesh and blood*. Taylor & Francis.
Hubbard, B. (2016, July 10). A Saudi morals enforcer called for a more Liberal Islam. Then the death threats began. *The New York Times*. https://www.nytimes.com/2016/07/11/world/middleeast/saudi-arabia-islam-wahhabism-religious-police.html
Hunt, A. (1996). *Governance of the consuming passions: A history of sumptuary law*. Macmillan Press.
Johnson, E. (2008). *The headscarf ban in Turkish universities is a safeguard or violation?: Analysis of the ECHR judgment in Leyla Sahin V. Turkey*. ProQuest.
Joseph, S. (2005). Learning desire: Relational pedagogies and the desiring female subject in Lebanon. *Journal of Middle East Women's Studies, 1*(1), 79–109.
Knauss, P. R. (1987). *The persistence of patriarchy: Class, gender, and ideology in twentieth century Algeria*. Greenwood Publishing Group.
Landes, J. B. (2003). *Visualizing the nation: Gender, representation, and revolution in eighteenth-century France*. Cornell University Press.
Layish, A. (1996). The fatwa as an instrument of accommodation. In M. K. Masud, B. Brnkley Messick, & D. Powers (Eds.), *Islamic legal interpretation, muftis and their fatwas*. Harvard University Press.
MacMaster, N., & Lewis, T. (1998). Orientalism: From unveiling to hyperveiling. *Journal of European Studies, 28*(1), 121–135.
Mahdi, H. (2009). The hijab in Nigeria, the woman's body and the feminist private/public Discourse. *Institute for the Study of Islamic Thought in Africa (ISITA) working paper, 09–003*. http://buffett.northwestern.edu/documents/working-papers/ISITA_09-003_Mahdi.pdf
Mahmood, S. (2012). Sectarian conflict and family law in contemporary Egypt. *American Ethnologist, 39*(1), 54–62.
Makhlouf, C., & Obermeyer, C. M. (1979). *Changing veils: Women and modernisation in North Yemen*. Croom Helm.
Martel, J. (2014). *The one and only law: Walter Benjamin and the second commandment*. University of Michigan Press.
Massad, J. (1995). Conceiving the masculine: Gender and Palestinian nationalism. *Middle East Journal, 49*(3), 467–483.
Maududi, M., & Sloan, I. (2011). *Purdah and the status of woman in Islam* (Al-Ash'ari, Trans.). Ishi Press.

Mcclintock, A. (1995). *Imperial leather: Race, gender, and sexuality in the colonial contest* (1st ed.). Routledge.
McClintock, A., Mufti, A., Shohat, E., & others. (1997). *Dangerous liaisons: Gender, nation, and postcolonial perspectives* (Vol. 11). University of Minnesota Press.
Mcdermott, B. K. (2013, February 4). *"Even BABIES must wear the burka": Saudi cleric says newborn girls should have their faces veiled to help ward off sex attacks*. Mail Online. http://www.dailymail.co.uk/news/article-2273308/Sheikh-Abdullah-Daoud-Saudi-cleric-sparks-outrage-calling-baby-girls-wear-burka.html
Mclaughlin, K. (2017, February 23). *Women set fire to face veils after village is liberated from ISIS*. Mail Online. http://www.dailymail.co.uk/~/article-4251918/index.html
Mellinkoff, R. (1993). *Outcasts: Signs of otherness in Northern European art of the late middle ages* (Vol. 32). University of California Press.
Mernissi, F. (1991a). *The veil and the male elite: A feminist interpretation of women's rights in Islam*. Perseus.
Mernissi, F. (1991b). *Women and Islam: An historical and theological enquiry*. Blackwell.
Michaels, P. A. (1998). Kazak women: Living the heritage of a unique past. In H. Bodman & N. Tohidi (Eds.), *Women in Muslim societies*. Lynne Reinner Publisher.
Mir-Hosseini, Z. (2007). The politics and hermeneutics of hijab in Iran: From confinement to choice. *Muslim World Journal of Human Rights, 4*(1). https://doi.org/10.2202/1554-4419.1114
Moore, R. I. (2008). *The formation of a persecuting society: Authority and deviance in Western Europe 950–1250*. John Wiley & Sons.
Mosse, G. L. (1988). *Nationalism and sexuality: Middle-class morality and sexual norms in modern Europe*. University of Wisconsin Press.
Murphy, R. F. (1964). Social distance and the Veil1. *American Anthropologist, 66*(6), 1257–1274.
Nagel, J. (1998). Masculinity and nationalism: Gender and sexuality in the making of nations. *Ethnic and Racial Studies, 21*(2), 242–269.
Naghibi, N. (1999). Bad feminist or bad-hejabi? Moving outside the hejab debate. *Interventions: International Journal of Postcolonial Studies, 1*(4), 555–571.
Najmabadi, A. (2005). *Women with mustaches and men without beards: Gender and sexual anxieties of Iranian modernity*. University of California Press.
Nancy, J.-L. (2003). Deconstruction of monotheism a. *Postcolonial Studies: Culture, Politics, Economy, 6*(1), 37–46.
O'Connor, K. (2005). Lycra, girdles and leggings: The immaterial culture of social change. In *Clothing as material culture*. Berg.
Pasha-Robinson, L. (2017). Women liberated from Isis in Syria take off face veils and burn them. *The Independent*. https://www.independent.co.uk/news/world/middle-east/women-liberate-isis-syria-burn-veils-burqa-hijab-take-off-islamist-jihadis-state-deir-ezzor-a7596116.html
Pearson, A. (2014, July 17). *"Ban the burka": Why is the veil so divisive?* The Week UK. https://www.theweek.co.uk/uk-news/59525/ban-the-burka-why-is-the-veil-so-divisive
Pettman, J. (1996). *Worlding women: A feminist international politics*. Routledge.
Quataert, D. (1997). Clothing laws, state, and society in the ottoman empire, 1720–1829. *International Journal of Middle East Studies, 29*(03), 403–425.
Robson, R. (2013). *Dressing constitutionally: Hierarchy, sexuality, and democracy from our hairstyles to our shoes*. Cambridge University Press.
Roded, R. (2011). Jennifer Heath (ed.), the veil: Women writers on its history, Lore and Politics. *Nashim: A Journal of Jewish Women's Studies & Gender Issues, 21*, 207–209. https://doi.org/10.2979/nashim.21.207
Rubinstein, R. P. (1986). Color, circumcision, Tatoos, and scars. In M. R. Solomon (Ed.), *Psychology of fashion*. Lexington Books.
Rugh, A. B. (1987). *Reveal and conceal: Dress in contemporary Egypt*. American University in Cairo Press.
Saeed, A. (2006). *Islamic thought: An introduction*. Routledge.
Said, E. W. (1985). Orientalism reconsidered. *Cultural Critique, 1*, 89–107.

Said, E. (1994). *Orientalism*. Vintage.
Said, E. W. (2003). *Orientalism* (25th Anniversary Ed with 1995 Afterword Ed edition). Penguin Books.
Sanday, P. R. (2003). *Women at the center: Life in a modern matriarchy*. Cornell University Press.
Schimmel, A. (1992). *Islam: An introduction*. SUNY Press.
Sedghi, H. (2007). *Women and politics in Iran: Veiling, unveiling, and reveiling*. Cambridge University Press.
Sedgwick, M. J. (2006). *Islam and Muslims: A guide to diverse experience in a modern world*. Nicholas Brealey Pub.
Shachar, A. (2001). *Multicultural jurisdictions: Cultural differences and women's rights*. Cambridge University Press.
Sharma, U. M. (1978). Women and their affines: The veil as a symbol of separation. *Man, 13*, 218–233.
Sheen, D. (2014, July 23). *Israel's War against Gaza's women & their bodies*. Muftah. http://muftah.org/israels-war-gazas-women-bodies/
Siddiqi, M. Z. (1996). The sciences and critique of Hadith. In P. K. Koya (Ed.), *Hadith and Sunnah: Ideals and realities*. Islamic Book Trust.
Simmel, G. (1957). Fashion. *American Journal of Sociology, 62*, 541–558.
Spivak, G. C. (1988). Can the subaltern speak? In *Marxism and the interpretation of culture*. Bay Press.
Sponsler, C. (1992). Narrating the social order: Medieval clothing laws. *Cliometrica, 21*(3), 265.
Stowasser, B. F. (1994). *Women in the Qur'an, traditions, and interpretation*. Oxford University Press.
Swedenburg, T. (1990). The Palestinian peasant as national signifier. *Anthropological Quarterly, 63*, 18–30.
Taher, A. (2006). Veil teacher was obeying a fatwa. *The Sunday Time*. https://www.thetimes.co.uk/article/veil-teacher-was-obeying-a-fatwa-tfcjg6vh6tk
Tohidi, N. (1994). Modernity, Islamization and women in Iran. In *Gender and national identity*. Zed Books.
Tohidi, N. (1998). Guardians of the nation. In H. L. Bodman & N. Tawhīdī (Eds.), *Women in Muslim scoieties: Diversity within unity*. Lynne Rienner Publishers.
Vivian, B. (1999). The veil and the visible. *Western Journal of Communication, 63*(2), 115–139.
Watt, G. (2013). *Dress, law and naked truth: A cultural study of fashion and form*. Bloomsbury Publishing Plc.
Webb, W. M. (1912). *The heritage of dress*. Times Book Club.
Whisner, M. (1982). Gender-specific clothing regulation: A study in patriarchy. *Harvard Women's Law Journal, 5*, 73.
Winter, M. (2009). Ulama' between the state and the society in pre-modern Sunni Islam. In M. Hatina (Ed.), *Guardians of faith in modern times: Ulama in the Middle East*. Leiden.
Woodward, K. (2004). *Questioning identity: Gender, class, nation*. Routledge.
Woodward, S. (2005). Looking good: Feeling right–aesthetics of the self. In *Clothing as material culture* (pp. 21–40). Berg.
Woodward, S. (2007). *Why women wear what they wear*. Berg.
Yarbrough, L. (2014). Origins of the ghiyār. *Journal of American Oriental Society, 134*(1), 113–121.
Young, W. C. (1996). *The Rashaayda Bedouin: Arab pastoralists of Eastern Sudan*. Harcourt Brace College Publishers.
Yuval-Davis, N. (1980). The bearers of the collective: Women and religious legislation in Israel. *Feminist Review, 4*, 15–27.
Yuval-Davis, N. (1993). Gender and nation. *Ethnic and Racial Studies, 16*(4), 621–632.
Yuval-Davis, N. (1997). *Gender & nation* (Vol. 24). Cambridge University Press.

Chapter 3
Proper and Improper: The Regulation of Veiling in Secular Europe

In 2003, Sirine Yahhiaten, a 17-year-old French Muslim girl, was obliged to change schools because her attire was considered not to be appropriate (Ramdani, 2013). Sirine did not wear a Muslim headscarf, but a long skirt with sweatpants underneath and a hair band that covered her hair. One day the school principal called her to inquire about her attire. While waiting to speak with the principal, the school's secretary told her that she should not wear sweatpants under her skirt because of the French law banning 'religious symbols'. "She told me that my skirt was too long and students walking behind me could fall because of its length, so she said that I was posing a threat to the security of the students. As for the headband, she said it prevents me from hearing well during the class" (Naili, 2014). As Sirine refused to change her attire, she was obliged by the head of the school to attend study period class every day. "Every time I entered the school, someone was waiting for me to accompany me to the study period class since I was no longer allowed to have any contact with other students. I was not allowed to go out during class breaks. I was given exercises to do but I was never given make-up material for the courses that I had been missing" (Naili, 2014). As an agreement could not be reached, she was obliged to find another school which did not consider a 'long skirt' as an 'ostentatious religious symbol'. But students in public institutions are not the only ones who have suffered for the legal regulation of the headscarf in many European countries. Rabha Chatar, a 40-year-old French woman and mother of three, was forbidden to accompany her children to school because she was wearing a full-face veil (Naili, 2014). Although she tried to challenge the ban in the French Court, her claim was dismissed because of the French law on secularism which prohibits the wearing of 'ostentatious' religious symbols. In Germany, a judge banned a woman from appearing in Court veiled. The woman, of Syrian origins, was presenting a divorce proceeding in the district Court in Luckenwalde, Brandenberg. Not only did the judge not proceed with her case, but she also warned of possible legal action, ordering the claimant to appear in person against her husband (Dearden, 2017). These are not the

G. Baldi, *Un-Veiling Dichotomies*, Boundaries of Religious Freedom: Regulating Religion in Diverse Societies,
https://doi.org/10.1007/978-3-030-79297-8_3

only cases of Muslim women who have been forbidden to wear the veil. Discussions about headscarf regulation have touched almost all private and public institutions in the west: from FIFA's 2010 headscarf ban for Iranian women soccer players (McElroy, 2010), to Disneyland's disputes over the wearing of the headscarf (Finnigan, 2012), women's veil regulation encompasses many aspects of (Muslim) women's life, from education to work, from sport to recreational activities.

The regulation of the practice of veiling, which has mainly focused on discourses about integration (Bader, 2010), cultural differences (Klausen, 2005), multiculturalism (Saharso, 2003) and gender equality (Benhabib, 2002a, b) has taken different forms in different European countries disclosing different understandings of secularism, state neutrality, state-church relations and gender equality. In this chapter, I consider veil regulation in three different European countries (the UK, Germany and France) and at the European Court of Human Rights (ECtHR) to show how different modes of secularism and state-church relations have operated a differentiation between 'proper' and 'improper' religious symbols which has led to a common incapacity of European western countries to deal with the matter of the female veil, failing to accommodate different religious sensitivities in the secular public sphere.

While France applies the principle of *laïcité*, a strict and radical form of secularism, the UK implements multicultural policies, and Germany applies a form of religious pluralism where the manifestation of Christian symbols is privileged over others. The difference between those countries lies in the 'visibility of religion'. While some takes a more tolerant approach, where the state plays a passive role and (usually) allows the manifestation of religious symbols in the public domain, others presupposes the active role of the state in advancing the principle of neutrality and hence in prohibiting any religious symbols in the public sphere, relegating them to the private domain. In essence, some European countries such as the UK and Germany tend to tolerate the expression and manifestation of religious symbols in the public sphere, reducing the interference of the state in the private life of the individual, while others, such as France, actively interfere in the private life of individuals as arbiter of social cohesion and neutrality. In light of this, while the French assimilationist model grants citizenship by excluding cultural and religious differences (*ius soli*), the German ethno-cultural model is based on descent (*ius sanguinis*), imposing specific requirements on immigrants. The multicultural UK on the other hand (presumably) promotes religious diversity by recognising cultural differences (Sauer, 2009). European countries also differ in the way in which the headscarf ban has been framed: while in France the veil has been forbidden in the name of a crusade to save secular values since the headscarf has been seen as a symbol that could challenge France's social cohesion (Brems, 2006), in Germany eight *Länder* (regions) have prohibited the veil in name of 'religious pluralism' and the protection of its Christian roots (Schiffauer, 2006), and in the UK, where the state tried to implement a more flexible approach towards religious difference, the *Begum* case (2006, 2007) re-opened the discussion about multiculturalism and the recognition of religious differences.

However, while the regulation of the practice discloses different state-church relations and modes of secularism(s), it also reveals important similarities, which I will further analyse in the next chapter. Firstly, the process of secularization has produced a privatization of religious beliefs which has led to the banning of the Muslim veil and the exclusion of many Muslim women from the European public sphere. Secondly, in all the legal decisions I take into consideration, secularism is understood as a synonym of 'neutrality', 'modernity', 'democracy', 'nationhood', and 'gender equality', which have become essential categories of the formation of modern western nation states (Taylor, 2007; Walzer, 1984). Thirdly, the legal and political debate regarding the admissibility of the female veil in the secular European public sphere reveals a particular preoccupation with the definition of what constitutes religion and whether the veil is a 'proper' religious symbol: by defining veiling as a political symbol that endanger western secular values, not only European judges did not feel that their decisions limited the right of many Muslim women in Europe, but they constructed the veil through oppositional categories such as Christian and Islamic symbols, 'acceptable' and 'unacceptable', 'proper' and 'improper' religious practices. This, in turn, has led to a monolithic understanding of the (Muslim) religious subject, which has arguably advanced the respect for plurality and the principle of gender equality that are enshrined in the European Convention on Human Rights (ECHR). More importantly, as I will further analyse in the next chapter, by defining the 'proper' religious symbol through the distinction between faith and manifestation, *forum internum* and *forum externum*, the secular state re-defines the line between the secular and religious spheres and between state neutrality and religious manifestation, operating in this way a reconfiguration of religious practices and sensitivities (Agrama, 2010).

This reconceptualization has been rendered possible through the juridical notion of *public order*, an exception to the 'freedom of thought, conscience, and religion' enshrined in Article 9 of the ECHR. The Article states that "1) Everyone has the right to freedom of thought, conscience and religion; this right includes freedom to change his religion or belief and freedom, either alone or in community with others and in public or private, to manifest his religion or belief, in worship, teaching, practice and observance. 2) Freedom to manifest one's religion or beliefs shall be subject only to such limitations as are prescribed by law and are necessary in a democratic society in the interests of public safety, for the protection of *public order*, health or morals, or for the protection of the rights and freedoms of others" (*Italics added*). The notion of public order, which is an integral part of the western concept of religious liberty, allows modern states to limit personal freedoms and to intervene in the private sphere of the individual in the name of a common good. Historically, the notion derives from the French Civil Code and has been used to resolve conflicts between laws (e.g. foreign laws within a territorial nation-state) or contradictory legal principles (Husserl, 1938): it is therefore an expression of domestic sovereignty which should help to solve "relations among private persons from different states, […] primarily [in the field of] commercial and personal status law" (Agrama, 2012, p. 95). Hence, the notion of public order can justify the withdrawal of a state from specific terms of international Convention to which it is signatory because certain international laws clash with national laws, values or norms. Because of its link with the legal and political assets of a country, public order is a notion that changes from place to place and in different historical periods: as Mahmood (2015) points out, the ambiguity that characterises the notion of public order is isomorphic of the ambiguity that characterises the concept of religious liberty. In light of this, it is not surprising that public order, although invested with different meanings, figures prominently in all the legal decisions over the wearing of the veil. The analysis of the European legal decisions concerning the practice of veiling shows that the doctrine of public order has been used and abused by both proponents and opponents of the veil, as a mean of inclusion or exclusion, and as a useful tool to defend the rights of the majority at the expense of minorities (Mahmood, 2015): contrary to western and human rights law's claim to safeguard plurality in the name of an abstract notion of 'public order', European states have enacted regulations that profoundly limit women's agency while strengthening particular (Christian) majoritarian sensitivities at the expense of religious minorities. In the dispute between Muslim women's individual right to manifest their religious beliefs and the demands of secular European states, the ECtHR, which should ensure that member states respect the individuals' fundamental freedoms, has allowed and upheld the banning of the headscarf in many European countries, excluding many veiled Muslim women from the European public sphere.

The regulation of women's bodies and the limitation of their personal freedoms thus becomes the *emblem* of the intrinsic contradiction in human rights discourse in general and liberalism in particular. In fact, if, on the one hand, liberal secularism operates a separation between spiritual and temporal, private and public, then on the other, the private life of the individual becomes extremely regulated. In this sense, secularism and western positive law act to eradicate differences and to protect a specific 'secular citizen' through the control of women's body, which reveals a western incapacity to think in terms of juridical plurality. Therefore, although the secular/liberal system is accepted unconditionally as the best asset for the respect of plurality and the development of women's rights and gender equality, in reality it acts to assimilate differences into the homogeneity of western societies. In the case of the headscarf ban, secularism, instead of upholding principles able to unite citizens (Gunn, 2004), works to divide citizens based on their religious beliefs, contrary to its claim to be the best system to deal with cultural and religious differences.

3.1 *Burkinis*, Face Veils and *hijab*: *laïcité* in France

In 2011, a few days before the '*burqa* ban' came into force in France, Kenza Drider, a 32-year-old French citizen who wore a *niqab,* a body covering that reveals only the eyes, declared on national TV that neither the state nor any mosque could order her how to dress. Oddly, a full-face veiled woman had become the public face of the country's '*burqa* brigades' who claimed that their personal right to freedom of religion and gender equality had been severely limited by the new law on *laïcité* which prohibited the wearing of 'ostentatious' religious symbols (Willsher, 2011).

The French concept of *laïcité* is a strict and radical form of the secularism that had been incorporated into French law in the nineteenth century. The principle derives from the 1905 Act on the separation of church and state: while the term *laïcité* does not appear in the 1905 Act, Article 2 of the *Loi de séparation des Églises et de l'État* clearly points out that 'the state does not recognize, salary or subsidize any religion'. Although from its inception the French notion of state/church separation presented tensions between the principle of religious freedom (Article 1 states that 'The Republic assures the freedom of conscience') and the principle of separation between the state and the church enshrined in Article 2, the *Conseil d'État* (the highest juridical institution in France) considers the Act as delivering a general legal framework which provides the fundamental notion of secularism and state neutrality at the base of the French legal system and the 1958 French Constitution (Article 1 states that 'France is an indivisible, secular, democratic and social Republic') (Joppke, 2007).

While France has inherited the discourse on women's veiling from its colonial past (where women's unveiling represented France's successful assimilation of Algerians into French citizens), in twentieth and twenty first century France, the veil re-emerges as linked to the concept of *laïcité*, state neutrality, the notion of *vivre ensemble*, and the defence of women's rights (presented as an achievement of secularism).

After the colonial period, the turmoil concerning the Islamic veil re-emerged in 1989 with the *Creil Affair*. The case concerns three teenage girls who were expelled from a school in Creil, in the north of Paris, because they refused to remove their headscarves. The case reached the *Conseil d'État,* which issues recommendations to the government on specific issues, held that "the wearing by students of signs through which they intend to express their religious belonging to a religion is not per se incompatible with the principle of laïcité if it constitutes an exercise of freedom of expression and a manifestation of belief" (*Conseil d'État* opinion No. 346.893, 1989, p. 5). The *Conseil* made a differentiation between students wearing religious symbols, considered compatible with the French notion of *laïcité*, and actions that could be considered opposed to the principle of secularism (such as proselytism, missing classes for religious reasons etc.). Based on the *Conseil d'État*, only certain religious symbols conflict with the principle of secularism and could amount to provocation, proselytism or propaganda: for this reason, after a review of French legislation, the *Conseil d'État* concluded that pupils were not permitted to wear religious, philosophical and political symbols which were considered "ostentatious" or an act of "provocation" or propaganda (*Conseil d'État* opinion no. 346.893, 1989, p. 5). The vague opinion of the *Conseil* inevitably created difficulties in establishing what constituted an 'ostentatious' religious symbol. This is exemplified by the fact that between 1989 and 2003 the *Conseil* reversed 41 of 49 cases of expulsion of veiled girls from French public schools (McGoldrick, 2006). The *Conseil d'État* expressed this difficulty in its opinion (no. 130394, 1992) on the *Kherouaa* case (1992), in which three girls were expelled from school because they refused to remove the veil after the enactment of the college's internal rules which included a ban of any religious, political or philosophical symbols. In the case, the

Conseil re-established students' fundamental rights to express their religious beliefs but argued that "this freedom does not permit students to show signs of religious adherence which, by their nature [...] constitute an act of oppression, of provocation, proselytism or propaganda" (*Kherouaa, Kachour, Balo et Kizic, Recucil des Arrets du Conseil d'Etat*, 1992, para 390). For the *Conseil*, students have the right to show religious symbols only if this does not endanger the health and security or does not jeopardise the normal functioning of the school.

Immediately after, in 1994, the former Minister of Education in France, Mr. Francois Bayrou, sent a note to every public school specifying that the wearing of discreet religious symbols was acceptable, while 'ostentatious' religious symbols should be banned as they constitute a breach of the freedom of the other and of the principle of secularism (Parekh, 2000). A few year later, in 1995, the *Conseil* delivered a decision on a case regarding the expulsion of young girls from school because they were veiled which seems to contradict its previous decisions in the *Kherouaa* case (1992). Following the Ministry of Education's note, the *Conseil* declared that the wearing of the veil violated the school dress policy and the principle of *laïcité*: for the *Conseil*, the veil "is incompatible with the proper conduct of physical education classes; [and] that the decision definitively excluding these [...] pupils was taken on account of the unrest caused by their refusal in the life of the establishment" (*Conseil d'État*, 1995, Rec.159981, on the *Dogru* case). However, only 1 year after, in 1996, the *Conseil* seemed to adhere again to its previous decision in the *Kherouaa* case (1992), quashing the decision of the Lille Administrative Court which had upheld the expulsion of veiled Muslim girls from a school in Lille. Based on the *Conseil's* reasoning, "pupils [...] [who] intended to express their religious beliefs cannot be regarded as a sign which, by its nature, is ostentatious or demanding, and which would in any case be an act of pressure or proselytism" (R. 170,208).

The confusion concerning what constituted an 'ostentatious' religious symbol led to the enactment of many ministerial circulars between 1989 and 2004 that aimed to give guidance on whether certain religious symbols were irreconcilable with the French principle of *laïcité*.[1] Notably, the pre-2004 debate over the wearing of the veil discloses a particular preoccupation with the definition of what constitutes religion, especially Islam, and whether the practice of veiling was an Islamic (religious) or an Islamist (political) symbol. For Alain Juppé, the former head of the Union for Popular Movement (a centre-right party) "the wearing of the veil is not the manifestation of piety or modesty [but] a militant act sustained by a veritable fundamentalist propaganda" (as cited in Fernando, 2017, p. 688). Similarly, Francoise Hostalier, the former Secretary of Education, declared that "to wear the Islamic veil is not a religious gesture but a political gesture" (in Fernando, 2017, p. 690). What is of interest in the debate is not only the political and legal

[1] It is worth noting that the French Universalist principle of laicity should be based on the principle of equality between different religions without any difference between majoritarian and other religions. However, although the French government claims neutrality under the principle of *laïcité*, it has accommodated many Catholic and Jewish religious practices while refusing to accommodate Muslim ones (Fernando, 2014b).

preoccupation to define what is religion, to which I will return in the next chapter, but also the designation of the veil as a political symbol, which has allowed schools and tribunals to ban the practice without feeling that it limited the personal rights of religious liberty of veiled Muslim women and girls.

The idea that veiling is a political symbol because the practice is not kept in the private sphere, where religious feelings (supposedly) belong, is clear also in the Stasi Commission Report (*Commission de reflexion,* 2003), commissioned by the former President of France, Jacques Chirac, to inquire into the application of the principle of laicism in the country. The report suggests banning all religious, political and philosophical symbols from any educational institution in the country, and proposes sanctioning pupils who do not conform to the regulation. The report (2003) points out that laicity is "a value shared by all, at the heart of the Republican pact" (p. 16): it is "the guarantee of individual freedom [and a] 'cornerstone of national unity'" (p. 36). Notably, the report refers to the Muslim headscarf as a "permanent guerrilla war against laicity" (section 3.2.2), an element able to disrupt the peace of the educational environment: for the Commission (2003),

> "the headscarf is too often a source of conflicts, divisions, and even suffering. The visible aspect of a religious sign is perceived by most people as contrary to the educational mission: to offer a neutral space where critical conscience may grow" (p. 57).

Indeed, without any logical or empirical evidence, the Commission established that the headscarf was a denial of women's freedom, arguing that "objectively, the veil stands for the alienation of women" (p. 58). It points out that "young women are victims of a form of sexism that manifests itself through various social pressures and physical, psychological or verbal abuse. They are forced to cover themselves to the extent of becoming asexualized and to lower their gaze in the presence of men; if they do not respect these measures, they are stigmatized as 'whores'" (p. 46). Implicitly, then, the Commission (2003) juxtaposes Islamic backward and chauvinist practices (such as veiling) with secular French emancipatory norms, depicting Muslim women as passive subjects to which is prohibited any kind of agency by backward religious norms that violate their rights. Based on the Stasi Commission (2003), Muslim women are "victims of the pressure exerted by the family or the neighbourhood and, for this reason, they need to be protected" (p. 46). Macmaster and Lewis (1998) note that this orientalist characterization of Islam as patriarchal and Muslim women as oppressed and in need of being saved by civilized western norms mirrors the work of French colonial scholars who tried to unveil Muslim women in order to justify their imperialist interests. Clearly, the representation of Muslim women as silenced subjects without agency has served the purpose of ideology (Althusser, 1972) within the French effort to assimilate Muslims into French citizens through the privatization of different identities and the exclusion of any sign of religious difference from the public sphere. By excluding any visible sign of difference, the report's aim seems to be to constitute a 'docile subject' (Foucault, 1981), obedient to the state and the values of the French Republic. In agreement with previous decisions of the *Counseil d'État* on the necessity to ban 'ostentatious' religious symbols, the report also defines which symbols should be considered 'ostentatious' and so a 'provocation', avoiding the vagueness of the *Conseil*'s decisions: the Muslim veil, large crosses and the Jewish *kippa* should be forbidden as they are considered 'ostentatious', and so unacceptable, while small crosses or the star of David are considered 'discrete symbols', and so acceptable (*Commission for the reflexion*, 2003, p. 59). Finally, the report proposes to offer wider food options to accommodate members of different religions in public institutions, and to introduce the two most important Muslim and Jewish holidays into the national school system.

A few weeks after the release of the Stasi Commission Report, former President Chirac, in a public speech, declared *laïcité* a 'common good', essential to preserve the public sphere from the divisive nature of religions (Bowen, 2007). He noted that *laïcité* is "the privileged place for meetings and exchanges, where everyone can come together bringing the best to the national community. It is the neutrality of this public space that enables different religions to harmoniously co-exist" (Bowen, 2008, p. 41). Although he re-established the difference between 'ostentatious' religious symbols (to be banned) and other (accepted) symbols, he did not address the wearing of political symbols (which was an integral part of the Stasi report), neither did he accept the proposal to accommodate religious groups' claims (such as food options or religious holidays).

Instead, a few months after the president's speech, the French government passed a law that prohibited the wearing of any 'ostentatious' religious symbol in public schools (*Loi n.* 2004–228, 2004). The law entered into force in September 2004: on the first day of school, 240 girls went to school wearing the veil; 170 of them were forced to remove the veil and between 50 and 60 girls were expelled from public schools due to their refusal to comply with the legislation (McGoldrick, 2006). The law seemed at odds with the previous decisions of the *Conseil d'État:* while, for the *Conseil*, the problem was not the veil *as such*, but the modality in which it was worn, the new regulation regarded the manifestation of all religious symbols as a 'provocation'. After the passing of the new law, the *Conseil* seemed to take a more radical position on the wearing of the headscarf in its decision on the case of Faiza Silmi, a Moroccan citizen living in France from 2000, married to a French citizen and a mother of three, who had applied for French citizenship in 2004 (Hirschl, 2011). Faiza's application was denied based on Article 21 (2) of the 1804 French Civil Code, which provides that

> "an alien or stateless person who marries and whose spouse is of French nationality may, after a period of two years from the marriage, acquire French nationality by way of declaration provided that, at the time of the declaration, the community of living, both affective and physical, has not come to an end and the French spouse has kept his or her nationality. The foreign spouse must also prove a sufficient knowledge of the French language, according to his or her condition" (French Civil Code, Article 21.2).

The government rejected her application because, upon her arrival in France, she started to wear a *niqab* which was inconsistent with the values of French society and the principle of gender equality. Ms. Silmi appealed to the *Conseil d'État* which upheld the government decision, arguing that the claimant "adopted a radical practice of her religion, incompatible with the essential values of the French community" (*Cousel d'État* 2008, R. 286798): for this reason, she failed to assimilate into French culture as required by Article 21 (2) of the French Civil Code and Act no. 2003–1119 of 26 Nov. 2003, which allows the government to deny citizenship on the grounds of a non-linguistic lack of assimilation with French culture. The case reveals not only the difficulty of establishing whether the new law is restricted to public schools or includes public places (Bowen, 2007), but also the extent to which the French principles of neutrality and secularity justify the prohibition of any religious symbol that can 'disrupt' the peace of the society, whereas different religious characteristics are erased in the name of a formal (but not substantial) equality (Hirschl, 2011). Clearly, the new law specifically affected veiled Muslim girls who were excluded from the public educational system, violating the principle of equality and the right to equal educational opportunities, leading, as Human Rights Watch (2004) highlighted, to a ghettoization of many veiled Muslim girls in the name of neutrality.

Although the French law attracted many critiques and protests, in 2008 France's ban had the blessing of the ECtHR in the case *Dogru v France* (2008). The case concerns the expulsion of a young girl because she refused to remove the veil during physical education class. In 1999, before the 2004 law entered into force, Ms. Dogru failed to participate in 38 physical education classes because her *hijab* was not allowed: the school teacher claimed that she was denied participation because of safety reasons, but she refused to answer on how the veil could endanger Ms. Dogru's or other students' safety (*Dogru v France* 2008). When the school expelled her, she tried to compromise by asking to wear a hat, but her offer was refused. The ECtHR did not find any violation of Article 9 of the ECHR and upheld the decision of the school and the French government to expel the student. The Court added that even if a violation of freedom of religion had been found, the interference was still justified by prescribed law, or by a legitimate aim necessary in a democratic society. The ECtHR found that, although at the time of the facts no law prohibited the wearing of the veil, the expulsion reflected domestic laws based on non-binding ministerial circulars, and that the aim was legitimate and necessary to protect the freedom of others and public order in the school (*Dogru v France,* 2008). However, as in other cases decided at the ECtHR, the Court never explained how the mere wearing of the veil could create a threat to public order or the freedom of others, nor why Ms. Dogru was not allowed to wear a hat in physical classes. The Court found that a limitation of Ms. Dogru's rights was necessary to preserve the secular character of French public educational institutions, but failed to explain how the veil could violate the principle of secularism. Despite the lack of empirical proof of the 'danger' of Ms. Dogru's veil and the absence of a national law that forbade the veil at school at the time of the facts, the ECtHR upheld the decision of the French national Courts to exclude Dogru from school because of her failure to respect the principle of *laïcité*.

Immediately after the ECtHR's decision in *Dogru v France* (2008), former President Nicolas Sarkozy, strong of the ECtHR support of France's crusade against the veil, addressed the parliament on the matter of the full-face veil, highlighting that as "it is not a religious practice but a patriarchal habit that neglects women's freedom and liberty", the *burqa* "is not welcomed on the French territory" (Liberation, 2009). For Sarkozy, the *burqa* is a "problem of liberty [and] dignity of women [as the item] is not a religious symbol" (liberation, 2009). Immediately after Sarkozy's speech, a parliamentary Commission was established to inquire about the wearing of the face veil on French territory in order to "better understand the problem and to find ways to fight against this affront to individual liberties"(Joppke, 2013, p. 21). Although the Commission did not recommend a "general and absolute prohibition of the integral veil in public space" (*Assemblée Nationale,* 2009, p. 187), in 2010 the French National Assembly passed a law which prohibits wearing the face veil (*Loi* 2010–1192, 2010). Those who do not obey the law will pay a fine of €150 and/or they will be required to complete a citizenship education course. The ban was justified in name of the principle of *laïcité,* human dignity and public order.

The *burqa* ban, however, was not constructed on solid bases. While the principle of *laïcité* was a central notion in the 2004 ban of religious symbols, as the *burqa* has not been considered a religious symbol, it falls outside of the ambit of *laïcité*. Indeed, the notion of 'human dignity' used to justify the ban of the full-face veil is also weak. In fact, in western thought, the notion of 'human dignity' is linked to the notion of personal choice and self-determination. Although many women declared they had autonomously chosen to wear the full-face veil, the French government saw in the *burqa* women's voluntary servitude focusing on "protecting the dignity of the person, if necessary against the person herself" (as cited in Joppke, 2011, p. 8). In fact, Francoise Hostalier, UMP deputy, declared that "society must protect its members, even if they voluntarily torture, mutilate, or impose on themselves an undignified appearance" (as cited in Joppke, 2011, p. 8). Although in secular/liberal thought the understanding of dignity is linked to that of 'freedom of choice', the law has banned the face veil based on the idea that the dignity of the individual should be protected by the state even if the individual does not want it: in this view, the notion of individual choice, and consequently of 'human dignity', loses any meaning. In the *burqa* ban, the notion of the protection of public order, an established notion in French public law which includes the concepts of security, peace, and public health, also emerges as extremely weak. On a matter of security, forbidding the *burqa* would imply that the manifestation of religious liberty *per se* is a threat to France: indeed, the fact that someone should always be identifiable clashes with the usual face coverings (such as masks in carnivals and folklore festivals, helmets etc.).

Called to give its opinion on the so called '*burqa* ban', the *Conseil d'État* stated that a general prohibition would give a new meaning to the concept of public order which "rests on a minimal foundation of reciprocity and of essential guarantees of life in society" (*Conseil d'État,* 'Study of possible legal grounds for banning the full veil', 2010, p. 26). For the *Conseil*, the only justifiable ban could be on the basis of public security. However, this could only be possible in "particular circumstances" (p. 30) as "public security does not justify imposing on everyone the obligation to have one's face uncovered during all times and in all places" (p. 30). The *Conseil* justified the ban on the ground of "public safety considerations and the fight against fraud," and allowed the prohibition "for purposes of identity checks and the performance of certain official procedures such as, marriage and voting" as the full-face covering represents a "denial of access or delivery of these services" (p. 27). Although the *Conseil* pointed out that a blind legal ban on any face covering garments may result in a "considerable legal uncertainty" (p. 19), it upheld the law after clearing it from all the legal obstacles.[2]

The idea that the burqa ban is essential to be recognized and avoid fraud is even more paradoxical in view of the spread of the Covid-19 pandemic and the law on facemask. While the wearing of face-masks has been justified for health reasons (as per art. 2 of the 2010 Law),[3] it has re-ignited the debate about the *burqa* ban and the necessity to show one's face to interact with other individuals in the society. Fatima Khemilat, a fellow at the Political Science Institute of Aix-en-Provence, explained that "if you are Muslim and you hide your face for religious reasons, you are liable to a fine and a citizenship course where you will be taught what it is to be 'a good citizen'. But if you are a non-Muslim citizen in the pandemic, you are encouraged and forced as a 'good citizen' to adopt 'barrier gestures' to protect the national community" (Bostock, 2020). Similarly, Oliver Roy, an important French scholar, pointed out that "if you cover your face for Islam, it's not the republic. If you cover your face for a reason not to do with Islam, it's acceptable" (Bostock, 2020). The irony of the *burqa* ban *vis-à-vis* with the compulsory mask-wearing imposed during the Covid-19 emergency, shows that the 2010 ban on face-covering was not really about security and concerns about face concealment in public spaces, but about the visibility of the (Muslim) 'other'.

This is clear in the '*burkini affair*': in summer 2016, 30 towns of the French Mediterranean Riviera banned the *burkini*, a full body swimsuit, from any public beaches based on the idea that the garment is linked to Islamic extremism and a "threat to good morals and secularism" (Myers, 2016). The issue started with a decree enacted by the mayor of Villeneuve-Loubet which stated that "of all the common beach areas, access to swimming is prohibited to anyone that does not have a dress, respectful of morality and the principle of secularism, and compliance with hygiene and safety rules adapted in swimming maritime public domain. Wearing clothes, while swimming, having a connotation contrary to the principles mentioned above is strictly prohibited on the beaches of the town" (art. 4.3). The '*burkini* ban' caused a wide public outcry, which resulted in a legal claim filed by French human rights organizations before the Nice Administrative Court, asking for the abolition of the decree on the basis of Article L. 521–2 of the Administrative Code of Justice, which allows a Court to "order any measure necessary to safeguard a fundamental

---

[2] In 2012, two women made a complaint to the UN Human Rights Committee which declared that the 'burqa ban' is a violation of fundamental human rights. For the Committee, France's 'burqa ban' was not proportionate to France's claim of security and it ordered France to review the law (Miles, 2018); however, nothing has changed.

[3] Article 2 of the 2010 law on the prohibition of concealing face in public spaces, specifies that "-The prohibition…shall not apply if such clothing is prescribed or authorised by legislative or regulatory provisions, is authorised to protect the anonymity of the person concerned, is justified for health reasons or on professional grounds, or is part of sporting, artistic or traditional festivities or events."

freedom" (*Loi* 2000–597, 2000). The Court established that the decree did not violate any fundamental rights and dismissed the petitioners' claim. For the Court the aim of the decree was proportionate, in light of the recent terrorist attacks in Nice, to maintain public order and to eliminate extremism (Breeden & Blaise, 2016). The decision was appealed to the French *Conseil d'État,* which ruled that the ban violated fundamental freedoms.

In France, the *hijab* ban (including all the forms the ban has taken) was legally imposed without any proof of how the simple wearing of the veil could be so dangerous that a society must limit Muslim women's individual rights. For Scott (2007), the *burqa* ban and the *affaire du foulard* represents the failure of France's efforts at assimilation. It indicates that French Muslims are asked to keep a low profile and to avoid behaviours that may be seen as related to their religious identity. But it also indicates a discrepancy between the practice and the interpretation of *laïcité*. In the French system the term refers to the separation between the state and religious organizations as well as the neutrality of the state towards religions (including religious beliefs and practices). Initially, religion was not blindly banned while the manifestation of religious symbols was decided case-by-case in conformity with the law concerning the manifestation of religious beliefs in public institutions. Over time, however, French authorities have increasingly constructed the veil as a threat to French *laïcité*; this, in turn, has fuelled misunderstandings regarding Islam and the veil which, instead of resulting in peace and harmony between different religions, have actually increased social tensions, as recent attacks in France demonstrate. The long lasting problem in France with any kind of Muslim women's covering indicates that, far from saving social cohesion, the concept of secularism has implied the gradual disappearance of religion and religious identities from the public sphere (McGoldrick, 2006). It is therefore unlikely that the new meaning conferred on *laïcité* in France would lead to a real integration of the Muslim community. The increasing radical meaning given to the notion of *laïcité* has also changed the meaning of the concept of 'neutrality' which has slowly started to be understood as a synonym of 'unity', whereas only through "non- identification with the particular" (Joppke, 2007, p. 317) can the state legitimately require citizens to be in the service of the common good.

Finally, the link drawn by French judges and politicians between the veil and women's sexuality is of particular relevance if we think about the tension between universalism (of human rights) and particularism (of France), pluralism (of the many meanings of the practice) and singularity (as the meaning attached to the veil). Gender equality has become one of the main arguments in France in favour of the women's veiling ban whereas women's sexuality has become intrinsically linked to a discourse of territorial border control and 'deviant sexual norms' (such as polygamy, arranged marriage etc.) which has become the dividing line between the citizens of France and its (alien) Muslim population. The foundational French republican principles (*Liberté, égalité, fraternité*) have been discursively linked to sexual liberation and equality while laicism has increasingly been associated with women's equality in a binary contraposition with Islamic symbols. In light of this, rather than saving Muslim women from a patriarchal culture that oppresses them, the French bans reveal the sexual regulation and normalization of Muslim French immigrants in their public and private sphere. In other words, in France, the discourse on the veil has been framed both as a matter of religion (through the binary understanding of religious v secular spheres) and as a matter of personal choice: this, however, as Fernando (2014b) wonderfully highlights, has rendered it impossible for Muslim veiled women to frame the practice on the ground of freedom of conscience (as a ban would constrain the exteriority and not the interiority of the subject), as well as a religious obligation (as Islam does not oblige women to wear the veil).

3.2 Germany and State Neutrality

While in France the principle of *laïcité* is applied to students and teachers, in Germany students' freedom to manifest their own religion has never been in doubt. Unlike in France, German secularism is based on the notion of religious pluralism, where the Protestant and Catholic religions occupy an important place. Articles 136 and 137 of the German Basic Law regarding freedom of conscience and religion integrates the principle of separation between the church and the state while recognizing the freedom of religion of different religious aggregations. Based on the 1949 Constitution, religious communities can acquire the status of public-law corporations, which provides them with a certain legal protection (Kastoryano, 2004).[4] The Muslim community in Germany applied to acquire the status of 'corporation' in 1977 in order to be publicly recognised and to acquire an equal religious status before the law (Vocking, 1995). However, Muslim applications have always been rejected due to the religion's lack of a hierarchical organized structure. Despite Germany's religious pluralism, Islam and, in particular, the Muslim veil, have been at the centre of a passionate debate for years. In April 2018, the North Westphalia regional government, pushed by the Austrian decision to ban the headscarf in primary schools, proposed a law to ban the veil on girls under the age of 14 (Welle, 2018). One year before, in 2017, a veiled Muslim woman was denied divorce because she was veiled during the legal proceedings (Dearden, 2017). In the same year, the German parliament passed a law concerning the partial banning of the *burqa,* while existing regional law on state neutrality allows federal states to forbid the manifestation of any religious symbols in judicial offices and educational institutions (Dearden, 2017).

The headscarf debate in Germany has been fuelled by the *Ludin* case (2003) which concerns an Afghan woman who applied to become a teacher in a primary school in the province of Baden-Württemberg. After the claimant had successfully

[4] This status provides far-reaching rights, such as the right to levy taxes from members of the community and to organize a parish, the right to employ people under a belief-oriented labour-law, the right to nominate members to broadcast-councils, tax reductions for property placed under public property law, etc. (Rohe, 2004).

passed all the required exams, the school rejected her application due to a lack of suitability for the required position (BVerfGE 108, 282 (284), 2 BvR 1436/02, para. 3). The rejection was motivated by the fact that Ms. Ludin was wearing a headscarf and she refused to remove it. She argued that the "headscarf is not only a characteristic of her personality but is also an expression of her religious conviction. According to the precepts of Islam, wearing a headscarf is part of her Islamic identity" (BVerfGE 108, 282 (284), 2 BvR 1436/02, para. 4). The competent school authority (Stuttgart School Supervisory Authority-SSA), however, established that the veil's symbolism is not only religious but also political: for this reason, the school authorities considered it incompatible with the principle of state neutrality, based on the fact that young children may be easily influenced and negatively impacted. For the SSA, Article 33 (3) of the Basic Law ('Equal Citizenship- Public Service'),[5] which establishes equal civil and political rights for individuals belonging to different religions, does not preclude the consideration that a specific religious affiliation could lead to a lack of qualification for working in the civil service (BVerfGE 108, 282 (285), 2 BvR 1436/02, para. 5). Although the SSA admitted that the manifestation of religious symbols is protected by Article 4 of the Basic Law ('Freedom of Faith and Conscience'), its denial of Ms. Ludin's claim was based on the idea that "[t]he religious freedom of the complainant is limited by the fundamental right of the students to negative religious freedom, the parent's right of upbringing from paragraph 2 of Article 6, as well as by the state's obligation to religious and worldview neutrality" (BVerfGE 108, 282 (285), 2 BvR 1436/02, para. 5). Ms. Ludin appealed the SSA's decision at the Stuttgart Administrative Court, which rejected her claim based on the idea that "[w]earing a headscarf for religious reasons by a teacher constituted a lack of qualification in the sense of section 11, paragraph 1 of the Baden-Württemberg's Law on State Civil Servants" (BVerfGE 108, 282 (285), 2 BvR 1436/02, para. 6) as the freedom of a teacher to express her religious beliefs clashes with the principle of state neutrality and pupil's negative freedom.

Ms. Ludin appealed to the Baden-Württemberg Court of Administrative Appeals, claiming that the prohibition against wearing the veil infringed her rights under Articles 4 (1) ('Freedom of faith and of conscience, and freedom to profess a religious or philosophical creed, shall be inviolable'), 4 (2) ('The undisturbed practice of religion shall be guaranteed') and Article 33 (3) ('Neither the enjoyment of civil and political rights, nor eligibility for public office, nor rights acquired in the public service shall be dependent upon religious affiliation') of the German Basic Law. The Baden-Württemberg Court of Administrative Appeal considered the

[5]Article 33 [Equal citizenship – Public service] states that "(1) Every German shall have in every Land the same political rights and duties. (2) Every German shall be equally eligible for any public office according to his aptitude, qualifications and professional achievements. (3) Neither the enjoyment of civil and political rights, nor eligibility for public office, nor rights acquired in the public service shall be dependent upon religious affiliation. No one may be disadvantaged by reason of adherence or nonadherence to a particular religious denomination or philosophical creed" (Basic law).

motivations of Ms. Ludin to be irrelevant and reiterated that, as the Baden-Württember Constitution clearly states that public schools are committed to the teaching of Christian and western values, non-Christian teachers should be subjected to certain limitations (VGH Baden-Württemberg, NJW 54 (2001), 2899). As the headscarf constitutes a religious symbol "which the observer [in the school classroom] cannot avoid" (BVerfGE 108, 282 (287), 2 BvR 1436/02, para. 11), "[w]earing a headscarf while teaching could influence the students' religiosity and could lead to conflicts within the affected classrooms" (BVerfGE 108, 282 (287), 2 BvR 1436/02, para. 11). Implicitly, then, Ms. Ludin's veil has been seen as the symbol of a 'conflict of cultures', something dangerous that threatens Baden-Württemberg constitutional values. As a matter of fact, the chairing judge of the Federal Constitutional Court argued that this was not "about a piece of cloth," but rather about the "coexistence of different religions and cultures in Germany" (Hauptmeier, 2003). Clearly, German judges have drawn a dividing line between Christianity, understood as a fundamental western cultural value, and Islam, understood as a backward religion, indicating a privilege of Christianity over other religions. This is also evident in the opening of the parliamentary debate in Baden-Württemberg when it was pointed out that the local Constitution should be honoured and that "youth are to be raised in the fear of God [...] [and] Children will be raised on the basis of Christian and Western educational and cultural values" (Landtag von Baden-Württemberg, 1997, p. 1632). The Federal Administrative Court in Berlin upheld the decision of the lower Courts, explaining that "[t]he right of the teacher to act according to her convictions must retreat from the competing religious freedom of the students and parents while teaching. Neither the requirement of toleration nor the principle of practical harmony compel the conclusion that the parent's right to the upbringing of their children and the religious freedom of the parents and the children must be repressed in favour of a teacher who wears a headscarf" (BVerfGE 108, 282 (289), 2 BvR 1436/02, para. 14).

After a long battle, in 2003 Ludin's appeal reached the German Federal Constitutional Court (GCC), which declared that the specific legal regulations were insufficient to justify banning the veil (BVerfGE 108, 282 (303), NJW 56 (2003), 3111 (3114), 2 BvR 1436/02, para. 49). Indeed, the GCC established that the decision of Baden to ban the veil clashes with Article 33 (2), which establishes equal access to public offices, and Article 4 of the German Basic Law,[6] which grants the unconditional guarantee of religious freedom (BVerfGE 108, 282 (297), 2 BvR 1436/02, para. 38).

The GCC approached the case differently from the previous courts and took into consideration three main aspects in relation to the headscarf: the meaning of the practice; the relation between the veil and the state; and possible empirical evidence of the proselytizing power of the veil. Regarding the meaning of the veil, the Court established that the veil, unlike the crucifix, is not a religious symbol: "the headscarf

[6] It is worth pointing out that access to employment in civil service could be limited by 'subjective criteria' as established in the Law on Guidelines for Employment in the Civil Service [*Beamtenrechtsrahmengesetz*] and the Laws on State Civil Servants [*Landesbeamtengesetzen*].

worn by Muslim women is often perceived as a statement of very different values and ideas: beside expressing the wish to adhere to a dress code that is perceived to be imposed by religion, the headscarf can also be understood as a symbol of clinging on to traditions of the country of origin/parent culture" (BVerfGe, 2003, para 50–51). While the Court admitted that

> "in the most recent times, [the headscarf] is increasingly seen as a political symbol of Islamic fundamentalism that expresses the separation from values of western society [...] according to the findings of fact in the oral hearing, this is not the message that the complainant wishes to convey by wearing the headscarf" (BVerfGe, 2BvR, at Par. II (5) a). The Court added that "the interpretation of the headscarf may not be reduced to a symbol of the social repression of women. Rather, for young Muslim women, it can also be a freely chosen means to conduct a self-determined life without breaking with their culture of origin" (BVerfGe, 2BvR, 2003, at Par. II (5)).

Concerning the relationship between the veil and the state, the Court (BVerfGe, 2003) observed that "a governmental order to install religious symbols in a school cannot be compared to/put on a par to allow teachers to dress in a way that can be interpreted as being religiously motivated" (para 54). Thus, the Court has drawn a clear dividing line between the notion of a state that tolerates the wearing of the veil (such as Germany) and a state that imposes limitations on public officials such as teachers in public schools. In essence, the Court made a distinction between the 'state' and the 'teacher' who is acting for the state: "the state, which accepts the religious statement implicit in the wearing of the veil by a teacher, does not thereby identify with this statement" (BVerfGe, 2003, para 15). Hence, for the Court, religious neutrality applies to the state itself and not to representatives of the state (BVerfGE 108, 282 (299–300), 2 BvR 1436/02, paras. 42–43). The Court also concluded that irrespective of pupils' negative freedom of religion, students and parents cannot avoid any confrontation with other faiths and religious symbols (BVerfGE 108, 282 (301–02), 2 BvR 1436/02, para. 46).

The GCC then analysed whether the veil could have proselytizing effects on young pupils and concluded that no empirical evidence of the veil's negative influence on young children has been found. Through the distinction between abstract and concrete danger, the Court concluded that the mere possibility of a conflict cannot limit the individual's fundamental rights (BVerfGE 108, 282 (301–02), 2 BvR 1436/02, para. 46). The GCC concluded that Ludin's limitation of access to public employment represents an infringement of her rights under Articles 33 (2) (3), 4(1) and (2) of the Basic Law (para 75) and based on the notion of 'open neutrality', a concept linked to the ECtHR's preference for an 'inclusive neutrality' because less limiting of personal rights (Greer, 2000).

The decision of the GCC was based on 5 to 3 votes. The dissenting judges' opinion focused on the relation between the state and civil servants: "whoever wishes to become a civil servant freely chooses to side with the state" (BVerfGe, 2003, Jentsch, Di Fabio & Mellinghoff, dissenting, para 77). For the dissenting judges, "the majority did not take sufficient account of the structural difference" (para. 79) between a civil servant and a normal citizen. For this reason, "[u]ncompromisingly insisting on wearing a headscarf while teaching in a public school, as the complainant has done, is not compatible with the [constitutional] imperative of moderation and neutrality required of a civil servant" (para 102). Notably, for the dissenting judges, the display of the crucifix in public schools was admissible as it is considered a cultural symbol, and not strictly a religious symbol, in contrast with the veil, which has been constructed as a symbol of political Islam and women's subjugation, not as a sign of religious piety.

However, while the German Constitutional Court quashed the decision of Baden-Württemberg to limit the access of veiled women to public schools based on a lack of juridical bases, it reinstated the principle of Federal Independence: in Germany, federal states (also called *Länder*) are also granted the power to pass new laws in relation to the public school system. Hence, federal states have the power to prohibit the wearing of religious, political and philosophical symbols and to re-define the balance between state neutrality and religious manifestation in public schools as long as those limitations are in line with fundamental freedoms. What was a victory for Ms. Ludin was a defeat for many Muslim women after her case. The decision sparked a passionate debate in the country; for many, Ms. Ludin, in her role of teacher in a public school, embodies values contrary to western ones. Ms. Annette Schavan (CDU), former Baden-Württemberg Minister of Culture, highlighted that the Muslim veil is "a symbol of cultural division and part of a history of repression of women" ("German State Plans Headscarf Ban," 2003). Surely, Ms. Ludin represented a disturbance due to her insistence on and persistence in wearing the veil which contradicts the view of Muslim women as submissive and silent: Ms. Ludin wanted to see and to be seen.

The aftermath of the judgement witnessed many *Länder* (including Baden-Württemberg, Bavaria, Hesse, Lower Saxony, Saarland, and most recently Bremen and North Rhine-Westphalia) adopting laws that prohibited women from wearing the headscarf in public schools, discriminating between Christian and Islamic religious symbols. In 2004, Baden-Württemberg enacted a law prohibiting teachers from manifesting any political, philosophical or religious beliefs that could challenge the principle of state neutrality in any public schools.[7] Notably, paragraph 38 (2) of the law clearly states that manifestations of Christian or other traditional western beliefs do not contravene the law, as these manifestations fulfil the educational mandate enshrined in the Constitution.[8] As the Administrative Court considered the new Baden-Württemberg law unconstitutional because it differentiates between 'proper' and 'improper' religious symbols, Baden-Württemberg, followed by other *Länders*, changed Article 38 of the state's education law, adding that

> "teachers are not allowed [...] to give external statements of a political, religious (or) ideological nature, which could endanger or disturb the neutrality of the Land toward pupils or parents or [...] the political, religious or ideological peace in the school [...]. Especially impermissible is an external behaviour which could create the impression on the part of pupils or parents that a teacher opposes the equality (principle) according to Article 3 of the Basic Law, basic liberty rights, or the liberal- democratic order [...]. The representation of

[7] See amended law of April 1, 2004, GVBI. Baden-Wüttemberg 178 (2004).

[8] See Federal Administrative Court's Judgement of June 24, 2004–2 C 45.03.

Christian and occidental values or traditions corresponds to the educational mandate of the [Land] Constitution and does not contradict the required behaviour according to sentence 1".

Notably, the legal adviser of Baden-Württemberg denied that the change in the law constituted a *privilegium Christianum* as, based on his reasoning, Christian symbols express a simple 'historical privilege' of Christianity (Joppke, 2007). In other words, Christian symbols were not seen as an "expression of an identification with religion" but "of a national identity," which carries an 'historical value' (Joppke, 2007, p. 333). To demonstrate his point, he took as his example the city emblem of Munich, a monk: "nobody could say that the city of Munich is in any way favouring a religion here; instead, it is only performing its tradition" (Joppke, 2007, p. 333). Hence, while the *hijab* has been banned, catholic nuns could continue to teach in public schools; "the nun's dress is, of course, admissible, because it corresponds to a historical formation" (Joppke, 2007, p. 333). Baden-Württemberg's decision was followed by the decisions of other *Länder* to ban the veil in public schools as the item was seen to threaten the principle of state neutrality and the Christian roots of the country. Germany's Christian roots are to be found in the Constitution of diverse *Länder*. The Constitution of Bavaria (one of the most conservative regions), for instance, states that reverence to God is one of the main educational goals of public education while the Baden-Württemberg Constitution specifies that "youth are to be raised in the fear of God [...] Children will be raised on the basis of Christian and Western educational and cultural values".[9] The privilege given to Christianity derives from a 1975 Constitutional Court decision which stated that in the region of Baden, children "were educated on the basis of Christian and occidental educational and cultural values".[10] Indeed, the preamble of the German Constitution opens with a reference to the responsibility of German people towards God.

The contraposition between Christian and Islamic symbols has been at the centre of the headscarf debate in Germany. Unlike in France, where all 'conspicuous religious symbols' are banned, German anti-veiling laws do not prohibit the display of religious symbols, but only political symbols, locating Christianity in a privileged position. While it is difficult to reconcile Germany's concept of neutrality with the privileging of a particular creed, as it would entail a discrimination between different religions, shifting the meaning of the cross from religious to cultural symbol and of the veil from religious to political symbol, Germany managed to justify adopting different forms of treatment towards Christianity and Islam and limiting Muslim women's fundamental rights without perceiving this as a limitation of their religious liberty. In Germany, unlike in France, the state and the church collaborate in specific areas (such as the health sector and childcare), Christian religion is taught in public schools, and Christian churches are recognized by the state as public corporations.

[9] Plenarprotokoll 12 / 23 20.03.97, (Stuttgart, 1997) 1630–32.

[10] 55BverfGE 41, 29 ("Simultanschule"), decision of 17 December 1975; the quote is from Article 16 of the 1953 constitution of Baden-Wurttemberg.

Clearly, the matter of state neutrality in Germany is quite vague. In the *Ludin* case, the GCC gave two different meanings of state neutrality in public schools: the first allows every religious symbol to be displayed, ensuring religious pluralism, while the second excludes any religious symbol to avoid possible conflicts (irreligious neutrality) (BVerfGe, 2003, para 64–5). Although the 1949 Constitution is inspired by Christian tradition,[11] and the country does not apply strict secular policies, the required neutrality of the state should be interpreted in a way to give equal status to all religious affiliations. In the case of Germany, it is unclear why different religions do not enjoy the same rights and whether the neutrality of the state requires the banning of religious symbols from schools. While in France 'neutrality' signifies the invisibility of any religious symbols, in Germany neutrality has taken another meaning which seems to differentiate between religious affiliations. Henceforth, while in France the principle of neutrality requires the suppression of religious expression of its citizens, now stripped of any particularity, by contrast, in Germany, citizens should conform to Judeo-Christian values and norms. The banning of the veil, along with the visibility of Christian symbols and the invisibility of Islamic ones, indicates that Germany violates constitutional equality principles: this, in turn, amounts to a defeat of neutrality where 'us' and 'them' cannot be part of the same 'occidental-Christian' tradition.

Hence, on the one hand German neutrality embraces a plurality of religions, while on the other, it understands itself as a secularized product of Christianity: this has led to the idea that in a country whose roots are so linked to the Christian tradition (which implies a specific idea of what religion is), equality between religions will be difficult to achieve. Clearly, the recent debate over the wearing of the veil mirrors a wider national imagination which excludes Muslim women by rendering them invisible, revealing the inability to accommodate Islam within the German Christian tradition.

3.3 'Is Multiculturalism Bad for Women?': The *Begum* Case in the UK

In her debated essay 'Is Multiculturalism Bad for Women?' Susan Okin (1999) highlights the tensions between feminism and multiculturalism, claiming to be sceptical on issues that justify gender inequality in the name of religious/cultural specificity. For Okin (1999), many cultural/religious/ethnic minority groups which are nowadays demanding 'minority rights' carry patriarchal values that often limit women's choice and their possibility of agency: hence, upholding minority groups' rights would carry the risk of undermining women's rights. In a similar vein, Honig

[11] Art. 2 of the Grundgesetz, the Federal Constitutional Court considers the great German churches as comprising of the Lutherans and the Roman-Catholics, through the interpretation of the term *Sittengesetz* (moral law). Decision of 10 May 1957, BverGE 6, 389.

(1999) warns of the "fragile gains of feminism [which] may be attenuated by heightened multicultural sensitivities" (p. 35). In relation to the Muslim headscarf, these scholars see in the French ban the disclosing of an inherent contradiction, namely prohibiting the practice of veiling while 'quietly permitting' it in name of 'cultural rights'. But the relation between multiculturalism, veiling and women's rights is particularly interesting in the British context.

England has tried to accommodate different cultures and religions through a multicultural secular system where different groups (such as religious, ethnic, cultural etc.) are entitled to formulate legal claims based on their diversity. This, in turn, entails a 'politics of recognition of differences' able to respect individual fundamental rights and to accommodate different identities in the public sphere. Yet, the debate over the headscarf has not spared the UK where the discourse over the veil has focused precisely on the recognition of diversity. The *Begum* case (2004, 2005, 2006) is a compelling example of the tension between 'recognition' and 'avoidance', 'acceptable' and 'unacceptable' religious practices and their link with the notion of citizenship and gender equality: in the case, judges oscillate between the desire to uphold neutral policy which creates homogeneity in the public sphere, and the need to accommodate differences into hybrid identities (Taylor, 1994). More importantly, the *Begum* case not only divided public opinion, but it also re-opened the discussion about multicultural policy in the country.

Shabina was a young student at Denbigh High School, where 75–80% of pupils were Muslims. The school, in view of its recognition of the multicultural/multi-faith environment, has imposed a uniform code in accordance with parents, pupils, and three local *Imams* which requires young Muslim girls to wear a *shalwar kameez,* a long tunic wrapped over a pair of trousers. One day, Shabina arrived at school with a *jilbab* (a long dress that covers the whole body except for the face), claiming that the *shalwar kameeze* did not comply with the requirement of her faith. The Head of School's Assistant noted that when Shabina entered school with a *jilbab* many young students felt "threatened" as the garment was "associated with extreme views and it would identify them as belonging to extreme Muslim sects" (*Shabina v. Denbigh High School* EWHR 2004 para. 51). As a compromise was impossible, Shabina was expelled and she sued the school based on religious discrimination: in 2004 the Administrative Court dismissed her claim, while she won in the appeal. The Court of Appeal held that the school did not take into account that Shabina had the right to wear religious dress even if those differ from the majority of believers (2005 EWCA Civ 199). Noting the difference between the British political system and other European countries', the Court of Appeal established that the limitation of the claimant's fundamental freedoms could not be justified under Article 9 (2) of the ECHR and that the school, in deciding about the appropriate students' uniform, did not take into consideration Article 9 of the ECHR, which protects the manifestation of religious beliefs. Finally, the case reached the House of Lords (UKHL 15, 2006) which quashed the decision of the Court of Appeal and ruled in favour of the school. The House of Lords held that the school had the right to introduce a uniform policy taking into consideration that the institution had tried to accommodate different cultural and religious traditions in choosing the best uniform for the school's pupils;

in this view, the limitation of Shabina's personal freedom was considered proportionate and necessary.

The judges and Lords focused on various issues: firstly, they considered whether Shabina had been excluded or if she 'excluded' herself by refusing to remove the *jilbab*. In the Administrative Court, Bennett J argued that Shabina had not been excluded: rather, she had excluded herself by choosing not to wear the school uniform, as she was aware of the school uniform policy when she started at the school. For this reason, the limitation was justified by art. 9 (2) of the ECHR as the school's decision to allow the *shalwar kameeze* was a means of inclusion. The Court of Appeal rejected this argument: Brooke LJ noted the existence of various interpretations of Islamic law in relation to female clothing, suggesting that Shabina's freedom to manifest her religion had been limited ([2006] UKHL 15, para. 28). The House of Lords, however, agreed with the outcome of the Administrative Court, stating that Denbigh High School did not intend to exclude Shabina (para. 38). The Lords recalled the decision in *Spiers v Warrington Corporation* ([1954] 1 QB para. 61) concerning the expulsion from school of a girl because she was not properly dressed. In the decision, Lord Goddard CJ stated that "the headmistress did not suspend this child at all. She was always perfectly willing to take her in; all that she wanted was that she should be properly dressed" (para. 66). For this reason, their Lordships believed that the act of expelling Shabina could not amount to an 'exclusion' for the purpose of sec. 64 of the School Standards and Framework Act 1998,[12] as she was never directed to stay away from school: rather, she was encouraged to return to school with the correct uniform and so it was Shabina that excluded herself. The position of the House of Lords regarding Shabina's 'voluntary contracting out' of the protection of Article 9 remains, however, quite controversial. It is difficult to define a situation as 'voluntarily chosen', as I will argue in the final chapter; indeed, it is arguable whether individuals should give up their jobs or change school in order to manifest their religion or whether the 'voluntary contracting out' could safeguard individual rights and freedoms. Their Lordships did not consider that "enrolling a child at a particular school is underpinned by informed consent and unconstrained choice [and they] appear to ignore the difficulties involved in sending a child to a different school" (Gies, 2006, p. 385–86). They also did not consider the emotional challenge of a young girl changing school in order to be able to manifest her religious beliefs.

In order to understand whether Shabina had been denied her right to education resulting from 2 years' interruption due to her position towards the school uniform

[12] Section 64 of the Act provides for the "power of head teacher to exclude pupils. (1) The head teacher of a maintained school may exclude a pupil from the school for a fixed period or permanently (2) The head teacher may not exercise the power to exclude a pupil from the school for one or more fixed periods such that the pupil is so excluded for more than 45 school days in any one school year. (3) A pupil may not be excluded from a maintained school (whether by suspension, expulsion or otherwise) except by the head teacher in accordance with this section. (4) In this Act "exclude", in relation to the exclusion of a child from a school, means exclude on disciplinary grounds (and "exclusion" shall be construed accordingly)."

policy, their Lordships took into consideration Article 2 of the First Protocol of the Convention. They concluded that, although 2 years of interruption is a source of regret, there was not an infringement of Article 2 as Shabina has chosen not to comply with the school policy, explaining that Article 2 is infringed when a claimant has been unable to have an education: as Shabina could study in another school that accepted the wearing of the *jilbab*, her right to education was not infringed. In fact, based on the English and the ECHR jurisdiction, freedom of religion could be limited if it falls within the scope of the Steadman analysis which recognizes limitation of personal freedoms in cases in which the individual has voluntary subjected itself to restriction or s/he has a choice to alter her/his position (Malik, 2008).

The House of Lords also considered whether Shabina's freedom of religion had been violated. By referring to the *Sahin* case (*Sahin v Turkey*, 2005) concerning the expulsion of a university student from a university in Turkey because veiled, the House of Lords argued that a certain margin of appreciation was allowed when considering section 2 of Article 9 which imposes limitations to the manifestation of religious beliefs when necessary. Lord Bingham noted that Article 9 makes a distinction between the right to hold a belief and the right to manifest a belief, which can lead to considerations over the 'rights and freedoms of others' ([2006] UKHL 15 para. 99). It is exactly this principle of respecting the 'freedom of others' that has activated the 'margin of appreciation' in previous cases decided at the ECtHR. Although the margin of appreciation is a principle of ECtHR jurisprudence[13] and so is not an option for national Courts in European countries, the United Kingdom has applied the principle in deciding over Shabina's case. Without any reference to the substantial differences between Turkey and the UK, Lord Bingham stated that

> "a domestic Court should accept the decision of Parliament to allow individual schools to make their own decisions about uniforms. The decision does not have to be made at a national level and national differences between Turkey and the United Kingdom are irrelevant [...] [i]n applying the principles of *Sahin v Turkey* the justification must be sought at the local level and it is there that an area of judgment, comparable to the margin of appreciation, must be allowed to the school" (para. 64). This point was also highlighted by Lord Hoffman who stated that the school was "in the best position to weigh and consider [...] [its] wish to avoid clothes which were perceived by some Muslims (rightly or wrongly) as signifying adherence to an extremist vision of the Muslim religion and to protect girls against external pressures" ([2006] UKHL 15; para. 65).[14]

However, as in other cases related to the wearing of the veil in Europe, the Lords failed to provide evidence of the pressure on others and to prove that banning the veil could be the best choice to protect other young girls. Indeed, the Lords failed to prove that the limitation of Shabina's freedom was 'necessary in a democratic

[13] The margin of appreciation plays an important role in remitting certain kinds of judgements to democratically elected officials who are said to know the particular context of their country better. It is usually employed by the ECHR when there is not a formal European consensus on particular topics or where the issue is particularly controversial (Arai & Arai-Takahashi, 2002).

[14] This argument has been, however, dismissed by many scholars (Davies, 2005).

society' as required by the Strasbourg jurisprudence. Instead, the Lords focused on whether the school had made a reasonable decision regarding the pupils' uniform, avoiding discussion about the possibility of implementing a less restrictive dress code policy.

The Lords' analysis of Article 9 (2) should focus on the claimant's substantive rights and not on whether the school had followed the correct legal procedure. The Lords explained that the school had consulted students, parents and three local *Imams* before adopting the school uniform. At the time, no objection had arisen from families or *Imams* in terms of Islamic requirements as the *shalwar kameez* was deemed to respect the Islamic requirement of modesty. The importance given by the Lords to a few designated religious authorities is striking as it shows a lack of recognition of the diversity of Muslims. As a matter of fact, when, in 2003, the school asked the Muslim Council of Britain which was the appropriate dress code for Muslim women, the Council answered that there was not a recommended style as long as the value of modesty was observed. Does Shabina not have the right to choose which authority to follow or how to express the Islamic value of modesty?

Indeed, by focusing on the importance of the school's consultation with the Muslim community and the pupils' families, the House of Lords gave great importance to the group aspect of freedom of religion, rather than to Shabina's autonomous choice. This in some ways narrowed the possibility for Shabina to negotiate her claim based on her personal choice, although her claim was also unsuccessful on a ground of autonomous choice. The House of Lords took into consideration whether Shabina, at that time 14 years old, had freely chosen to wear the *jilbab*: for Lord Scott, "the confrontational nature of the peremptory manner in which the *jilbab* issue was raised with the school was very unlikely to have been chosen by Shabina, not yet 14 years of age" (UKHL 15, para 80). By taking a distance from the ECtHR's view that sees veiling as an oppressive practice imposed on women (as in the *Sahin* and *Dahlab* cases, for instance, to which I will return) the House of Lords discussed Shabina's 'free choice'. The Lords emphasized that Shabina had worn the *shalwar kameeze* without any problem for 2 years prior her dispute with the school: implicitly, then, the Lords asserted that Shabina could not autonomously change her mind and so she was not free to choose what was better for her. Baroness Hale pointed out that "if a woman freely chooses to adopt a way of life for herself, it is not for others, including other women who have chosen differently, to criticize or prevent her" (UKHL 15, para. 96). In the meantime, however, she expressed a particular preoccupation with the 'free will' of young Muslim girls in the UK pointing out that "if a Sikh man wears a turban or a Jewish man a *yamoulka*, we can readily assume that it was his free choice to adopt the dress dictated by the teaching of his religion" (para 94). The sentence is quite contradictory as it is not clear how a man is free to choose his garments if they are 'dictated' by religious beliefs while a woman is not. By referring to Raday, an ex-member of the UN Committee on the Elimination of Discrimination Against Women, Baroness Hale advocated the necessity for schools' neutrality to enhance the principle of gender equality: for Raday, "'mandatory policy that rejects veiling in state educational institutions may provide a crucial opportunity for girls to *choose the feminist freedom* of state education over the patriarchal dominance of their families" (Raday as cited in UKHL 15; [2007] para. 98).[15] It seems that Baroness Hale operated a separation between gender and culture, implying that they are two concepts in opposition and so needing to be balanced by the state.[16] Clearly, Shabina's case has been played around the rhetoric of choice. This, however, has been used to hide western chauvinism towards non-liberal cultures as in the west women are also constrained by a specific idea of womanhood. In the discourse concerning the banning of the veil, western clothes are constructed as expressing a freedom of choice and Islamic ones a complete lack of choice: Brown (2006) sees in this construction the need for western culture to define itself in contraposition with other cultures: "we need fundamentalism, indeed, we project and produce it elsewhere, to represent ourselves as free" (p. 189).

Notably, in the House of Lords' decision, Shabina's claim oscillated between individual and community rights. On the one hand, the recognition of 'her' kind of Islam as a religion, which carries the fundamental right to be protected, while on the other, her continuous defence of her choice to wear the *jilbab* as an 'autonomous choice'. Hence, while Shabina's claim for recognition of a specific interpretation of Islam raises the question of Islam (plural) identities, it only becomes possible as long as wearing the *jilbab* is her autonomous choice. This, however, leads to the counter-argument of the school: first, it seems that Shabina was the only Muslim girl in the school who complained about the policy (reinforcing the idea that she embraced extremist views). Second, the fact that Shabina was pushed to present the *jilbab* as a choice reinforces the argument that she could have chosen differently, avoiding excluding herself. If, as Düttmann (2000) argues, recognition is the recognition of what it is already recognized, Shabina's *jilbab* was pre-recognized as a symbol of extremist Islam: in this view, Shabina automatically becomes an individual who threatens the peace of the school by wearing clothes that symbolize extremists and intolerant ideals. As the *jilbab* was pre-recognized as a symbol incompatible with western/liberal values of tolerance, Shabina could not defend her choice on a ground of a personal and autonomous choice, nor she could claim minority religious rights, as British judges and school authorities did not recognize the *jilbab* as a normal manifestation of the Muslim faith.

Indeed, while the Court expressed a particular preoccupation with the fact that when Shabina arrived at school wearing a *jilbab*, she was accompanied by her two older brothers who had often spoken for her, judges and Lords also spoke for Shabina, defining whether she had freely chosen to wear the *jilbab*. I will return to women's freedom of choice in the last part, but for the moment it is worth noticing the Lords' assumption that the law should 'save' a young girl (in the case, Shabina) from Islamic radicalism, otherwise she should pay a price for her choice. This is well explained by Lord Hoffman's speech which clearly pointed out that "people sometimes have to suffer some inconvenience for their beliefs and choices" ([2006]

[15] *Italics added.*

[16] This view ignores that the very concept of gender equality is the result of a particular (western) culture (Salecl, 1994).

UKHL, para 50). In the same view, Lord Bingham stated that the claimant had *chosen* to study in a secular institution, presupposing a rational abstract self-mastering individual free from any constraints without any reference to whether Shabina could obtain the same education in another school. Hence, the Lords did not find any interference with Shabina's freedom of religion as she has 'voluntarily' chosen to put herself in a situation that she knew would limit the manifestation of her religious beliefs. Notably, by seeing Shabina as responsible for her own beliefs and convictions, the Lords made a distinction between different kinds of discrimination which, in turn, define the very category of religion: in other words, unlike sex, ethnicity or gender, religion is something that the individual can choose and not an integral part of the individual which forms its very interiority. The notion that religion is a matter of personal choice and that the individual is responsible for its own beliefs is well explained by Lord Bingham who stated that

> "the Strasbourg institutions have not been at all ready to find an interference with the right to manifest religious belief in practices or observance where a person has voluntarily accepted an employment or role which does not accommodate that practice or observance and there are other means open to the person to practice or observe his or her religion without undue hardship or inconvenience [...]. There is [...] no evidence to show that there was any real difficulty in [Shabina Begum attending another school that permitted the wearing of a *jilbab*], as she has in fact done and could no doubt have done sooner had she chosen" (para 24–5).

The reasoning, however, contradicts previous decisions. In the case *Noah v. Desrosiers* (2008), in which a claimant was not employed in a hairdressing salon because she refused to remove her veil, the employment tribunal found that Desrosiers has indirectly discriminated against the claimant, although she could find a job in another salon. For the Court, the salon's rule prohibiting the headscarf was a burden for the claimant which did not justify the achievement of a legitimate aim. If we also apply this logic in the *Begum* case, then Shabina had been discriminated against by the school.

Another controversial point for the Lords' decision is the way in which Shabina's desire to wear the *jilbab* was presented:

> "on 3 September 2002, the first day of the autumn term, the respondent (then aged nearly 14) went to the school with her brother and another young man. They asked to speak to the head teacher, who was not available, and they spoke to the assistant head teacher, Mr. Moore. They insisted that the respondent be allowed to attend school wearing the long garment she had on that day, which was a long coat-like garment known as a jilbab. They talked of human rights and legal proceedings. Mr. Moore felt that their approach was unreasonable, and he felt threatened" ([2006] UKHL 15, para. 10).

Hence, while western European countries celebrated Human Rights as an important achievement, trying to enforce one's own personal human right is seen as threatening and confronting behaviour (Mikhail, 2008).

The *Begum* case illustrates the difficulty in defining the scope of freedom of religion in a multicultural society and, at the same time, the challenge posed to a liberal/multicultural/secular society in a global era. In the British context, this is mirrored in the various religious claims, such as the accommodation of Sikhs wearing turbans (*Mandla v Dowell Ue,* 1983), or the accommodation of a Muslim teacher's timetable to allow them to pray in the Mosque on Friday (*Copsey v Devon –Clays,* 2005). In all these claims, applicants required 'exceptional rules' by arguing that what seemed to be neutral was in reality a privilege for specific groups of citizens. While the Race Relations Act 2000 gives an example of rule-exception accommodation, cases of accommodation of religious minorities show the difficulty in accommodating very different claims, especially when a monolithic and fixed notion of religion and belief is given. In fact, unlike claims related to the accommodation of cultural, gender or ethnic minorities, religious minorities' claims challenge the private/public divide at the base of secular/liberal thought. Liberal/secularism, as it is clear from the case analysis, tends to protect religious liberty in the private sphere and to limit this right in the public sphere. The fear is that the manifestation of different religious identities would undermine the ability of the individual to identify itself with the state and so it will threaten the relation between the individual and the state (Malik, 2008).

The *Begum* case should be placed, therefore, as representative of the tension between liberal and multicultural political visions on the accommodation of different religious minorities. Specifically, the case shows the difficulty in drawing a line between religion and ideology, and between 'accepted' and 'unaccepted' religious practices. This dichotomous understanding of religion hides the many ways in which Muslims practice Islam and reduces both the Islamic religion and the Muslim religious subject to a monolithic and fixed entity.

Liberal and multicultural settings have been deeply criticized in relation to the accommodation of religious minorities. For some, liberal theory does not recognize the existence of important cultural diversity (Kymlicka, 1995b). For others, it is the nation-state itself which aims at creating a united (imagined) political community that is threatened by cultural differences (Parekh, 2001). Tully (1995) notes that the application of liberal theory in the nation-state, based on the uniformity of constitutional principles, is threatened by the juridical accommodation of religious minorities that challenge the fixed identity of the state. While multicultural scholars (Kymlicka, 1995a; Taylor, 1992) pose a particular emphasis on the individual as the base of group minority rights, those theories encounter a fundamental problem, namely, that to be defined as a minority, communities should highlight their differences from the common identity, culture and traditions of a country in order to make a particular claim (Mahmood, 2015): this, in turn, would lead to the exacerbation of differences and, as in the *Begum* case, to the exclusion of certain (unaccepted) differences.

As western liberal nation states are constituted by a clear and explicit constitutional settlement, different identities and definition of citizenship become problematic. The accommodation of different religious minorities has important implications in relation to the equal treatment of all citizens irrespective of different cultures, traditions or religious affiliations. Yet, to treat citizens equally means also to recognize the differences between citizens (Malik, 2010).

Shabina's case clearly deals with the accommodation of diversity, based on the recognition of her diversity. This, in turn, entails a recognition of identities and differences, which is inevitably linked to the concept of 'inclusion' and 'exclusion'. Both the school and Shabina argued for the importance of recognizing different religious identities in the public sphere. Shabina sees in the *jilbab* the public manifestation of her religious identity: the *jilbab*, she writes, "represents Islam as way of life rather than Islam as a few personal rituals and actions. It is a public expression of Islam as a way of life or ideology" (as cited in Thomassen, 2011, pp. 326). Shabina's point is that she cannot privatize her religious beliefs as they are part of her identity. On the other hand, for the school, the point to take into consideration is which religious identities should be recognized and therefore protected by law. This was also the position of the House of Lords which, in upholding the school's decision, implicitly chose between different religious beliefs (e.g. acceptable religious beliefs v unacceptable religious beliefs). The Lords, unlike the judges in the Court of Appeal, did not recognize that different interpretations of Islamic law correspond to different sartorial practices. Instead, they preferred to take the position of the school for whom the *jilbab* "would lead to divisiveness within the school and would threaten cohesion within the school" (UKHL 15, para 84). In this view, the school recognized certain differences (ethnic, religious, class, gender etc.), but not all. Hence, for the school, the problem was not religious difference *as such*, but the content of Shabina's difference as the school authorities saw in Shabina's *jilbab* an intrinsic link with Islamic extremism. The rejection of Shabina's difference by the school and the Court shows that the recognition of religious differences is constructed to create specific social hierarchies, whereas western values acquire a universal character which allows the law to protect only certain differences that conform to western secular sensitivities. As I shall show in the last part, since the manifestation of ('inappropriate') religious symbols is understood as a failure of the project of western modernity, the solution is the elimination of visible differences in name of assimilation to western/secular/liberal universal values. In light of this, multicultural policy as applied in the UK does not recognize differences; rather, it 're-organizes' and 'manages' certain differences which carry detrimental effects for different religious minorities.

Returning to Okin's (1999) provocative question on whether multiculturalism is bad for women, it seems to me that a more accurate analysis of the recognition of differences between and within women should be made. The *Begum* case shows a failure of multiculturalism to accommodate the differences between Muslim women, presupposing not only a specific notion of womanhood, but also a monolithic and fixed law and religious subject which arguably defended Shabina's desire to express her religious beliefs by wearing a *jilbab*. The analysis of the *Begum* case highlights the way in which hierarchies are established in western multicultural/liberal/secular countries in order to assimilate differences into the homogeneity of western societies: this, however, has given to certain groups of women the burden of limiting their rights in the name of common shared values.[17] What is of particular interest is not whether multiculturalism is opposed to women's rights, but how

[17] For a detailed discussion of 'multiculturalism vulnerability' see Shachar (2001).

multicultural policy constructs specific binary oppositions between different notions of religion and womanhood: while western women are defined as autonomous free agents, Muslim women are seen as subjugated to patriarchal religious rules. This binary opposition has led inevitably to the establishment of a hierarchy among western and non-western women whereas the western concept of women's freedom and agency becomes paramount in the understanding of whether multiculturalism is bad for women. In the case of the banning of the veil, universal western values of autonomy have operated in a way to exclude and oppress Muslim women, instead of liberating them. In this sense, multiculturalism is not a system that includes different religions, cultures and ethnicity but, increasingly, a way to ghettoize different religions that are deemed to be compatible with the western way of thinking while excluding others that are deemed incompatible.

3.4 Upholding Dichotomies: Reading the ECtHR Legal Decisions Over the Practice of Veiling

The turmoil caused by the juridical regulation of the Muslim veil has reached the ECtHR which has been called to decide on whether the European banning of the Muslim veil respects the individual's fundamental rights, enshrined in the ECHR. While in recent years the ECtHR has decided on many cases concerning the wearing of the veil, I consider *Dahlab v Switzerland* (2001), Sahin v Turkey (2005) *and* SAS v France (2014) particularly exemplificative of secular/liberal paradoxes concerning women and religious freedom in secular Europe. All the applicants claimed an infringement of their rights under art. 8, 9, 10 and 14[18] of the

[18] Art. 8 'Right to respect for private and family life 1. Everyone has the right to respect for his private and family life, his home and his correspondence. 2. There shall be no interference by a public authority with the exercise of this right except such as is in accordance with the law and is necessary in a democratic society in the interests of national security, public safety or the economic well-being of the country, for the prevention of disorder or crime, for the protection of health or morals, or for the protection of the rights and freedoms of others.' Art. 9 'Freedom of thought, conscience and religion 1. Everyone has the right to freedom of thought, conscience and religion; this right includes freedom to change his religion or belief and freedom, either alone or in community with others and in public or private, to manifest his religion or belief, in worship, teaching, practice and observance. 2. Freedom to manifest one's religion or beliefs shall be subject only to such limitations as are prescribed by law and are necessary in a democratic society in the interests of public safety, for the protection of public order, health or morals, or for the protection of the rights and freedoms of others.' Art 10 'Freedom of expression 1. Everyone has the right to freedom of expression. This right shall include freedom to hold opinions and to receive and impart information and ideas without interference by public authority and regardless of frontiers. This Article shall not prevent States from requiring the licensing of broadcasting, television or cinema enterprises. 2. The exercise of these freedoms, since it carries with it duties and responsibilities, may be subject to such formalities, conditions, restrictions or penalties as are prescribed by law and are necessary in a democratic society, in the interests of national security, territorial integrity or public safety, for the prevention of disorder or crime, for the protection of health or morals, for the protec-

ECHR. However, through a considerable emphasis on state neutrality and the defence of secular values, along with the distinction made by art. 9 between faith and its manifestation (to which I will return in the next chapter), the ECtHR has widened the 'margin of appreciation', leaving considerable discretion to member states to define what kind of religious manifestations are allowed in the secular public space. The ECtHR recognises that each member state has a different concept of secularism and the state-church relationship varies widely within Europe: for the ECtHR judges, "where questions concerning the relationship between State and religions are at stake, on which opinion in a democratic society may reasonably differ widely, the role of the national decision-making body must be given special importance" (*Sahin v Turkey*, 2005, para 101). However, this (apparently) neutral position to protect the plurality of European views on state-church relations actually hides a European desire to assimilate different religious practices and sensitivities into the homogeneity of Christian/secular European culture.

This is well shown in the case *Dahlab v Switzerland* (2001) decided at the ECtHR. Ms. Dahlab was a teacher in a primary school in Switzerland. After a period of deep spiritual searching she converted to Islam and started to wear the *hijab*. She wore the veil for 4 years; during that time there was no complaint from her young students or their families. When students asked her why she was wearing long clothing and covering her head, she used to answer that it was to keep her ears warm. After 4 years, an inspector visited the school and reported that Ms. Dahlab was wearing 'Muslim' garments. The Director General of Public Education asked her to remove the veil: when Dahlab refused, alleging her right to wear the headscarf, she was dismissed. She appealed the decision in the Swiss Court which, upholding the decision of the school, found Ms. Dahlab's request conflicted with the norms of a Christian country and prohibited the wearing of the headscarf based on a law on the state's neutrality. The domestic Court pointed out that it was impossible for the law to cover all state school teachers' behaviours and that some margin was allowed in circumstances where the conduct would be regarded by the average citizen as being of minor importance. Ms. Dahlab appealed at the ECtHR which, in line with the Swiss Court, pointed out that Switzerland was pursuing a legitimate aim to ban the *hijab* in public schools in the name of gender equality (as the veil has been seen by the judges as a chauvinist practice imposed on women by the Koran) and state neutrality, considered an expression of state's secularism.

In the case, the ECtHR found that the principle of *laïcité* could be interpreted in such a way as to allow states to restrict personal freedoms and it emphasized the importance of weighting "the requirements of the protection of the rights and liberties of others against the conduct of which the applicant stood accused" (*Dahlab v*

---

tion of the reputation or rights of others, for preventing the disclosure of information received in confidence, or for maintaining the authority and impartiality of the judiciary.' Art 14 'Prohibition of discrimination The enjoyment of the rights and freedoms set forth in this Convention shall be secured without discrimination on any ground such as sex, race, colour, language, religion, political or other opinion, national or social origin, association with a national minority, property, birth or other status.'

Switzerland, 2001, p. 12): suddenly, the right-holder woman has become the accused. In fact, instead of weighting the rights of Ms. Dahlab to wear the *hijab* with the rights and freedoms of others, the ECtHR presented an (imaginary) undefined 'other' in need of protection from the 'wrongdoing' of Ms. Dahlab. The Court presupposed that, because Ms. Dahlab was working with young children and the student-teacher relationship is a powerful one, her *hijab* could have 'proselytizing effects'. However, the Court did not find any coercive or proselytizing action carried out by the applicant to induce students to behave or believe in the same way she did. Indeed, it is not clear what kind of 'bad influence' or 'proselytizing effects' Ms. Dahlab was exercising on 'vulnerable children' since she did not even tell them that she had converted to Islam: in other words, it is unclear how Ms. Dahlab could violate the negative religious freedom of young children when she was not involved in any preaching or missionary activities. Moreover, in 4 years, it should have been possible to produce further evidence from students who had suffered as a result of her wearing the *hijab*. Many of those children were probably exposed to religious rituals by parents, relatives and other figures of authority; consequently, it is difficult to understand how Ms. Dahlab would defy the authority figures of a child's life. Furthermore, many Muslim children attended the school and they might have asked why a teacher who dressed like them had been dismissed. Those children, who probably suffered from mistrust or discrimination, may have received the message that stereotypes about Muslims are valid (Killian, 2003). Moreover, if it is true that we live in a pluralistic society, how can we justify the fact that, when the individual works in public places she has to comply with 'liberal' values?[19] If wearing a *hijab* creates tensions and conflicts, as stated in the Strasbourg decision, then the parties should take measures to reconcile and not to prohibit group manifestations; in this view, allowing the manifestation of any religious symbols at school could decrease the psychological pressure (supposedly) exercised by the wearing of the headscarf.

The weakness of the accusation of proselytism moved against Ms. Dahlab is evident when comparing the case with *Kokkinakis v Greece* (1993), decided at the ECtHR. The case involved two Jehovah's Witnesses who were charged with the criminal offence of proselytizing after knocking on the doors of diverse Greek Orthodox priests in order to try to convince them of the truth of their religion in a country where it is illegal.[20] The Court held that the conviction of the Greek national Court against Mr. Kokkinakis was a breach of Article 9 of the ECHR because the simple attempt to convince others to convert to a religious belief cannot be considered a breach of freedom of religion (*Kokkinakis v Greece*, 1993). Notably, the Court distinguishes between 'proper' proselytism, which is protected by Article 9, and 'improper' proselytism which may be prohibited as incompatible with the freedoms of others. Based on the Court's reasoning,

---

[19] In *Kokkinakis v Greece,* (1993, para 31), and in the case of *Manoussakis and Others v. Greece* (1996, para 44), the ECHR clearly stated that pluralism is an important feature in a democratic society.

[20] In Greece proselytism is forbidden by constitution. For this reason, Mr. Kokkinakis was judged guilty by the Greek Court (see Art. 13. 2 of the Constitution of Greece).

> "[proper proselytism] corresponds to true evangelism, which a report drawn up in 1956 under the auspices of the World Council of Churches describes as an essential mission and a responsibility of every Christian and every Church. [...] [In contrast, improper proselytism] represents a corruption or deformation of it. It may, according to the same report, take the form of activities offering material or social advantages with a view to gaining new members for a Church or exerting improper pressure on people in distress or in need; it may even entail the use of violence or brainwashing; more generally, it is not compatible with respect for the freedom of thought, conscience and religion of others" (*Kokkinakis v Greece*, 1993, para 48).

Oddly, for the ECtHR, Ms. Dahlab's clothing represented a greater threat to liberty than Mr. Kokkinakis's attempt to proselytize: in fact, the former was considered by the ECtHR as a 'proper' form of proselytism whiles the latter was not. The position that the ECtHR has adopted in the *Kokkinakis* case is difficult to reconcile with the one taken by the Court in the *Dahlab* case as she did not pursue any proselytising activities. In this view, although the Court took into consideration the principle of proportionality and necessity, it applied them inconsistently. While, for the Court, it was not necessary to regulate proselytizing actions such as that committed by Kokkinakis in a country where this action was considered illegal by the domestic laws, in Switzerland, removing a woman from a public space because she had started to wear the veil was presented by the ECtHR as a necessity to save the principle of 'state neutrality'. Thus, the principles of proportionality and necessity, as applied by the ECtHR, do not restrain western/liberal paradoxes; rather, they allow them to be perpetrated. In fact, if the rule of law is ultimately a promise of predictability, the very idea that one has to wait and see *how* the Court will in each case employ the tests of proportionality and necessity is paradoxical. This paradox reveals that in order for the 'sovereign nation-state' to remain strong and unified, certain performances of some rights have to be limited. In the event, a Muslim woman's dress choice is more threatening than a Christian man's speech.

The fact that a woman who never tried to proselytize was *removed* from the public space just because her image did not conform to the western conception of liberated woman is a significant feature: not only does it reveal that in liberalism the individual emerges as an abstract entity who, while enjoying the *allowed* freedoms, is also subjected to the state's rules, but it also unmasks the intrinsic paradoxes of positive and Human Rights law. In fact, if the individual has 'equal rights' those rights can be regulated more or less depending on how abstractly or concretely the individual is perceived to be using these rights. The protection afforded to the individual by the rules of law –certainty, predictability – follows this pattern. If Kokkinakis's proselytizing is protected, it is because 'he did nothing but speak' with the intention to convert another who is free to accept or not; if Ms. Dahlab was removed from sight it was because she demonstrated, performed, acted out her right to be different, which carries illocutionary force. In other words, Kokkinakis' proselytizing speech benefits the model of the Christian/secular/'human' protected as an abstract equal citizen from the state; by contrast, Dahlab, whose body already assigned her to the order of an asset for concrete societal reproduction, engaged in a performative speech-act that has to be regulated by the state. Otherwise she should be removed from the public space; she should disappear. In essence, by presenting her with the alternative 'unveil or lose your teaching job', the law has hidden Dahlab much more efficiently than any veil could ever do. For the veil, as all clothes do, does not hide but *presents* humans to each other, whereas the *persona juridica*, in modern law, isolates people from each other and connects them to the state.

Sahin v Turkey (2005) is another case decided in the Strasbourg Court which discloses a specific relation between the individual and the state. The case is particularly controversial due to the narrow interpretation of the notion of freedom of religion given by the Court; the imposition of a radical form of secularism; the implications on Muslim women's right to education; and the inadequate application of the doctrine of the margin of appreciation. In 1998, Istanbul University released a circular prohibiting students from wearing the headscarf (along with 'long beards') during lectures and examinations. A few months later Sahin, in her fifth year of medical school at Istanbul University, was denied access to a written examination because she was veiled, and disciplinary measures were imposed as a result of her failure to comply with the circular. One year after, she was also suspended for 6 months by the Dean of the Cerrahpa Faculty of Medicine for taking part in a demonstration concerning the right to wear the headscarf in Turkey. As no university in the country allowed the wearing of the veil, Sahin was forced to move to Vienna University in order to complete her studies. She applied to the Istanbul Administrative Court, claiming her right to wear the *hijab* in the university; the Court, however, dismissed her application. She also lodged a complaint against the Turkish government, claiming that the headscarf ban in higher education violated her rights under Articles 8, 9, 10 and 14 of the ECHR and Article 2 of Protocol No.1. The case reached the ECtHR in 2005 when the Grand Chamber decided that the university's refusal to allow her to wear a headscarf did not violate Article 9 of the ECHR on freedom of thought and religion and confirmed the decision of the Fourth Section of the Court of June 2004. In reaching this conclusion, the Court considered (i) whether the ban represented a breach of Article 9, (ii) whether the ban was prescribed by law, and (iii) whether Turkey pursued a legitimate aim, (iv) which was necessary in a democratic society.

The ECtHR found that the ban on wearing the veil applied by the university was sought to "preserve the secular nature of the institution concerned" (*Sahin v Turkey,* 2005, para 116) and so was considered admissible. The Court established that the ruling of the Turkish Constitutional Court to ban the headscarf in universities was a sufficient basis for the prohibition in light of the Turkish Supreme Administrative Court decision which held that the headscarf was incompatible with Turkey's secular values and "fundamental principles" (*Sahin v Tuerkey,* 2005, para 78). Recalling *Karaduman v. Turkey (1993)* and *Dahlab v. Switzerland* (2001) to justify the interference with Sahin's rights, the ECtHR argued that in a democratic society the state is entitled to restrict the manifestation of a religious belief, when incompatible with the freedom of others, and to maintain public order and safety. However, while in the *Dahlab* case the veil was seen as a 'powerful external symbol' which could have proselytizing effects on very young children, in the *Sahin* case the ECtHR failed to give evidence that wearing a headscarf in a higher educational institution could "pressure students who are not wearing the *hijab*" (*Sahin v Turkey,* 2005, para 111).

As Sahin was a university student, and not a teacher in a primary school like Dahlab, the argument that veiling can be seen as a tool for proselytism is extremely weak.

In the *Sahin* case, the ECtHR showed a confused reasoning: although the Court stated that there was no interference with Article 9 (1), the Commission considered whether the interference was justified under Article 9 (2). The Court found that the interference was motivated by two main principles: secularism and gender equality. According to the ECtHR, the decision of Istanbul University to ban the *hijab* was motivated by the need to protect the rights of others and public order, in accordance with Article 9 (2), which justifies restrictions on freedom of religion. However, based on Article 13 of the Turkish Constitution, fundamental freedoms and rights can be restricted only by a parliamentary Act and not by an institution such as a university. Despite the absence of statutory bases to ban the headscarf in universities, the Court accepted as a legal basis the transitional section 17 of law No. 2547 which states that "choice of dress shall be free in institutions of higher education, provided that it does not contravene the laws in force" (*Sahin v Turkey,* 2005, para 88). Through this choice, it was not difficult for the Grand Chamber to understand the restriction on wearing Islamic headscarves merely as an internal rule of Istanbul University, rather than a limitation of personal freedoms (Altiparmak & Karahanogullari, 2006a). Again, the ECtHR particularly emphasized the role of state neutrality and the Court's responsibility to interpret domestic law in respect of European plurality, relegating its role to examining whether the domestic laws were in line with the ECHR (Altiparmak & Karahanogullari, 2006a).

By widening the 'margin of appreciation', the ECtHR stated that "it is the principle of secularism, as elucidated by the Constitutional Court, which is the paramount consideration underlying the ban on the wearing of religious symbols in universities" (*Sahin v Turkey*, 2005, para 116): this, in turn, would maintain not only public order but also pluralism in the university. Even if Sahin declared that she embraced the principle of secularism, the Court, without any analysis of Turkey's interpretation of secularism, the actual circumstances, or whether the headscarf was a danger for social order, discharged Sahin's claim, obliging her to change country in order to obtain a university degree (Evans, 2001, p. 306). In other words, by stressing the principle of secularism, the Court not only limited Sahin's individual rights of freedom of religion, but it also assumed the duty to define which Islamic symbol was appropriate in Turkish universities: Muslim students could "manifest their religion in accordance with habitual forms of Muslim observance" (*Sahin v Turkey,* para 159). The Court, however, failed to explain which religious duties were allowed and why the headscarf could not be considered an 'habitual' Islamic practice: hence, the argument was quite weak in its legal reasoning (Altiparmak & Karahanogullari, 2006b).

The ECtHR decision to ban the veil in order to 'save' Turkish secular values was supported by two problematic assumptions: *Sharia* is a substantively static and unchangeable revealed legal system, and the values of *Sharia* law are illiberal and incompatible with western secular democratic principles. Hence, rather than trying to understand whether wearing a headscarf in the university violated Article 9 of the Convention, it seems that the judges focused on the question of how to incorporate/

accommodate Islam within 'secular' societies. In the case, the Strasbourg Court felt the need to retell the master narrative of the rise of the secular state in Turkey and the supposed difficulties in convincing Muslim religious groups to accept the privatisation of their religion. With the defeat of the Ottoman empire, the Kemalist 'secular' revolution (1924) started a western-style modernization process in the attempt to establish a strong nation-state. Kemalists wanted to 'civilize' and 'modernize' Turkish society, understood as backward for its inability to embrace western secular modernity (Göle, 1996). The new secular/republican[21] project put a great emphasis on women's emancipation and their unveiling as a necessary condition for the modernization of the nation. Although Mustafa Kemal never legally banned the veil, he strongly discouraged the practice: in this way, Turkish women's hair became the symbol of a new nation, an (apparently) de-Islamised, westernized, and modernized nation-state. In the 1980s, as a result of the secularization process operated by subsequent governments, the veil started to be legally prohibited in public offices. For women who were wearing the veil, this represented a denial of their presence in the public sphere. After years of passionate debate, the ban was lifted in 2013, but at the time of the ECtHR's decision over *Sahin*'s case, the ban was still in force. According to the ECtHR, since the formation of the secular nation-state in Turkey, the country has been constantly struggling with political and religious forces that try to overthrow the secular, liberal, state. In fact, the abolition of the caliphate and the formation of the Turkish Republic were described by the Court as if they were actual problems: "the Constitutional Court underlined that the principle of secularism is the major force of shifting Turkey from *umma*- based country toward a nation-based republic" (in Ulusoy, 2007, p. 422). Thus, it seems that instead of judging Sahin's claim, the Court was preoccupied with judging the challenge posed by political Islam to the Turkish 'secular' Republic. The Court stated that

> "in a country like Turkey, where the great majority of the population belong to a particular religion, measures taken in universities to prevent certain fundamentalist religious movements from exerting pressure on students who do not practice that religion or on those who belong to another religion may be justified under Article 9 (2) of the Convention [...] the Court does not lose sight of the fact that there are extremist political movements in Turkey which seek to impose on society as a whole their religious symbols and conception [...] The regulations concerned have to be viewed in that context and constitute a measure intended to achieve the legitimate aims referred to above and thereby to preserve pluralism in the university" (*Sahin v Turkey,* 2005, para 115).

It seems that the approach of the ECtHR sets forth a general rule for Turkey which implies that, because in the country the majority of the population is Muslim, it is essential to ban the *hijab* in order to protect the freedom of others, public order, and the principle of secularism and gender equality. However, by focusing on the history

[21] It is important to point out that Turkish model of secularism, even if based on western concepts of *laïcité'*, created a sort of hybrid in which a particular kind of Islam was accommodated within the state's institutions and subjected to state regulations. The Presidency of Religious Affairs, for instance, is a state institution whose duty consists of dealing with the affairs of Sunni and appointing *imams* (Davison, 2003).

of Turkey and the (supposed) existence of extremist religious movements attempting to overthrow the secular state, the ECtHR made a mistake: it "substituted Turkey for the University of Istanbul and Islam for the headscarf" (Altiparmak & Karahanogullari, 2006b, p. 279). This is well explained in the dissenting opinion of Judge Tulkens.

> "[...] while everyone agrees on the need to prevent radical Islamism, a serious objection may be nevertheless be made to such reasoning. Merely wearing the headscarf cannot be associated with fundamentalism and it is vital to distinguish between those who wear the headscarf and 'extremists' who seek to impose the headscarf as they do other religious symbols. Not all women who wear the headscarf are fundamentalists and there is nothing to suggest that the applicant held fundamentalist views. She is a young adult woman and a university student and might be reasonably expected to have a heightened capacity to resist pressure, it being noted in this connection that the judgement fails to provide any concrete example of the type of pressure concerned. The applicant's personal interest in exercising the right to freedom of religion and to manifest her religion by an external symbol cannot be wholly absorbed by the public interest in fighting extremism" (*Sahin v Tuekey,* 2005, dissenting opinion Judge Tulkens, para 10).

Although, in the case, the Court defined the wearing of the veil as a symbol of affiliation with religious/political movements, it failed to justify the existence of extremist Islamist groups in the university and to explain the relation between the claimant and those groups. Hence, what is at stake in the *Sahin* case is not the fact that someone could feel threatened by Sahin's headscarf, but the (supposed) threat to the structure of the secular Turkish Republic.

To emphasize the impossibility of reconciling the Republic's secular, liberal and democratic values with 'extremist' (Islamist) religious movements in Turkey, the Court referred to the *Refah* case (2003), a political party which was banned. Refah Partisi, an Islamic political party founded in 1983, participated in the first national election in 1991, gaining growing consent until 1998, when the Constitutional Court of Turkey officially banned the party for violating the constitutional secular principle of the separation between religion and the state: in 2003, the ban was upheld by the ECtHR based on the premise of a general incompatibility of an Islamic-based-politico-legal system with secular western democracy. In fact, for the ECtHR, Refah was allegedly attempting to introduce *Sharia* law which "would oblige individuals to obey [...] static rules of law imposed by the religion concerned" (*Refah v Turkey*, 2003, para 70). In the case, the Strasbourg Court concluded that:

> "*Sharia*, which faithfully reflects the dogmas and divine rules laid down by religion, is stable and invariable [...]. Principles such as pluralism in the political sphere or the constant evolution of the public freedoms have no place in it. The Court notes that it is difficult to declare one's respect for democracy and human rights while at the same time supporting a regime based on *Sharia*, which clearly diverges from Convention values, particularly with regard to [...] its rules on the legal status of women and the way it intervenes in all spheres of private and public life in accordance with religious precepts [...]. Refah's policy was to apply some *Sharia* private law rule to a large part of the population in Turkey [namely Muslim], within the framework of a plurality of legal systems. Such a policy goes beyond the freedom of individuals to observe the precepts of their religion [...]. This Refah policy falls outside the private sphere to which Turkish law confines religion and suffers from the same contradictions with the Convention system as the introduction of *Sharia*" (*Refah v Turkey*, 2003, para 19 and 72).

Clearly, in the Court's view, a political party whose actions seem to be aimed at introducing *Sharia* along with other religious legal systems in relation to family law (as is the case in modern Israel) fails to comply with the democratic ideals that motivate the Convention. It is clear from this case that western judges tend (erroneously) to see *Shari'a* law as shaped by a dichotomy between traditionalists and modernizers that focuses on the 'clash' over the constitutional structure of the state and whether this structure can be legitimated by *Sharia*, which is imagined as a fixed body of law. Interestingly, the *Sahin* case reveals a common view among Islamists and liberals that the matter falls under *Sharia* law, which is misrepresented as a comprehensive and transparent code of unalterable revealed law. As I have argued in the first chapter through Diamantides' analysis (2012) of sovereignty formation, both liberals and Islamists aim at creating a universal(ist) law capable of binding the individual to a fixed and monolithic identity. The history of Islam, as well as a deeper analysis of classical Islamic jurisprudence, shows a flourishing plurality of Islamic laws which correspond to a plurality of sartorial practices and numerous ways in which to live and understand Islamic precepts.

In the case, and by referring to the *Refah* case, the ECtHR accepted the Turkish Court's conception of *Sharia* law as a non-negotiable code whose authority lies outside the human horizon and, certainly, outside the authority of a modern nation-state. In the *Refah* case (2003), the Court also observed that "there was already an Islamic theocratic regime under Ottoman law" (para 125) and that this system was dismantled with the introduction of the republican regime in Turkey. The Ottoman empire applied a legal system (namely the 'Millet system') based on religious identity where every religious group responded to different laws in relation to family law (Shahar, 2012). The 'Millet system' was a confessional system based on the recognition of different religious groups rather than territorial jurisdiction. In contrast to the liberal/modern definition of freedom of religion which is based on an individualist notion of equality, the 'Millet System' based freedom of religion on collective terms (Mahmood, 2012). In light of this, the Court's ignorance of the 'Millet system' in the *Sahin* case is astonishing: it confused *Refah* neo-Ottomanism, which called for a plurality of legal systems, with Islamic fundamentalism, which calls for the establishment of a unique, fixed, territorial *Sharia* law. Clearly, the ECtHR has identified 'religion' as a force that aspires to regulate human life and to subordinate secular to religious values: as I will further argue in the next part, all the European decisions to ban the veil rely on the assumption that religion should be relegated to a small private sphere in order to safeguard a wider secular public sphere. However, by defining religion as a simple private belief, not only has the Court circumscribed the role and place assigned to religion and religious practices but it has also imposed a narrow definition of religion on other cultures (Nielsen, 1999).

This is particularly evident in France, a country that, along with Turkey, has applied a radical form of laicity. Although, in the last decade, many young Muslim girls have tried to challenge legally the French headscarf ban, the ECtHR has always upheld the irremovable decisions of French national Courts. In 2010, the French government decided to ban the concealment of the face in public places (also known as the '*burqa* ban') (*LOI No. 2010–1192)*. This latest ban was challenged by a young girl in the case *SAS v France* (2014) decided at the ECtHR. The case is of particular interest as the ECtHR's judges justified the ban in a different way to previous cases, further widening the application of the 'margin of appreciation'. The case concerned a young French girl who wore the *burqa* or *niqab* based on her personal convictions. The claimant stressed that no one from her family had exerted any pressure on her to wear a specific garment; that she did not wear it 'systematically' (adding that she might not wear it when she goes to the doctor or when she meets friends and she wants to socialize); that, by wearing the veil, she did not want to annoy anyone but to "feel at inner peace with herself" (*SAS v France*, 2014, para 10–2); and that she did not have any problem with taking off her *niqab* for security reasons (in banks, airports etc.) and showing her face if required by a public officer. Her request was not to wear the *niqab/burqa* always, but when she needed to, based on her spiritual inclinations. She claimed that the ban interfered with her fundamental rights as it could not be proved that it was a legitimate aim to protect 'public safety' or to 'ensure respect for the minimum requirements of life in society'. For her, the ban was based on a purely visual form of communication which does not consider the rights of minorities, and on chauvinist and paternalistic stereotypes of Muslim women. In the case, the Human Rights Centre of the University of Ghent presented an empirical study on the uses of the veil. The research points out that women who wear a face veil in Belgium understand it as 'part of a life project that considers Islam as a lifestyle' and that the *burqa* does not limit communication between people: indeed, the report adds that the "profile that emerges from the studies of women who wear the face veil in Europe, is not one of 'submissive' women" (Written Submission by the Human Rights Centre of Ghent University, 2014, p. 4).

The French government reiterated that the ban was within the limitations established by art. 9 (2) of the Convention and that it was justified as it pursued a legitimate aim within a democratic society. For the French government, the ban was necessary to ensure identification; to protect the rights and freedoms of others; and to prevent fraud. Moreover, the government reiterated the importance of the face in human interaction, as its concealment would break 'the social tie' and manifest a refusal of the principle of 'living together' (*SAS v France,* 2014, para 81) and gender equality (as the concealment of women's face has been understood as a denial of women's existence) (*SAS v France*, 2014, para 82).

The ECtHR declared inadmissible the applicant's claim under art. 3, 11,[22] and 14, and did not find any violation by the government of art. 8 and 9 of the Convention. Although, for the first time, the ECtHR dismissed the idea that the veil is a limit to gender equality, it approved France's '*burqa* ban' based on the principle of 'living together': "the respect for the minimum requirements of life in society […] [can be associated with the legitimate aim of the] protection of the rights and freedoms of others" (*SAS v France*, 2014, para 121).

---

[22] Art. 3-'No one shall be subjected to torture or to inhuman or degrading treatment or punishment', Art. 11- 'Everyone has the right to freedom of peaceful assembly and to freedom of association with others, including the right to form and to join trade unions for the protection of his interests'. European Convention on Human Rights art 3 and 11 (art 14 *supra*).

The notion of 'living together', at the basis of the decision, is a principle which is not covered by art. 9 (2) and it encounters many problems when applied in a legal reasoning. Although the Court recognised the "flexibility of the notion of 'living together' and the resulting risk of abuse," (*SAS v France*, 2014, para 122) it nevertheless widened the margin of appreciation in relation to the manifestation of religious symbols in the French public sphere without examining whether the '*burqa* ban' was necessary in France. However, the idea that an individual needs to be 'available' for contact and communication as an obligation imposed by the state and against the individual's will contradicts the 'right to private life' enshrined in Article 8 of the ECHR:[23] by understanding the veil as a mere communicative barrier (*ibid*, para 52), the Court imposes a specific sociability on the individual's public sphere. Indeed, the fact that 'living together' implies that people need eye contact encounters strong empirical and normative objections,[24] taking into consideration that a number of social and sporting activities involve the wearing of clothing that conceals the face (such as motor-cycling, carnivals, folkloristic events etc.).

These, however, are considered exceptions of the law. Exactly because the law recognizes these exceptions, it shows that people can also live together with face covering (as in many other societies). Therefore, the '*burqa* ban' did not aim at liberating women or favouring human interaction. Rather, the ECtHR upheld a law that affects a specific minority in France without any empirical proof that the *burqa* limits people's interaction. As Nußberger and Jäderblom (SAS v France, 2014), the dissenting judges, argued, the concept of 'living together' "sacrifices concrete individual rights guaranteed by the Convention to abstract principles" (para A.2). This, in turn, has opened the door for the imposition of specific practices on minorities under the concept of 'living together,' instead of pursuing the aim of building a democratic and pluralist society. It seems, therefore, that the Court has blindly upheld a specific idea of secularism and 'living together', as intended by the French government.

Clearly, in cases concerning the practice of veiling, the ECtHR has allowed the coexistence of different state-church relations by widening the doctrine of the margin of appreciation, giving to it a new meaning. While the doctrine of 'the margin of appreciation', which allows European member states a certain freedom in the protection of individual rights enshrined in the ECHR, is not included in any text of the European Convention (Yourow, 1998), it has been used by the ECtHR in cases where there is an absence of consensus across Europe, such as in the field of morals and religion (see *Wingrove v UK*, 1996; *Kokkinakis v Greece*, 1993). However, as Evans (2008) observes, the margin afforded to member states has been narrowed or widened in relation to specific subject matter: while in cases regarding freedom of expression (art. 10) or homosexual conduct in private (art. 8) the ECtHR has narrowed the margin of appreciation giving a higher level of protection to claimants, in

[23] Art. 8 establishes the right to "respect private and family life, his home and his correspondence".

[24] It is worth noting that only the *burqa* conceals the eyes, while other kinds of face-covering, such as the *niqab*, usually show the eyes.

cases involving religious manifestation the ECtHR has excessively widened the margin of appreciation, leaving states a great discretionary power to limit the individual's fundamental rights.[25] By claiming to protect specifically European state-church relations, the ECtHR shows a new use of the doctrine which appears at times incompatible with the defence of individual fundamental rights. In theory, the margin of appreciation should be applied after carefully considering whether the measures taken by a country interfere with the individual's fundamental human rights: indeed, limitations of fundamental rights are permitted as long as the aim is proportionate and necessary. In the analysed cases it is unclear how a veiled woman could interfere with the freedom of others and be a danger to public order or to the 'peace of the society': it is exactly this lack of clarity about the real danger represented by the veil that has led to one group prevailing over another (or a majority over a minority). Certainly, the Court never properly analysed the incompatibility of the veil with the principle of secularism (Bleiberg, 2005) and did not really show a different reasoning based on specific context where the ban had been imposed. It did not distinguish between the fact that Dahlab was a teacher in a primary school and Sahin a student in the university, and nor did it analyse whether different interpretations of secularism, gender equality, and neutrality could lead to a violation of an individual's right of religious freedom. Since the principles of necessity, proportionality and state neutrality have been applied differently in different cases concerning the right to religious freedom (compare, for instance, the *Dahlab* and *Kokkinakis* cases), it seems that at the heart of these decisions is a specific (political) interpretation of the Islamic veil *as such* which has led to framing the veil as a defence of public order.

The understanding of the veil as a threat to western values is exemplified by European member states' decisions to ban the practice of veiling: those decisions are founded on the 'unproved' idea that the veil could endanger western/liberal values of secularism and gender equality. As a matter of fact, in all European decisions concerning the practice of veiling, gender equality and women's sexuality have been indissolubly linked to discourses of identity and territorial borders. By defining veiling as a 'political symbol' or an 'improper (chauvinist) religious symbol', and by locating the practice in clear contraposition with Christian symbols, European Courts have banned the veil without perceiving it as a limitation of Muslim women's fundamental freedom.

However, by defining the practice of veiling as something intrinsically alien to western values, western/secular/liberal human rights law, instead of protecting Muslim women's fundamental rights, and contrary to its democratic and pluralist values, has upheld national political decisions that have excluded many Muslim women from the European secular public sphere. In light of this, European decisions concerning the practice of veiling are not neutral as they disclose the European desire to assimilate different religious practices into the homogeneity of Christian/

[25] For the ECtHR "it is not possible to discern throughout Europe a uniform conception of the significance of religion in society" (*Otto-Preminger-Institut v. Austria*, 1995, p. 19).

secular European societies. The force of these decisions lies in their ability to re-define the balance between state neutrality and the right to religious liberty and between the public and the private sphere. Those decisions disclose all the tensions and the intrinsic paradox of secularism: while on the one hand secularism presupposes a separation between public and private, then on the other, it seeks constantly to trespass the boundaries that it tries to establish. An example is the 2003 Stasi Commission which clearly defined which religious symbols are protected by the law (small crosses or star of David, etc.) and which are not (*hijabs, yarmulkes*, and large crosses, etc.) (Fernando, 2014a). Hence, contrary to western law's claim to safeguard the plurality and diversity of the European population, it actually acts to eradicate differences in the name of creating a monolithic western/secular subject of law and religion. As I will show in the next part, what is missed in the contemporary discourse regarding the veil is a deep problematization of secular forms of power that allows the secular state to introduce restrictions to personal freedoms without perceiving them as violence but as a safeguard of the place assigned to religion (Cavanaugh, 1995): those restrictions are not neutral as they shape a specific law and religious subject.

References

Agrama, H. A. (2010). Secularism, sovereignty, indeterminacy: Is Egypt a secular or a religious state? *Comparative Studies in Society and History, 52*(3), 495–523.

Agrama, H. A. (2012). *Questioning secularism: Islam, sovereignty, and the rule of law in modern Egypt*. University of Chicago Press.

Althusser, L. (1972). *Lenin and philosophy, and other essays*. Monthly Review Press.

Altiparmak, K., & Karahanogullari, O. (2006a). After Sahin: The debate on headscarves is not over. *European Constitutional Law Review, 2*, 268–292.

Altiparmak, K., & Karahanogullari, O. (2006b). European Court of Human Rights: After Sahin: The debate on headscarves is not over, Leyla Sahin v. Turkey, Grand Chamber Judgment of 10 November 2005, Application No. 44774/98. *European Constitutional Law Review, 2*(2), 268–292.

Arai, Y., & Arai-Takahashi, Y. (2002). *The margin of appreciation doctrine and the principle of proportionality in the jurisprudence of the ECHR*. Intersentia nv.

Bader, V. (2010). *Secularism or democracy?: Associational governance of religious diversity*. Amsterdam University Press.

Benhabib, S. (2002a). Citizens, residents, and aliens in a changing world: Political membership in the global era. *Public Worlds, 10*, 85–119.

Benhabib, S. (2002b). *The claims of culture: Equality and diversity in the global era*. Princeton University Press.

Bleiberg, B. (2005). Unveiling the real issue: Evaluating the European Court of Human Rights' decision to enforce the Turkish Headscarf Ban in Leyla Sahin v. Turkey. *The Cornell Law Review, 91*, 129.

Bonnie, H. (1999). In J. Cohen, M. Howard, & M. C. Nussbaum (Eds.), *My culture made me do it*. Princeton University Press.

Bostock, B. (2020). France has made wearing face masks compulsory in public, while maintaining a controversial ban on burqas and niqabs. *Business Insider*. https://www.businessinsider.com/france-face-masks-compulsory-burqas-niqabs-banned-criticism-muslims-2020-5

Bowen, J. R. (2007). *Why the French don't like headscarves: Islam, the state, and public space*. Princeton University Press.
Bowen, J. R. (2008). Why did the French rally to law against scarves in school? *Associées, Droit et Société, 68*(1), 33–52.
Breeden, A., & Blaise, L. (2016, August 26). Court overturns 'Burkini' Ban in French Town. *The New York Times*. http://www.nytimes.com/2016/08/27/world/europe/france-burkini-ban.html
Brems, E. (2006). Above children's heads: The headscarf controversy in European schools from the perspective of children's rights. *International Journal of Childrens Rights, 14*(2), 119.
Brown, W. (2006). Tolerance as/in civilizational discourse. In W. Brown (Ed.), *Regulating aversion: Tolerance in the age of identity and empire*. Princeton University Press.
Cavanaugh, M. W. T. (1995). "A fire strong enough to consume the house": The wars of religion and the rise of the state. *Modern Theology, 11*(4), 397–420.
Constitution of Greece. (n.d.). Retrieved May 4, 2016, from http://www.hri.org/docs/syntagma/artcl25.html
Davies, G. (2005). United Kingdom: Banning the Jilbab: Reflections on restricting religious clothing in the light of the court of appeal in SB v. Denbigh High School. Decision of 2 March 2005. *European Constitutional Law Review, 1*(03), 511–530.
Davison, A. (2003). Turkey, a "secular" state?: The challenge of description. *The South Atlantic Quarterly, 102*(2), 333–350.
Dearden, L. (2017). Muslim woman banned from wearing headscarf in court. *The Independent*. https://www.independent.co.uk/news/world/europe/muslim-woman-court-headscarf-banned-germany-divorce-luckenwalde-burqa-neutrality-law-case-eu-a7849881.html
Diamantides, M. (2012). Shari'a, faith and critical legal theory'. In M. Diamantides & A. Geary (Eds.), *Islam, law and identity*. Routledge.
Düttmann, A. G. (2000). *Between cultures: Tensions in the struggle for recognition*. Verso.
European Court of Human Rights. S.A.S v France, Application no. 43835/11Written submission by the Human Rights Centre of Ghent University. (n.d.). Retrieved September 16, 2016, from http://www.hrc.ugent.be/wp-content/uploads/2015/11/SAS.pdf
Evans, C. (2001). *Freedom of religion under the European Convention on Human Rights* (Vol. 1). Oxford University Press.
Evans, M. D. (2008). *Religious liberty and international law in Europe* (Vol. 6). Cambridge University Press.
Fernando, M. L. (2014a). Intimacy surveilled: Religion, sex, and secular cunning. *Signs: Journal of Women in Culture and Society, 39*(3), 685–708.
Fernando, M. L. (2014b). *The republic unsettled: Muslim French and the contradictions of secularism*. Duke University Press.
Fernando, M. L. (2017). Intimacy surveilled: Religion, sex, and secular cunning. In D. L. Boisvert & C. Daniel-Hughes (Eds.), *The Bloomsbury reader in religion, sexuality, and gender*. Bloomsbury Academic.
Finnigan, D. (2012, August 15). Muslim woman files suit against Disney over headscarf dispute. *Washington Post*. https://www.washingtonpost.com/national/on-faith/muslim-woman-files-suit-against-disney-over-headscarf-dispute/2012/08/14/cf13432e-e655-11e1-9739-eef99c5fb285_story.html
Foucault, M. (1981). *The history of sexuality*. Penguin Books.
German state plans headscarf ban. (2003, November 11). *BBC News*. http://news.bbc.co.uk/2/hi/europe/3261147.stm
Gies, L. (2006). What not to wear: Islamic dress and school uniforms. *Feminist Legal Studies, 14*(3), 377–389.
Göle, N. (1996). *The forbidden modern: Civilization and veiling*. University of Michigan Press.
Greer, S. C. (2000). *The margin of appreciation: Interpretation and discretion under the European Convention on Human Rights* (Vol. 17). Council of Europe.
Gunn, T. J. (2004). Religious freedom and Laïcité: A comparison of the United States and France. *Brigham Young University Law Review, 2004*, 419.

Hauptmeier, C. (2003). *Wieviel Symbolkraft hat ein Stück Stoff?* Agence France Presse- Germany.
Hirschl, R. (2011). Constitutional law and religion. In T. Ginsburg & R. Dixon (Eds.), *Comparative constitutional law, research handbooks in comparative law* (pp. 422–435). Edward Elgar.
Husserl, G. (1938). Public policy and Ordre public. *Virginia Law Review, 25*, 37–67.
Joppke, C. (2007). State neutrality and Islamic Headscarf Laws in France and Germany. *Theory and Society, 36*(4), 313–342.
Joppke, C. (2011). Limits of restricting Islam: The French burqa law of 2010. *Migration Studies Unit of the London School of Economics, 25*.
Joppke, C. (2013). *Legal integration of Islam: A transatlantic comparison*. Harvard University Press.
Kastoryano, R. (2004). Religion and incorporation: Islam in France and Germany. *International Migration Review, 38*(3), 1234–1255.
Killian, C. (2003). The other side of the veil: North African women in France respond to the headscarf affair. *Gender & Society, 17*(4), 567–590. https://doi.org/10.1177/0891243203253541
Klausen, J. (2005). *The Islamic challenge: Politics and religion in Western Europe*. Oxford University Press.
Kymlicka, W. (1995a). *Multicultural citizenship: A liberal theory of minority rights*. Clarendon.
Kymlicka, W. (1995b). *The rights of minority cultures*. Oxford University Press Oxford.
Macmaster, N., & Lewis, T. (1998). Orientalism: From unveiling to hyperveiling. *Journal of European Studies, 28*(109–110), 121–135. https://doi.org/10.1177/004724419802810909
Mahmood, S. (2012). Religious freedom, the minority question, and geopolitics in the Middle East. *Comparative Studies in Society and History, 54*(02), 418–446.
Mahmood, S. (2015). *Religious difference in a secular age*. Princeton University Press.
Malik, M. (2008). Religious freedom and multiculturalism: R (Shabina Begum) v Denbigh high school. *King's Law Journal, 19*(2), 377–390.
Malik, M. (2010). "Progressive multiculturalism": Minority women and cultural diversity. *International Journal on Minority and Group Rights, 17*(3), 447–467.
McElroy, D. (2010, April 6). Iran demands Fifa lifts Olympic games football hijab ban. *The Telegraph*. https://www.telegraph.co.uk/sport/olympics/7559228/Iran-demands-Fifa-lifts-Olympic-games-football-hijab-ban.html
McGoldrick, D. (2006). *Human rights and religion: The Islamic headscarf debate in Europe*. Hart Publishing.
Mikhail, J. (2008). Dilemmas of cultural legality: A comment on Roger Cotterrell's 'The struggle for law'and a criticism of the House of Lords' opinions in Begum. *International Journal of Law in Context, 4*(4), 385–393.
Miles, T. (2018, October 24). *French ban on Islamic veil violates rights, say UN experts*. Independent.Ie. https://www.independent.ie/world-news/europe/french-ban-on-islamic-veil-violates-rights-say-un-experts-37452406.html
Myers, P. (2016). Burkini does not respect 'good morals,' earns French ban and subsequent overturn. *The Seahawk*. https://theseahawk.org/3756/news/burkini-does-not-respect-good-morals-earns-french-ban-and-subsequent-overturn/
Naili, H. (2014). 5 veiled Frenchwomen tell 5 stories of harassment. *Women's ENews*. https://womensenews.org/2014/11/5-veiled-frenchwomen-tell-5-stories-of-harassment/
Nielsen, J. (1999). *Towards a European Islam*. Palgrave Macmillan UK.
Okin, S. M. (1999). *Is multiculturalism bad for women?* Princeton University Press.
Parekh, B. C. (2000). *Rethinking multiculturalism: Cultural diversity and political theory*. Macmillan.
Parekh, B. (2001). Rethinking multiculturalism: Cultural diversity and political theory. *Ethnicities, 1*(1), 109–115.
Ramdani, N. (2013). *Veil row reignites in France after 15-year-old girl expelled from school for wearing a headband and long skirt which were considered ¿too religious¿ | Daily Mail Online*. Mail Online. http://www.dailymail.co.uk/news/article-2305314/Veil-row-reignites-France-15-year-old-girl-expelled-school-wearing-headband-long-skirt-considered-religious.html
Rohe, M. (2004). The legal treatment of Muslims in Germany. In B.-P. R. Aluffi & G. Zincone (Eds.), *The legal treatment of Islamic minorities in Europe* (pp. 83–107). Peeters.

Saharso, S. (2003). Feminist ethics, autonomy and the politics of multiculturalism. *Feminist Theory, 4*(2), 199–215.

Salecl, R. (1994). *The spoils of freedom: Psychoanalysis and feminism after the fall of socialism*. Routledge.

Sarkozy, N. (2009). *La burqa n'est pas la bienvenue sur le territoire de la République*. LIBÉRATION.

Sauer, B. (2009). Headscarf regimes in Europe: Diversity policies at the intersection of gender, culture and religion. *Comparative European Politics, 7*(1), 75–94.

Schiffauer, W. (2006). Enemies within the gates. The debate about the citizenship of Muslims in Germany. In T. Modood, A. Triandafyllidou, & R. Zapata-Barrero (Eds.), *Multiculturalism, Muslims and citizenship* (pp. 94–116). Routledge.

Scott, J. W. (2007). *The politics of the veil*. Princeton University Press.

Shachar, A. (2001). *Multicultural jurisdictions: Cultural differences and women's rights*. Cambridge University Press.

Shahar, I. (2012). Legal pluralism incarnate: An institutional perspective on courts of law in colonial and postcolonial settings. *The Journal of Legal Pluralism and Unofficial Law, 44*(65), 133–163.

Taylor, C. (1992). *Multiculturalism and "the politics of recognition": An essay*. Princeton University Press.

Taylor, C. (1994). *Multiculturalism: Examining the politics of recognition*. Princeton University Press.

Taylor, C. (2007). *A secular age*. Belknap Press of Harvard University Press.

Thomassen, L. (2011). (Not) Just a piece of cloth: Begum, recognition and the politics of representation. *Political Theory, 39*(3), 325–351.

Tully, J. (1995). *Strange multiplicity: Constitutionalism in an age of diversity*. Cambridge University Press.

Ulusoy, A. (2007). The Islamic headscarf problem before secular legal systems: Factual and legal developments in Turkish, French and European human rights laws. *European Journal of Migration and Law, 9*(4), 419–433.

Vocking, H. (1995). Organisations as attempts at integration of Muslims in Germany. In S. M. Gè & S. Jan (Eds.), *Muslims and Christians in Europe: Breaking new ground: Essays in honour of Jan Slop*. Kampten.

Walzer, M. (1984). Liberalism and the art of separation. *Political Theory, 12*(3), 315–330.

Welle, D. (2018). *German headscarf ban for children met with mixed response | DW | 09.04.2018*. DW.COM. http://www.dw.com/en/german-headscarf-ban-for-children-met-with-mixed-response/a-43307138

Willsher, K. (2011, April 10). "Burqa ban" in France: Housewife vows to face jail rather than submit. *The Guardian*. https://www.theguardian.com/world/2011/apr/10/france-burqa-law-kenza-drider

Yourow, H. C. (1998). The margin of appreciation doctrine in the dynamics of the Strasbourg jurisprudence and the construction of Europe. *Zeitschrift Für Europarechtliche Studien, 1*(2), 233–248.

Cases and Legal Documents

Assemblée nationale (2009), *'Proposition de résolution'*, no. 1725.

Assemblee nationale (19 June 2009) *Mission d'information sur la pratique du port du voile integral sur le territoire national*. N. 1725.

Baden-Wüttemberg 178, (2004) GVBI amended law of April 1.

'Basic Law for the Federal Republic of Germany', from https://www.btg-bestellservice.de/pdf/80201000.pdf
55BverfGE 41, 29 ("Simultanschule"), decision of 17 December 1975.
Bundesverfassungsgericht [BVerfG] [Federal Constitutional Court] (Sep. 24, 2003), 108 Entscheidungen des Bundesverfassungsgerichts [BVerfGE] 282, (F.R.G.) [the Ludin case].
BverGE Decision of 10 May 1957, 389.
Chassagnou v. France (1999) Application Nos. 25088/94, 28331/95 and 28443/95.
Conseil d'Etat (November 27, 1989), Avis no. 346.893.
Counseil d'Etat, (Mar. 10, 1995), Rec. Lebon 159981.
Counseil d'Etat (Nov. 27, 1996) Rec. Lebon 170208.
Conseil D'Etat. (2010) 'Study of Possible Legal grounds for Banning the Full veil: Report Adopted the Plenary General Assembly of the Conseil D'Etat' from http://www.aihja.org/images/users/1/files/fullveil.en.pdf
Conseil d'Etat (27 November 1989) Opinion No. 346.893 from www.conseil-etat.fr/ce/rappor/index-ra-cg03-O1.shtml
Conseil d'Etat, Rapport Public (2004), 337.
Conseil d'Etat, (2 November 1992) Kherouaa, Kachour, Balo ed Kizic, Recieil des Arrets du Conseil d'Etat 1002.
Conseil d'Etat et l Juridiction Administrative (2010) 'Etude Relative Aux Possibilités Juridiques d'Interdiction du Port du Voile Intégral', from http://www.conseil-etat.fr/Decisions-Avis-Publications/Etudes-Publications/Rapports-Etudes/Etude-relative-aux-possibilitesjuridiques-d-interdiction-du-port-du-voile-intégral
Commission de reflexion sur l'application du principe de laïcité dans la republique [Commission for the reflection on the application of the principle of laicism in the republic], Rapport au President de la Republique [Report to the president of the republic] (Laicism report), (11 December 2003.), from http://lesrapports.ladocumentationfrancaise.fr/BRP/034000725/0000.pdf. Accessed on 3 May 2007.
Copsey v Devon -Clays (2005) EWCA Civ 932.
Dahlav V Switzerland, (ECHR, 2001) Application 42393/98.
Dogru v France (ECHR 2008 and 2009) 27058/05, ECHR 1579, [2009] ELR 77, (2009) 49 EHRR 8.
Federal Constitutional Court, Decision of 10 May 1957, BverGE 6, 389.
French Civil Code, 'The Publication, Effects, and Application of Legislation in General', from http://www.wipo.int/wipolex/en/text.jsp?file_id=450530
German Federal Administrative Court's Judgement of June 24, 2004–2 C 45.03.
Goerlich, H. (1999). Distanz und Neutralitat im Lehrberuf – zum Kopftuch und anderen religiosen Symbolen. *NeueJuristische Wochenrchrifl, 32*(40), 2929.
Higher Constitutional Court, 'Judgment of the Second Senate of 24 September 2003 on the basis of the oral hearing of 3 June 2003–2 BvR 1436/02' from http://www.bverfg.de/entscheidungen/rs20030924_2bvr143602en.html
Is the HIJAB really COMPULSORY? (n.d.). Ummah. Retrieved December 4, 2015, from http://www.ummah.com/forum/showthread.php?261950-Is-the-HIJABreally-COMPULSORY
karaduma v Turkey, (1993) app no. 16278/90, D&R 74/93.
Landtag von Baden-Württemberg (20 March 1997), Plenarprotokoll 12/23, 1632.
Loi 2000-597 du 30 Juin 2000 relative au référé devant les juridictions administratives [Law 2000-597 of June 30, 2000 on the Relating to Summary Proceedings Before the Administrative Courts], JOURNAL OFFICIEL DE LA RÉPUBLIQUE FRANÇAISE [J.O.] [OFFICIAL GAZETTE OF FRANCE], Feb. 13, 2017.
Loi nº 2004-228 du 15 mars 2004 encadrant, en application du principe de laïcité, le port de signes ou de tenues manifestant une appartenance religieuse dans les écoles, collèges et lycées publics (FR).
LOI No. 2010-1192 du 11 Octobre 2010 interdisant la dissimulation du visage dans l'espace public, Journal Officiel (JORF) (FR).
Mahmood, S. (2009). Religious reason and secular affect: An incommensurable divide?. *Critical Inquiry, 35*(4):836–862.

Mandla v Dowell Ue [1983] 2 AC 548.
Manoussakis and Others v. Greece, (ECHR 26 Sept. 1996) Application No. 18748/91, IV RJD.
Noah v. Desrosiers [2008]. ET 2201867/07.
Opinion of the Conseil d'Etat No. 346.893, session of 27 November 1989. See www.conseil-etat.fr/ce/rappor/index-ra-cg03-O1.shtml. Accessed on 3 May 2007.
Otto-Preminger-Institut v. Austria (ECtHR 20 Sept. 1994), Appl. n No. 13470/87.
Plenarprotokoll 12 / 23 20.03.97, (Stuttgart, 1997) 1630–32.
Pretty v UK (2002), reported 2002-III.
R (Begum) v. Headteacher and Governors of Denbigh High School, [2004] EWHR 1389, [2005] EWCA Civ 199 2006 WL 690559, [2006] UKHL 15.
Refah Partisi (The Welfare Party) and others v. Turkey (ECHR 31st July 2001), Application nos. 41340/98, 42342/98 and 41344/98.
Sahin v. Turkey (ECHR 10 Nov. 2005), Application No. 44774/98.
SAS v. France (ECHR 1 July 2014) Application no. 43835/11.
Wingrove v UK (1996) 24 EHRR 1.
Young, James and Webster v. United Kingdom (1981) no. 7601/76; 7806/77 ECHR Application.

Chapter 4
Excluding *by* and *Through* Law: The Re-configuration of Religious Subjectivities in Secular Europe

In mid-August 2016, Rania El-Alloul was attending the hearing of her son who had been caught driving with a suspended licence in Montreal, Canada. During the hearing, Judge Eliana Marengo asked Rania to remove her headscarf, stating that "the courtroom is a secular place and you are not suitably dressed"(Osborne, 2016). When Rania refused, alleging her right to wear the veil because there was no ban on wearing religious items in the courtroom, the judge refused to hear the case of her 21-year-old son. The fact leads to the thought that western secular space is not neutral as it requires a specific form of attire in which hair is visible. The understanding that women should be un-veiled in the western secular sphere is mirrored in the European decisions that have banned the veil, whereas through the establishment of oppositional categories in the legal discourse on the veil (such as women's freedom v women's un-freedom, religious v secular, public v private etc.), European judges have imposed a specific form of female/secular attire to be displayed in the public sphere. This 'secular' form of attire is based on dichotomous categories and mirrored in the European decisions that have banned the veil. In Germany, a dichotomy has been established between Christian and Islamic symbols, where the first is understood as the metaphor for the western value of tolerance, while the latter is the symbol of backward and intolerant values. This dichotomy is mirrored in the French obsession with defining whether veiling is a proper or improper religious symbol, which is linked to the dichotomy between the secular and the religious sphere; while the discourse concerning veiling in the UK has been framed through the dichotomy between women's freedom and oppression. These dichotomies are also visible in the European Court of Human Rights (ECtHR)'s juridical decisions which have allowed and reiterated these polarizations, excluding many Muslim women from the European public sphere. From laic France to Catholic Germany and the multicultural UK, veiled Muslim women have been rendered invisible through the exclusionary power of western law, or they have been rendered visible in order to be

G. Baldi, *Un-Veiling Dichotomies*, Boundaries of Religious Freedom: Regulating Religion in Diverse Societies,
https://doi.org/10.1007/978-3-030-79297-8_4

rendered invisible from the European public sphere. This law's double movement of inclusion/exclusion should not be understood as a way to save western/secular values of democracy and tolerance, as European judges have claimed, nor has it advanced the principle of gender equality by un-veiling Muslim women: rather, those decisions are instances of the effects of the embeddedness of liberal/Christian/secular values in western and Human Rights law.

In order to understand how this embeddedness works, in this chapter I offer an analysis of the juridical dichotomies on which the legal decisions to ban the veil in Europe are based. Those dichotomies are embedded in the discourse concerning the regulation of the female headscarf, revealing how those oppositions are constitutive of a fixed legal and religious subject along with a specific relation between the individual and the sovereign. In particular, I examine three important dichotomies which emerge from the analysis of the European decisions to ban the veil: that between *forum internum* and *forum externum*, embedded in article 9 of the European Convention on Human Rights (ECHR), which is based on a specific ontological concept of the person and has the power to shape a specific notion of religion and the religious and legal subject; that between humanisation and de-humanisation encoded in Human Rights law, which unmasks Human Rights law's inability to protect the individual's rights from the state power; and that between public and private embedded in the right of religious liberty, which discloses a specific relation between the individual and the sovereign power.

Esposito (2015) reveals that, historically, the western legal subject has been constructed through dichotomous categories. In Roman law, the subject of law was framed through the division between slave and freeman, male and female, while in Christianity the subject was split between the soul and the body. Gauchet (1997) shows how the development of western secularity and the modern secular subject of law is intrinsically linked to Christianity and the dual nature of Jesus Christ: this is mirrored in St. Augustine's doctrine of the two kingdoms, which conceives the individual as obeying two different authorities (public/private, secular/religious, outward/inward) (Augustine, 1998; Calvin, 2008; Luther, 1962). This, in western/secular historical development, has led to an understanding of the human as split between its internal world (with an inner relation with God) and the external world, which has resulted in the Hegelian notion of the 'buffered self' (Hegel, 1991): an individual who has learned to judge the world objectively, being able to separate its internal from its external world. This specific western notion of the person has, historically, coincided with the subject of law: a split subject who oscillates between oppositional categories (such as person/non-person, humane/in-humane, external/internal etc.) (Esposito, 2015).

This split subject, I argue, is reproduced in the European decisions to ban the veil. Article 9 of the ECHR ('Freedom of thought, conscience and religion') makes a difference between faith and manifestation, internal and external, posing particular emphasis on a post-protestant understanding of religion as located in the conscience of the individual (Mahmood, 2013). The subject that emerges from the European juridical decisions to ban the veil is one who is split between faith and manifestation, and so able to separate its internal from its external world; a secular subject[1] constituted *by* and *through* the western/secular (privatist) definition of religion given by article 9 of the ECHR as solely located in the private sphere, and so separated from its manifestation. In light of this, the subject protected by western and Human Rights law is one who acts in a secular way, by which I do not mean simply non-religious practices, but practices that have been

> "discursively identified and valorized through the discourse of secularism (as distinct from the political doctrine) [...]. [A] practice is not secular because it stands in a particular relation to the political doctrine of secularism. Rather, the historical discourse of the secular, as predicated on the opposition religious–secular, is integral to the grammar of the concept"(Hirschkind, 2011, p. 639).

Far from being neutral, article 9 operates in such a way as to define specific religious and non-religious forms of knowledge and behaviour and to exclude others. In fact, it is thanks to the specific notion of the person (and not 'in spite of it', as Esposito would argue) as embedded in western and Human Rights law, that the law excludes certain individuals from its protection, or it includes them in order to exclude them. Since western and Human Rights law conceive the subject as split and oscillating between dichotomous categories, the subject of law is subjected to an inclusionary/exclusionary pattern (Esposito, 2012b). In other words, it is exactly the understanding of the individual as split into oppositional categories that results in the dialectic between personalization and depersonalization which, in turn, is related to the possibility of the subject to be recognised by the law and therefore to be protected (Esposito, 2012b). This shows that secularism is not a neutral position but a normative prescriptive model that favours certain forms of religion at the expense of others that are equally legitimate. In the case of the headscarf ban, it is thanks to the employment of the notion of the legal subject as split between *forum externum* and *forum internum*, that western and Human Rights law have excluded a certain category of people (veiled Muslim women), while privileging others, dividing, in this way, one who deserves the protection of article 9 from one who does not. In fact, in western law, only a life that is within the definition of personhood can be deemed sacred or qualitatively significant (Esposito, 2012b) and therefore entitled to the law's protection.

This process of inclusion/exclusion is also at work in Human Rights law, which is based on the same understanding of a split subject who is brought into life through its inscription within the pale of the law. I employ Esmeir's work (2012) on Juridical Humanity to show how human rights pose another dichotomy; that between humane and in-humane. Her exploration discloses the link between human rights and colonisation, showing how the imposition of modern positive law by British colonizers was a project of colonization which presupposed the inclusion of the human within the pale of (positive) law as an instrument of subjugation able to eliminate the past in the name of an eternal present, and thereby to deliver humanity. Esmeir (2012)

[1] For Hirschkind (2011), a secular individual "is one that depends on, one that cannot be abstracted from, the secularist narrative of the progressive replacement of religious error by secular reason – what Asad calls the 'triumphalist narrative of secularism'. A secular sensibility is one considered from the standpoint of its contribution to that progressive narrative" (pp. 641–642).

argues that Human Rights law, a combination of positive and natural law, replaced the legal positivism exported during the colonial period and took over its global power to deliver humanity through the inclusion of the individual within the pale of the law. By delivering humanity through the inscription of the individual within the law, the human becomes the *telos* and the *theological end* of the law. However, in this way, becoming the subject of human rights can ensure both a temporal humanity and its possible suspension because Human Rights law protects a *mask*, a 'human-yet-to-become' that forever needs state law in order to be human. In this way, Human Rights law's power allows a double movement: 'de-humanizing' and 're-humanizing' (Esmeir, 2006), whereas the subject of Human Rights law is a de-humanized subject waiting to be re-inscribed within the pale of the law in order to be re-humanized. The dichotomy between humanization and de-humanization embedded in Human Rights law is clear in the legal decisions concerning the practice of veiling, where Muslim women have been seen as subjects de-humanized by their backward culture and religion and therefore in need of being re-humanized by western law through the un-veiling of their bodies, exactly as British and French colonizers posed the un-veiling of women at the centre of the western project of humanization. In fact, European judges have seen "the un-veiling as equivalent to liberating women, just as the rhetoric of colonialism focused on women's oppression in colonized societies, attaining moral justification for eradicating the culture of colonized people" (Davary, 2009, p. 65).

The dichotomous contrapositions between faith and manifestation, humanization and de-humanization, inclusion and exclusion from the protective wing of the law, are linked to the dichotomy between public and private encoded in western and human rights understanding of the juridical notion of freedom of religion, which presupposes the paradoxical active interference of the state in regulating religious communities. In fact, from its inception, the notion of religious liberty was split into two spheres: the *forum internum* (inviolable) and the *forum externum* (regulated by the state). This is mirrored in article 9.2 of the ECHR which states that 'freedom to manifest one's religion or beliefs shall be subject only to such limitations as are prescribed by law and are necessary in a democratic society in the interests of public safety, for the protection of public order, health or morals, or for the protection of the rights and freedoms of others'.

In the case of the headscarf ban, article 9.2 has been used to regulate majority and minority religious rights through the notion of public order; a concept that changes from place to place and is linked to European early preoccupation with religious plurality (Mahmood & Danchin, 2014). As an instrument of sovereign power in between norm and exception, public order emerges as a semantic field which is often associated with the notion of public interest, public sentiments, and morality (Agrama, 2010)[2]: while this indicates that the notion of public order has served to protect the majoritarian view through the indeterminacy of its meaning(s),

[2] The notion of public order is not fixed: rather it changes based on specific context and historical period. It is a notion of state domestic sovereignty that enables states to overcome international law when a norm is in contrast with local legislation or public morality (Agrama, 2010).

it is also constitutive of a specific form of sovereignty and of a specific relation between the sovereign power, the law, and the individual's private sphere. In fact, it is through the notion of public order encoded in the right of freedom of religion, along with the difference made by article 9 between *forum internum* (inviolable) and *forum externum* (regulated by the state), that the law presupposes the active interference of the state into the private life of the individual. The western notion of religious liberty is not something that helps the individual to be free from state interference: rather, it is a legal vehicle of state interference (Danchin & Mahmood, 2014).

This is the paradox of the secular, that while on the one hand it claims a division between public and private, then on the other, it regulates the private life of the individual. In other words, while a secular system establishes an inviolable line of separation between public and private, secular and religion, then it continuously redefines the place of religion and religious sentiments in the secular European public sphere by constituting specific criteria of inclusion/exclusion through the definition of the *forum internum* as solely located in the conscience of the individual. Hence, while the secular state claims to treat all its citizens equally regardless of their religious affiliations, then it limits the private life of (certain) citizens by privileging the sensitivities of the majority. This paradox shows the prerogative of the modern political order in which the state does not fix but continually re-establishes the lines between the private and the public divide on which it is based by organising and managing different sensitivities and religious creeds (Danchin & Mahmood, 2014) through a double circular movement between norm and exception, humanization/de-humanization, person/non-person, public/private, faith/manifestation.

Secularism, then, emerges as a particular technology of governance[3] which ensures the sovereign state can regulate the private life of its citizens through the control and regulation of the visible. For Foucault (1981), the control of bodily practices by legal/political authority is a modern technique of discipline. Through this reading, the regulation of Muslim women's attire can be understood as an essential disciplinary tool of the new form of neo-liberal governmentality. The concept of secularism, widely used to justify the normative control of (Muslim) women's body, becomes one of the technologies of control employed by the state to discipline (different/non-homogeneous) bodies. In this view, secularism is used to keep women's body under the control of the state: in fact, from a secularist point of view, religious symbols mark differences in bodies that are supposedly neutral, rational and abstract. This technology of power is at work in European decisions to ban the veil and it is productive of political and legal polarizations that make possible the existence of an inclusionary/exclusionary pattern which is translated in the

[3] With the term 'technology of power' I refer to Foucault's (2012) understanding of the modern state which produces 'docile bodies' through disciplinary institutions such as schools, hospitals etc. He argues that the modern state "has to qualify, measure, appraise, and hierarchize, rather than display itself in its murderous splendor" (Foucault, 1981, p. 144). For Agamben (1998), this technology of power represents the expansion of western form of sovereign: "placing biological life at the center of its calculations, the modern State […] does nothing other than bring to light the secret tie uniting power and bare life" (p. 6).

dichotomy veiling/un-veiling, whereas only lives that are considered significant are protected by the law. As Esposito (2012b) argues, legal debate

> "hinges on determining the exact moment when a living being -or on defining what type of living being – can be considered a person, but never on the decisive value that this attribution entails "(p. 2).

In light of this, the European legal decisions concerning the practice of veiling emerge as a key to understand the extraordinary normalising and universalising power of secular/liberal forces. Those forces, when translated to a western and human rights architectural juridico-semiotic structure, render inevitable the exclusion of different forms of life, producing particular sensitivities, knowledge and behaviours along with a specific law and religious subject. Rather than the protection of a universal humanity, what emerges from European decisions to ban the veil is the imposition of a new universal law that in principle 'saves' the part of humanity that has yet to be allowed to enter into the arrangements of liberal law but, in reality, it reinforces its own absolute power and, as a transcendent Christian God did before, it controls and guides the individual by creating a specific secular subject who enjoys the abstract equality of a (supposedly) neutral secular state within the jurisdiction of the law.

4.1 (Un)Masking the (Christian/Secular) Legal Subject

The female headscarf has often been portrayed as a metaphor for a profound incompatibility between the 'east' and the 'west'; at times, the veil has been seen as the symbol of a political and violent Islam and linked to the recent terrorist attacks (Khalid, 2011); at other times, as a metaphor for women's subjugation to patriarchal culture/religion which is seen in contrast with secular democratic principles. Far from representing its factual plurality, the veil has been understood by western judges through dichotomous categories (public/private, religious/secular, free/unfree, body/soul, etc.) which are translated into the dichotomies of veiling/unveiling and inclusion/exclusion from the protective wing of western and Human Rights law. These binary dichotomies, in western history, have formed and informed the modern notion of the legal and religious subject through which it is possible to understand the process of inclusion/exclusion established by western secular law (Esposito, 2012b). It is through the understanding of the modern normative category of person as developed in western and Christian thought, an unquestioned assumption in today's debate concerning the veil, that it is possible to understand the exclusionary dimension of western and Human Rights law and the specific legal and religious subject that emerges from the European decisions concerning the practice of veiling. The very construction of the veiled woman as something other, from which society must be defended, is based on a specific understanding of religion and the religious and legal subject which, as I will argue in the next chapter, is at odds with the plurality of religious sensitivities that inhabit contemporary Europe.

From ancient Greek philosophy to Christian thought and Roman law, western history has been marked by the definition of 'person' as divided into two contraposed categories (e.g. mind and body, person and thing, *zoe* and *bios,* etc.) in which the latter is subordinated to the former (Esposito, 2012b). In Roman law, the notion of person was characterised by a binary division between person and thing, freeman and slave, where the slave was defined as a 'thing', a tool owned by the free man. Hence, the relation between person and thing is one of domination, as things exist to serve (or to belong to) the person. Esposito (2015) highlights that "a slave is a man, not a person: man is a term of nature, person is a term of civil law" (p. 81). Henceforth, in Roman law, a difference is made between *homo* (slave) and *persona* (which indicated the juridical capacity of a person, its juridical personality). Notably, the Roman juridical notion of person oscillated between different legal categories, so a person was at times a non-person, in the sense that at different point of its life s/he enjoyed the status of personhood or, *vice-versa,* of non-person. In fact, Roman law was marked by the establishment and definition of different oppositional categories to which different legal status were assigned: an example was the *filii in potestate* (children under the authority of the father), *uxores in matrimonio* (wives), *mulieres in manu* (women subjected to the power of others) etc. While Roman law differentiated between different legal categories, it also established a continuous movement from one category to another. For instance, before becoming *pater familias*, the man was a *filii in potestate*: hence no one, in Roman law, was a person by nature, neither slave nor free man, as everyone oscillated from one category to another, from person to thing and *vice-versa* (Esposito, 2012b). Paradoxically, Roman law, although founded on the opposition between persons and things, shaped an individual who continually oscillated between these two categories, creating at the same time a continuous state of exception (Esposito, 2015).[4] This 'state of exception', at the very basis of Roman law, "concerns the process of inclusion through the exclusion of what isn't included" (Esposito, 2012a, p. 23). As different juridical categories were defined in opposition to other categories, the result was an inevitable process of separation not only between slaves and freemen but also within the latter, producing a chain of infinite differentiation. Hence, while on the one hand the concept of person was conceived as a general category that encompassed the whole of humanity, then on the other, it is through this notion that humans were separated by a hierarchical division that constituted their very difference. In this view, the role of the law was to recognise in which category the human was placed at a specific point of its life and to regulate it according to specific legal principles (Esposito, 2012b). Hence, the juridical person "intersects at several points with the political category of sovereignty" (Esposito, 2012b, p. 83): this, in turn, produces processes of inclusion/exclusion, unity/separation.

---

[4] It is worth pointing out that in Roman law norms are not separated from their exceptions whereas the exception derives from the norms and norms from the exception (for instance, a father had an absolute power over his children, but not if the child was illegitimate or under 3 years of age) (Esposito, 2012a).

Christianity operated a shift from the Roman division between human and person, to an ontological division within the human or between two entities that form the human: from Christianity, western theological political thought reaches unity only by excluding one or more of its parts. Christianity's essential supremacy of the soul over the body is mirrored in the notion of the person, which is made in the image of God, its creator, exactly because of its dual nature (spiritual and corporeal). The concept of an individual split and oscillating between a metaphysical and a corporeal sphere is found in almost all Christian authors: while, for Augustine, only when the soul wins the endless struggle against the body's needs and desires, the 'city of God' will triumph upon the 'city of men'(Esposito, 2015, p. 36–7), for Thomas, reason should dominate a person's body and own actions (Serafini, 2017). Christianity, then, defines the human being as one who is able to maintain full control over its animal nature, "[a]nd the reason why human beings have an animal nature is so they can measure against it their sovereign status as a person" (Esposito, 2012b, p. 89). Since man was conceived in the image of God, natural law understood the individual as owning certain natural privileges.

With the papal revolution the individual started to be slowly defined as an abstract rational subject: one who is split between the mask of its legal personality and its real face. The various religious wars in Europe, culminating in the so called 'papal revolution', and the consequent fragmentation of the authority and unity of the Catholic Church, favoured the creation of important notions which have persisted to this day, and are the foundation of modern western law (David Kennedy, 1999). Firstly, the aftermath of the papal revolution witnessed a separation between spiritual and temporal power, where religion was relegated to the private sphere (Cavanaugh, 1995). This favoured the emergence of the modern western/liberal understanding of the state as a "form of public power separated from both ruler and the ruled, and constituting the supreme political authority within a certain defined territory" (Skinner, 1978, p. 353) where the policy of *cuius regio, eius religio* was applied (Cavanaugh, 2009). Secondly, this period witnessed the emergence of a new concept of 'Man': driven by rational judgments and individual reason, the new man was now independent from his Father and in the place of the Holy Spirit (Diamantides, 2014).

The various religious conflicts in Europe pushed the idea of the necessity to subordinate the religious domain to institutional political power in the modern nation-state. As Locke (1960) argued, a delimitation of the political and religious realm was necessary, as conflicts between political and religious powers were incapable of being resolved by rational means: the division between secular and religious power, then, was seen as a useful tool to establish the lowest common denominator between different Christian sects and to link the individual to the power of the state (Charles Taylor, 1998). The preoccupation with defining different spheres of influence is attested by the obsession of western philosophers with the proper definition of religion (Asad, 2003) which comes to be understood as a trans-historical and transcultural phenomenon, an illogical and un-real belief, a myth (Cavanaugh, 2009). Cavanaugh (1995) observes that "what is at issue […] is the creation of 'religion' as a set of beliefs which is defined as personal conviction and which can exist separately from one's public loyalties to the State" (p. 403). While the universalization of the concept of religion as a private belief neglects the particularities of different faith communities, the descriptive definition of religion has created a fundamental problem: by defining religion as a mere private/un-real/mythological belief, religion itself becomes a normative concept which acquires a specific meaning based on particular power relations (Asad, 2001). In other words, the definition of religion depends on who has the power to define it in different cultural and historical contexts.

The narrow understanding of religion as a personal, irrational, transcendent, and mythological belief was accompanied by the creation of a new rational knowledge, now 'desensualized' from human invisible experiences and understood as a precondition for moral actions (Keane, 2015). Locke (1960) defined 'person' as one who is the author of its own actions and thoughts, a 'moral agent' who is, at the same time, the subject of law and the object of judgement. In fact, in order for the subject to become a person and to judge itself, it is essential that s/he separates from itself, becoming at the same time the judge and the accused. Hence, instead of eliminating the split and duality that has accompanied western thought from its inception, philosophers of that time, with their insistence on the importance for human beings to take ownership of their selves, have reinforced the split of the individual in dichotomous spheres. 'Person' started to be identified with a rational subject who is able to separate from itself and to fully control its animal part.

The aftermath of the papal revolution did not produce a separation between Church and state power, or a decline in religiosity in the name of human reason. Rather, it simply transferred religious devotion from the realm of the Church to that of the world: this new religiosity, which in western history has been expressed in concepts such as secularization, modernization, nationalism, etc., (Inayatullah & Boxwell, 2003) becomes the foundation of modern/positive/western law. In fact, in western history, elements of the state's apparatus come to be secularized according to new sacred narratives. Hobbes (1991) describes the state as 'a mortal God' whose life is 'eternal' because the duty to protect the worldly life of the individual is given to the state. The state is transcendent in part for its sacredness,[5] due to its claim to protect the life of its citizens, and in part because it acquires the power to shape the individual's life and to create an obedient 'citizen' through the force of the law (Hobbes, 1991). Although the state is not a living human, to it is accorded the same sacrality of human life and for this reason, as Kantorowics (1957) reminds us, the Leviathan, the sovereign, is composed of two bodies, one transcendent and the other immortal; the genealogy of this duality is the transfer of the dual nature of Christ (mortal and eternal) into the sovereign body (Esposito, 2015, p. 38): with the *reductio ad unum* of the king's two bodies begins what we call 'modernity'. Cavanaugh (2009) observes that the modern notion of state undergoes a process of naturalization: "the secular nation-state [...] appears as natural, corresponding to a universal and timeless truth about the inherent dangers of religion" (p. 3). Since the state (or the Leviathan) claims eternal life, it is also entitled to defend itself by any means; this is translated into the expansion of the Leviathan's sovereign power. In fact, the

[5] For Emile Durkheim (1972) the state's sacredness is what defines society.

Leviathan is authorized to do whatever is necessary to maintain the commonwealth, including the use of violence: thus, secular violence becomes legitimated over religious violence. This is one of the paradoxes of the modern/secular/liberal concept of politics: "just as the violent act of enforcing law establishes conventions which then guarantee the validity of this performative act itself, so a state, by means of its funding gesture, sets up conventions which then retroactively give legitimacy to its creation" (Salecl, 1994, p. 91). The founding of western law and the mode of sovereignty, then, is intrinsically linked to a discourse of self-legitimation which also justifies acts of violence to enforce the law and to defend the state. The sovereign power (the *persona ficta*) embraces the absolute power able to dictate law and to contain or encompass any political decisions. In the western history of secularisation, the state had started to assign to religious practices and religious beliefs a proper place, creating the conceptual conditions to secure the loyalty of its citizens, irrespective of different religious allegiances.

The individual becomes thus split into two parts: one (outward) obeys to the sovereign power, while the other (inward) remains free. This split, as Esposito (2012b) argues, has been translated in contemporary Europe into the split between human being and citizen: the first is outside the protection of western positive and Human Rights law, while the second is protected by the law by virtue of its being a person (or *persona juridica*) (Esposito, 2012b). With the public/private divide and the emergence of the modern/liberal/secular form of government, each person comes to be split into two spheres that are impossible to reunite. As no one can be defined as a person before the sovereign, the subject always incurs the risk of being depersonalised. With the birth of the sovereign state, the notion of person becomes increasingly linked to that of sovereign (Esposito, 2012b) because it is the sovereign that decides upon the value of each life, as I will further argue in the next chapter.

The new form of government was accompanied by positivization of the law, as articulated by Hart (1997). Positive law conceives the individual as 'abstractly equal' to others. For Hobbes (1991), although egalitarianism may not be supported by nature, abstract equality is a precondition for political life. The concept of abstract equality, which is at the foundation of positive law, rests on the idea that every individual is equal before the law. With Hobbes' abstract equality the distance between *homo* and *persona*, split between natural and artificial, is reduced to a minimum: as all humans were considered to possess a rational will, independently of their differences, they were considered to have a legal personality (Esposito, 2012b). In this way, the human was split between its biological body and its juridical personality where the first is subordinated to the latter. However, as the individual is conceived in abstract terms, the legal subject inevitably emerges as a mask, a theatrical artifice, a product of mere institutional performances. This *persona*, or mask, comes to life as law's progenitor, but, at the same time, it also comes *before* the law and maintains its maker. In other words, Hobbes (1991) transformed the Roman separation between *homo* and *persona* into a fundamental separation between natural and artificial, between the mask and the face, fiction and reality. *Persona* started to designate who wears a mask while the mask designated the *persona* (Esposito, 2012b). *Persona*, then, is not the individual as such, but its legal status which changes based on power relations with others: this is what Esposito (2015) calls the 'western paradigm of the person' (p. 30–1) which separates people based on their social roles and the individual from its biological being through the contraposition between mind and body, person and things, *zoe* and *bios,* the mask and the human face. Here is another paradoxical split: the mask never fully adheres to the face, and nor does the legal person coincide with the human to whom it refers. As the individual is different from the mask s/he wears, there is always the risk of the individual's depersonalisation or of a *capitis diminutio* (the extinguishing of a person's legal capacity). In other words, the person does not coincide with the human as the juridical personality attached to the human being is superimposed and juxtaposed on the human (Esposito, 2012b).

Marcel Gauchet (1997) links the emergence of secular modernity to Christianity's historical development. For him, it is Christianity that created a dynamic which culminated in the emergence of the abstract autonomous individual of modern democracy and it is Christianity that allowed the emergence of an earthly absolute power as substitute for a withdrawn God. The separation between 'the divine' and 'the human' opened a space for human action and the rise of the modern notion of sovereignty. Christianity's attention to the concept of conscience encouraged individual interpretation and evaluation of sacred authority, furthering, in this way, the western/liberal concept of autonomy. This process, in turn, led to 'Christianity's own overcoming' which resulted in the modern Christian/secular/liberal political order and the relegation of religion as a private belief (Gauchet, 1997). Supiot (2007) finds that Christianity is the only religion in which God is perceived as law giver (as creator of the law of nature) but is, at the same time, bound by it: similarly, the modern/Christian/secular subject is creator and, at the same time, is subject to state law. This is the paradox of the modern western subject of law: that its intrinsic nature is both obedient and free and self-governing. In other words, while on the one hand the subject of law enjoys a freedom guaranteed by the state, then on the other s/he must be subjected to state power in order for her/his freedom to be protected.

In the 18th–nineteenth century another important change took place and a new form of governmentality[6] emerged in the shift from government (in which the state intervenes in specific areas), to governance (in which the state sets standards)

[6] Foucault (1991) defines governmentality as the 'art of government' which includes a wide range of control techniques. Governmentality, however, is not seen as a top-down form of power, but a variety of disciplinary social institutions and forms of powers which produces discourses that come to be internalised by the individual: in this way, the individual governs itself through a specific form of interiorised knowledge. Hence, for Foucault (1991), governmentality means "1. The ensemble formed by the institutions, procedures, analyses and reflections, the calculations and tactics that allow the exercise of this very specific albeit complex form of power, which has as its target population, as its principal form of knowledge political economy, and as its essential technical means apparatuses of security. 2. The tendency which, over a long period and throughout the West, has steadily led towards the pre-eminence over all other forms (sovereignty, discipline, etc) of this type of power which may be termed government, resulting, on the one hand, in formation of a whole series of specific governmental apparatuses, and, on the other, in the development of a whole complex of savoirs. 3. The process, or rather the result of the process, through which the state of justice of the Middle Ages, transformed into the administrative state during the fifteenth and sixteenth centuries, gradually becomes 'governmentalized'"(pp. 102–103). While Foucault

(Supiot, 2007) when the figure of the sovereign started to decline in the name of effective management and governance:

> "governance is to government what regulation is to rules and ethics to morals: a technique for standardizing behaviour that aims to close the gap between the law and the subject of law. The idea is to make human beings behave in a way that spontaneously conforms to the needs of the established order" (Supiot, 2007, p. 168).

Sovereign power becomes a 'functional power' implemented through a continuous monitoring and surveillance of the population (Supiot, 2007): these technologies of power, which are both disciplinary and normalising, are oriented towards biological processes affecting large part of the population (Foucault, 1981). The shift in the way in which power is exercised and manifested has privileged the biological life of the individual against the marginalisation of the human (Esposito, 2012b). This is exactly the logic of sovereign power, which is based on the inclusion of bare life through its exclusion (Agamben, 1998), as the life of the individual is subjected to sovereign violence and sovereign power to define the value of the human. This new form of sovereignty ad governmentality, which I will further analyse in the next chapter, presupposes a subject who is free and yet indissolubly bound to the law and the secular form of power; an individual who has the freedoms that the state allows and guarantees while, at the same time, for the sake of these freedoms, s/he must to obey static rules of positive law.

As positive law presupposes an individual able to turn desires into rights, the individual acquires his/her natural identity by having rights: hence, western law's development has transformed the individual into a *homo juridicus* (Supiot, 2007). Since the modern legal subject is included within the pale of the law because it is the bearer of a rational will, the *persona* does not have any meaning outside of the category of *ius* because humans acquired their personhood only within the law and only within a continuous movement between person and non-person, human and non-human, abstract and real person. This movement, which has accompanied western development, is mirrored in today's Human Rights law which, while claiming its universality, in reality protects a specific western/Christian/liberal citizen, excluding those who lack of the rights of citizens (Esposito, 2012b). In fact, Human Rights law, which derives from positive and natural law, upholds and expands the western Christian notion of person as subject of law (Esposito, 2012b). The link between the western notion of the person and human rights lies in the notion of human being as bearer of universal rights regardless of its race, gender or social condition (Esposito, 2012b). As, in human rights, the notion of citizen is what seems to separate law and humanity (as only citizens can enjoy human rights), the concept of person emerges as a semantic field that can overlap the sphere of law and humanity. In other words, the notion of human right can be conceivable only if we employ the western notion of personhood (Esposito, 2012b). However, if subjective rights are strictly linked to the western notion of person, then in order to have access to individual's rights, the

---

applies the notion of governmentality to different historical periods, he nevertheless links this notion to western/neo-liberal governmentality.

human should firstly be recognised as a person and be included within the pale of the law (Esposito, 2012b). Human Rights, then, represent not a limitation of the notion of the person, but its expansion "not to the fact that we have yet to enter fully into its regime of meaning, but to the fact that we have never really moved out of it" (Esposito, 2012b, p. 5). In fact, juridically, what is inside is defined by contrast to what is outside: hence, only one who is considered part of the political community can be included within the protection of the law (Esposito, 2012b). As Weil (1986) observes, a right is at the same time private and privative, as it can only protect a certain category of people, excluding those who do not fall into the western category of person where one who possesses rights is defined in contraposition to one who is deprived of rights. For Weil (1986), it is impossible for all people to enjoy the same rights: "the claim is both absurd and base; absurd because privilege is, by definition, inequality: base, because it is not worth claiming"(p. 64). In light of this, the western notion of person, which has led to the universalization of human rights, has been employed, in western history, to exclude certain categories of humans while privileging others, and to divide humans between those who have rights and those who do not. As Esposito (2012b) argues, the triumph of the western category of the person, at the centre of western and Human Rights law, represents the very failure of human rights as, rather than including the whole of humanity within the protection of the law, it discloses its exclusionary pattern because, by employing the notion of a split subject developed in Christianity and Roman law, it is unable to bridge the gap between the notion of humanity and that of citizenship.

4.2 Universalising Humanity: Human Rights and the 'Humane' Subject of Law

Amin Qasim, an Egyptian jurist considered an important scholar within Arab feminism during the British colonisation (Hatem Mervat, 2004) wrote:

> "Who do you understand a woman to be? Like a man, she too is a human being. Her body and its functions, her feelings, and her ability to think are the same as a man's. She has all the essential traits, differing only in gender"(Qasim Amin, 2000, p. 11).

Qasim disclosed a fundamental dichotomy that was at stake during the colonial period: that between humanity and in-humanity, where women's body was located at the centre of the colonial project to humanise a de-humanised population through their inclusion under the protective wing of western positive law. This split is reproduced nowadays in Human Rights law (Esmeir, 2006) and reiterates the western inclusionary/exclusionary dimension of western law by excluding certain categories of people while including others. Hence, Human Rights law does not solve western dichotomies through the inclusion within the law of a universal humanity: rather, in Human Rights law, the western dichotomy between inclusion and exclusion from the protective wing of the law has been translated into the dichotomy humanisation/de-humanisation.

I employ Esmeir's work (2006, 2012) on the colonial genealogy of Human Rights law to show how the split between the human and in-human established by colonial power, which mirrors the split between inside and outside the protection of the law, reproduces a split typical of Human Rights law, revealing the inability of Human Rights law to protect the whole of humanity, as it claims. In the European decisions to ban the veil, the split between humane and in-humane is constitutive of the fictionality of the legal person and emerges as an instance of the (in)visibility of the human in front of the law; however, while the European juridical decisions that I have taken into consideration picture a 'de-humanized' female, victim of chauvinistic religious law, who must be re-humanized as an abstract individual, at once legislator and subject of law, they also invite us to see what there is behind the mask of the modern legal subject, namely, the female veiled body, in its plurality.

Esmeir's analysis (2012) reveals how the concept of humanity encoded in Human Rights law has profound roots in the work of colonial jurists. She explains how the imposition of the new, modern, positive law during the British occupation of Egypt (1882–1956) was a precise project of colonization which presupposed the inclusion of the human in the law as an instrument of subjugation able to eliminate the past in the name of an eternal present, and thereby to deliver humanity. Her work shows how the new legal reforms, alongside the adoption of positive law, claimed to deliver Egyptians from their 'inhuman' existence under a 'despotic', 'lawless' and 'in-humane' pre-colonial past.[7] In order to deliver humanity, the new law confined the past to a place unrelated to the present: this 'absolute now' created not only the 'human' but also the 'in-humane' backwardness of what preceded it. In order to deliver humanity and to save Egyptians from their backwardness, British colonizers imposed the positivization of the law, relegating religious laws (including *Sharia*) to matters of family law. Egyptian jurists, influenced by western law, also started to standardize aspects of Islamic family law resulting in a further limitation of Islamic scholars' legal interpretation (Hallaq, 2009; Massad, 2012). The rejection of the past and the creation of positivized and westernized juridical textbooks *in* and *for* the present were necessary to create a rupture with the former legal tradition. Consequently, Egypt witnessed a loss of traditional authority and the rise of a new authority embedded in obedience to a western, universal, positive, fixed legal order. The law becomes strictly bound to state power and the human has become chained to the universal power of law because law itself delivered humanity. Anghie (2005) highlights that

> "the existence of a distinction between the civilised and uncivilised was so vehemently presupposed by positivist jurists, that the state of nature –and therefore naturalism- became epistemologically incoherent because it lack[ed] this central distinction […]. [I]n crude terms, in the naturalist world, law was given; in the positivist world, law was created by human societies and institutions. Once the connection between 'law' and 'institutions' has

[7] As Festa (2006) argues, the encounter between colonizers and colonized produced emotions that could threaten the integrity of the colonizers. One way in which the colonizers' integrity could be reasserted was to define the colonizer/colonized relations in term of the asymmetry of sympathy: this, in turn, articulated a relation between the colonizers' sympathy and the colonized's suffering (p. 7).

> been established, it followed from this premise that jurists could focus on the character of institutions, a shift which facilitated the racialization of law by delimiting the notion of law to very specific European institutions"(p. 55).

For Esmeir (2012), positive and Human Rights law incorporate the 'human' in three ways: firstly, by claiming authorship and source to be human; secondly, by rendering the human the theological end of the law, and finally by defining the human according to the law. Consequently, "the new men are either the governed or the orderly governors; one becomes a new man by learning the art of being governed or of governing" (Esmeir, 2012, p. 69). With the colonial project humanity is no longer a category of birth,[8] but a juridical category that defines the legal subject itself as human/inhuman. As 'man is not born but made' (Pagden, 1986), humanity has become the *telos* of the new, modern, positive law which becomes the prerequisite for a new, universal humanity.

Thus, positive law emerged as a tool for the education of a new man and, along with it, a new 'woman'.[9] For Amin Qasim (2000), the inferior status of women was the main evidence of the backwardness of Egypt. He argued that British people were able to occupy Egypt because of the perfection of their species and because, thanks to the power of positive law, western European countries were able to move from despotic to democratic law, from chaos to order. He proposed extending the concept of humanity to women, although colonial officials argued that humanity has been delivered to all Egyptians, irrespective of their gender[10]: for the British, the humanity given to women was the result of a broader 'humanity project' in which the introduction of new legal reforms acted to elevate women from their animal status.[11] For the colonizers, what distinguished humans from animals was that the former, unlike the latter, had awareness that punishment is attached to the infringement of moral/legal rules: hence, only a subject who has awareness of its rights and duties could be defined as 'human' (Esmeir, 2012). One of the first legal reforms of British colonizers was the banning of the veil, understood as a symbol of an uncivilized and backward society and an in-humane practice imposed on women.[12] Yegenoglu (1998) observes that the obsession over the practice of veiling was "characterized by a desire to master, control, and reshape the body of the subjects

---

[8] Conversely, Fanon (1967) argues that humanity is not something that can be delivered or taken away, but a category of birth.

[9] As Miner (1892) points out "our task [...] included something more than new principles and new methods. It ultimately involved new men" (p. 28).

[10] Leila Ahmed (1992) coined the term 'colonial feminism' to describe feminism "used against other cultures in the service of colonialism" (pp. 150–152). In fact, in the western colonial discourse "the domesticated, subjugated, unenlightened Other as opposed to the liberated, independent and enlightened western self was used as a moral prop to legitimize colonial power relations" (Mohanty, 1988, p. 73). In this sense, as Said (2003) argues, orientalism "is not an airy European fantasy about the orient, but a created body of theory and practice" (p. 6).

[11] In Esmeir's work (2012), animality means 'absence of humanity', as defined by British officials (pp. 81–82).

[12] In the colonial period, Puritan English missionaries insisted that indigenous populations should learn English culture before converting to Christianity (Haefeli 2015).

by making them visible" (p. 12). This, in turn, has signified the imposition of western modernity which privileges the visible as a primary source of knowledge (Macdonald, 2006). For Massad (2012) "this project […] [intended to create the] Arab women (following European nationalist examples) as custodians of tradition and managers of the nation's moral life and that of its future generations" (p. 82). However, while, on the one hand, women were offered some education and knowledge of home economy, then on the other, their acquisition of rights was always asymmetric compared to men's (Massad, 2012). All in all, what Amin and the colonial officials shared was not only a specific concept of 'womanhood', but also the idea that humanity is a status that may be delivered or taken away.

In declaring Egyptian men and women as 'human', British colonizers combined coloniality, judiciality and humanity. The principle advocating a government of laws and not of men was central to the operations of the colonial state in Egypt. However, by defining and delivering humanity through law, the British never succeeded in determining the transition from pre-human to human or from violence to non-violence; since the law delivers humanity, it continues to contain the inhuman. In contrast with Arendt's work (1967), in which the juridical person and the human overlap and so the subject's de-humanization corresponds to the collapse of its juridical status, for Esmeir (2012) the juridical subject coincides with the human because law locates the human as a product of the law itself. Moreover, contrary to Agamben (2005), for Esmeir (2012), colonization did not suspend the law; rather, through colonization, law was expanded and it contained multiple legalities. Law, then, has become "a technology of colonial rule and modern relationship of bondage" (Esmeir, 2012, p. 285); it has not only delivered humanity, but it has also assured total domination through functional, utilitarian violence.

Esmeir (2012) sees the inclusion of the individual within the pale of the law not as an instrument aiming to protect, but as the vehicle of a 'functional', 'repressive' violence and domination. She unfolds the double face of the colonial project; if, on the one hand, the British aimed to eliminate the arbitrary, non-instrumental khedival legal system,[13] then on the other, they established an arbitrary distinction between 'humane', utilitarian, colonial violence and 'in-humane' pre-colonial violence. Through a systematic reconstruction of historical and legal documents, Esmeir (2012) unmasks the true face of the colonial project: *corvee* labour was not abolished, but regulated. Similarly, harsh punishments such as the use of the whip (no longer used in the Ottoman Empire) were not prohibited but allowed for those who refused to obey orders or convicts who refused to work (Esmeir, 2012): as "civilization must, unfortunately, have its victims" (Cromer in Baring, 2010, p. 44), the process of becoming human required certain sacrifices. In this way, British colonizers established a distinction between necessary suffering and wasteful pain, whereas juridical humanity aims to eliminate only 'unproductive' pain. In this regard, Esmeir (2012) does not see any distinction between 'arbitrary cruelty' and 'productive

[13] The Khedival-legal system was the Ottoman pluralist legal order grounded in the tradition of Islamic law. For an overview of the Ottoman legal system, (see Hunter, 1984)

cruelty'; the impossibility of that distinction reveals all of the law's violence as arbitrary and signals a collapse of ends into means. Hence, positive law, in the colonial period, emerged as embracing a split between the ideal of humanity and the factuality of its own violence.

The universalist and humanising claim of positive law can now be understood as a constitutive part of human rights discourse;[14] Human Rights law has replaced the 'metaphysical conceptions of natural law' and the universalistic claim of positive law. In the modern world, though universal categories have been challenged, human rights remains something sacred, universally just, and unquestionable (Douzinas, 2000; Otto, 1997). The history of human rights is not much concerned with the creation of a universal humanity (its object), but it is intrinsically linked to the interpretations that nineteenth-century European scholars gave to medieval Christian literature and to how the medieval concept of natural law as divinely inscribed ethics was translated into a secular device which inscribed the plurality of the world's culture into the transcendentality of western universal law. As per positive and natural law, Human Rights law is based on the idea of an original sense of rights, which inevitably relies on the notion of an authority, a transcendental order, the *imago dei* (Lévinas, 1993). Human Rights law, then, derives not only from western secularization of Christianity which led to the establishment of a specific form of sovereignty, but also from the western colonial past and the encounter with different forms of (Islamic) governance and legal systems.

Esmeir's work (2012) shows the profound colonial roots of Human Rights law. In particular, she reveals a link between colonial and Human Rights' assumptions: firstly, despite the difficulties in organizing pluralistic societies, the liberal democratic positivized order is considered the one able to produce the most equitable outcomes. Hence, Human Rights law, as well as positive law during the colonial period, is considered a universally valid global formula (Esmeir, 2006). The Universal Declaration of Human Rights aimed to announce an 'internationalization' of human rights and pave the way for a new international jurisdiction which would exist outside the borders of national countries while presupposing an individual within the pale of a new universal law.

Secondly, gender equality can be defined in global terms: "in other words women around the world can be considered one indivisible group, historically silenced and oppressed by men. Thus, the solution offered by international Human Rights discourse must be global (universal)" (van Hoecke, 2016, p. 49). Feminist legal theory has found the concept of abstract equality embedded in Human Rights law extremely problematic (Kotef, 2009; McNay, 2013). For many feminist scholars, human rights carries a patriarchal character exactly because it presupposes an abstract notion of the subject of law which is deeply informed by individualism (Salecl, 1994). Olsen (1992) highlights that the discourse of human rights does not resolve social conflicts, rather, it reformulates them: as human rights discourse defines a specific

[14] In the west, natural law (humanism) and positive law essentially agree that there is a stability of legal process (positivist) or legal value (humanist).

subject, along with a fixed idea of womanhood, it acts to use sexuality as a tool for social control, allowing new forms of sexual and gender violence. Similarly, Gilligan (1982) argues that Human Rights law presupposes an individual detached from society and, by so doing, it hides relations of power and domination. While the concept of abstract equality presupposes an individual bound to the sovereign power, the abstract concept of human rights allows political and legal authorities to determine who is 'human' and who is not, or who can rightly be threatened 'humanly' or 'inhumanly': "precisely because it is an inclusive category, 'the human' belongs to an exclusive universe that does not contain mere life" (Asad, 2003, p. 157). Thirdly, although Human Rights law aims to be universal, its identification and application does not exist independently from the legal institutions of the nation-state, nor does it exist independently from the individual's civil/political status; in other words, human rights do not exist independently from a specific form of sovereign power and a specific conceptualization of the subject of law (Esmeir, 2006).

In light of this, Human Rights law protects an already-given human and it claims jurisdiction over the declaration of its status: "Human Rights law, like modern law more generally, aspires to name, define, call into being, redeem the human" (Esmeir, 2006, p. 1544). Since the legal subject is a human and, at the same time, a human-yet-to-become, becoming the subject of human rights can ensure both a temporal humanity and its possible suspension. In fact, positive and Human Rights law aspire to constitute a 'human' who would not exist outside of the law and therefore would remain non-human: if it is true that there is no legal system without a legal subject, it is also true that there cannot be human rights without the 'human'. By defining the human through its inscription within the pale of the law, Human Rights law also defines the pre-human or the non-human that preceded it. Hence, as Esmeir (2006) points out,

> "becoming subjects of human rights ensures recognition of their (temporary) humanity and its (possible) suspension. A person is, therefore, at once a human and yet-to-be-human, a member of universal human kind and its de-humanized figure. This contradiction does not constitute a failure in logic but is related to the law's aspiration to call into existence, and by so doing to constitute a human who would otherwise remain non-human" (p. 1546).

In other words, the problem with this conceptualisation is that allows a double movement: dehumanizing and re-humanizing. For Weil (1986) the force of the law lies exactly in its dehumanizing function: as the law protects a mask, it does not protect the wearer of the mask, nor those who do not wear a mask, or those who have lost the mask. Moreover, because any government can violate one's legal status as a human, there is always the risk of being de-humanized: consequently, the concept of human as inscribed in the law is extremely fragile.

Clearly, the subject of Human Rights law is a Christian/secular/humane subject waiting to be rescued, 're-humanized', through its inscription within the pale of the law. The call to humanize de-humanized individuals responds to a desire to establish secular reason as the only true, universal form of humanity. This, however, has the power to exclude other humanities, as in the case of many veiled women in Europe. Hence, human rights do not signal the inclusion of all humans within the protective pale of the law (Esposito, 2012b); rather, it reiterates the dipositive of inclusion/exclusion typical of Roman law. The separation between human beings and rights, which characterised the Roman and Christian 'dispositive of the person' (Esposito, 2012b, p. 80), has accompanied western history and, although in slightly different terms, is very much part of contemporary Human Rights law. As Esposito (2012b) argues, from a juridical point of view, what is 'inside' the law is defined by contrast to what is 'outside': "the law allow[s] entrance only to those who fall into some category – citizens, subjects, even slaves – [...] insofar as they are part of a political community" (Esposito, 2012b, pp. 69–70). Henceforth, for those who have been excluded from the protection of the law because they are not part of any category, the only way to be included in the law is by breaking the law, rather than complying with it (Esposito, 2012b). Weil (1986) sees in the western notion of right (private and, at the same time, privative) the essence of the very exclusion of various categories of persons: "once assumed as an attribute [...] of subjects rendered such by possessing specific social, political, and racial characteristics, a right ends up coinciding with the dividing line that separates and opposes them to those who are deprived of it" (p. 64). Thus rights, unlike justice, belong to the person and reproduce the very dispositive of the person, always oscillating between binary oppositional categories of person/non-person, humane/in-humane etc. (Esposito, 2012b). In the case of the headscarf ban, European judges have 'de-humanized' veiled Muslim women in order to re-humanize them: through the force of the law, Muslim women have been un-veiled to be re-veiled with the mask of the abstract Christian/secular/humane subject of law and religion. Hence, as Esposito (2012a) argues, the failure of human rights does not lie in their inability to link the non-universal category of the citizen with the universal category of the individual *qua* human being, but in their inability to restore the association between rights and human life: this, in turn, depends on the meaning given to the notion of person in western and Human Rights law which results in the exclusion of part of humanity. This specific notion of the person as split into oppositional categories, is mirrored in article 9 of the ECHR, which presupposes an individual who is split between its internal and its external world, *forum internum* and *forum externum*.

4.3 On *forum internum* and *forum externum*: The Re-configuration of Religion and Religious Practices in the Secular Space

In the middle of the headscarf turmoil in France, Laïdi (2004), an important French political scientist, spoke in defence of the Government ban stating that "there are a thousand ways for a Muslim woman who aspires to wear the veil on the inside without wearing it on the outside" (in Zaki, p. 159). Laïdi expressed a simple secular way to understand religion as solely located in the conscience of the individual and so detached from its external manifestation, reiterating the dichotomy between *forum internum* and *forum externum*, public and private. This understanding, which carries the potentiality to exclude, rather than include, different religious subjectivities, is mirrored in art. 9 of the ECHR which makes a distinction between faith and its manifestation. According to the ECHR, religious freedom is not limited to belief, but it also extends to its manifestations and is "one of the foundations of a democratic society" (*Kokkinakis v Greece*, 1993, para 31); however, not every act based on religious belief is protected by article 9. In the ECtHR's decisions, the term 'practice' in article 9 (1) "does not cover each act which is motivated or influenced by a religion or belief" as the manifestation should be one of the "normal and recognized manifestations" of religion or belief that "actually express the belief concerned" (*Arrowsmith v the United Kingdom*, 1978, pp. 5, 19, 20). It is therefore unclear why the ECtHR's judges could not consider the veil a 'normal manifestation' which expresses a profound religious belief (Evans, 2001). In cases regarding the practice of veiling, the ECtHR has showed a confused reasoning: in 1993, the European Commission on Human Rights (ECmHR) established that the request by a Turkish public university to provide a photo without the veil to obtain a university degree does not raise any issue regarding article 9 and the claimant's freedom of religion (*Karaduman v Turkey*, 1993). Differently, in the *Dahlab* (2001) and *Sahin* cases (2005), the Court established that the veil is a religious symbol and so it deals with article 9, but it applies the appropriate exceptions to the article in order to ban the veil (as exceptions are relevant only when they fall under the protection of article 9) (*Dahlab v Switzerland*, 2001 p. 11; *Sahin v Turkey*, 2005, para 78): this confusion is mirrored in the obsession of European judges with defining whether the veil is a religious symbol.

Although the ECtHR and European national courts do not have the right to define what religion is, as it would be a violation of the principle of separation between state and religion (Renucci, 2005), the distinction between *forum internum* and *forum externum* made by article 9 of the ECHR discloses a specific (western/secular) definition of religion and the religious subject. In fact, the normative distinction between faith and its manifestation, which is taken as necessary in the legal reasoning (Cumper & Lewis, 2008), presupposes a religious individual whose faith is a simple private matter distinguishable from its manifestations (such as symbols, rituals, etc.). Not the judges, then, but the law establishes and sustains a specific conceptualization of religion and the religious subject as split between 'inward' and 'outward', *zoe* and *bios*, public and private, faith and its manifestation.

For Cavanaugh (2009), the separation between faith and its manifestation, at the heart of European juridical discourse over the veil, makes room for state action to identify and characterize different social spheres of competence such as 'religious' and 'secular' and to justify limitations of personal freedoms. In recent years the ECtHR's attitude has shifted in relation to cases that deal with religious freedom: previously, for the Court "the state has no direct role to play in the religious life of believers" (*Otto-Preminger-Institut v Austria,* 1995, p.19) which implied that different religious communities should not interfere in the public sphere and *vice-versa*. However, recently, through a growing emphasis on state neutrality and the protection of public order, the ECtHR has given states the power to decide which practices are to be considered 'religious' and so protected by the right to religious liberty.

This means that, for the Court, only the state can decide how to provide an appropriate space for religious diversity while advancing the principle of secularism. Since secularism is conceived as the only possible system to secure the autonomy of the individual "from others and from state power through its articulation of the autonomy of the state from cultural and religious authority" (Brown, 2008, p. 153), the state has the power to "either tolerate or ban particular cultural differences without being defined as partial" (Volpp, 2007, p. 574).

While the ECtHR has left the duty to define what religion is to member states,[15] it has at the same time advanced a specific understanding of religion as an individual, voluntary, private, intellectual conviction: something that the individual can choose to keep at home. Following the architectural structure of article 9, the discussed rulings uphold the inviolability of the *forum internum* as the locus of religious beliefs, while limiting the *forum externum* in the name of public order.

However, it is unclear whether the law protects beliefs that are autonomously chosen by the individual or beliefs that are unchosen (Mahmood, 2015). This confusion is clear in the rhetoric of choice at work in the *Begum* case (2006) in which the claimant was seen first as someone to be saved from her family and community and then as a person who should pay for her choice (wearing the *jilbab* and sustain her interpretation of Islam). Shabina, then, oscillated from a person who chooses her own belief (and so she should pay for her choice), to one who is subjected to the backward religious traditions of her oppressive family (and so in need of being saved); from a person protected by western law, to one from whom society must be defended. This confusion is also clear in two recent cases decided at the Court of Justice of the European Union (CJEU) in 2017. Both cases concern the right to wear a veil in the workplace (C-157/15 *Achbita,* 2017*;* C-188/15 *Bougnaoui,* 2017). In the *Bougnaoui* case (2017), Advocate General (AG) Sharpston stated that

> "to someone who is an observant member of a faith, religious identity is an integral part of that person's very being […] it would be entirely wrong to suppose that, whereas one's sex and skin colour accompany one everywhere, somehow one's religion does not" (para. 118).

Differently, AG Kokott, in *Achbita* (2017), argued that "the practice of religion is not so much an unalterable fact as an aspect of an individual's private life, and one, moreover, over which the employees concerned can choose to exert an influence […]. [A]n employee may be expected to moderate the exercise of his religion in the workplace" (para. 116).

Despite this (apparent) divergence, in both cases the AGs link religious liberty to the individual's autonomy, reinforcing the liberal concept of religion as something autonomously chosen by the individual. AG Sharpston links autonomy and religious freedom by drawing on the *Coleman case* (C-303/06, 2008*)* and defines beliefs as detached from communal rituals and symbologies, reinforcing the liberal position taken by diverse scholars who pose a great emphasis on the individual's

[15] Differently, in *Otto-Preminger-Institut v Austria* (1995), the ECtHR specified that 'it is not possible to discern throughout Europe a uniform conception of the significance of religion in society' (p. 50).

autonomy in the establishment of minority religious rights (Kymlicka, 1995; MaAdams, 2006). This reasoning echoes Kymlica (1995) for whom the meaning of individual autonomy lies in the individual capacity to maintain one's cultural institution and way of life: this inevitably expands the range of options among which an individual can choose by exercising its autonomy. The *Achbita* case (2017), in which the CJEU's understanding of religious freedom as a means to protect the autonomy of an individual's beliefs, inevitably leads to the idea that it is not religion *per se*, but the ability of the individual to 'manifest' a religious belief in a specific way that is at stake (McCrea, 2016). It follows that the task of European Courts is not so much to identify what religion is and to protect it, but to ensure that a specific liberal/secular way of understanding and experiencing religion is protected by article 9 (Baldi, 2018).

The confusion regarding what article 9 protects is mirrored in the comparison between the *Lautsi* (2011) and *Dahlab* cases (2001). In the *Lautsi v Italy* (2011) case, in which the claimant complained that the crucifix affixed in the classroom of a public school in Italy was a breach of the negative freedom of her children, the Grand Chamber constructed the crucifix as a "passive symbol", a representation of an *inner state*, which does not infringe the *forum internum* as it does not influence pupils' internal beliefs. Conversely, Dahlab's veil was considered a proselytising symbol that might infringe the pupils' negative freedom, despite her never having told her students that she had converted to Islam. In the *Lautsi* case (2011) the Court established that the crucifix did not endanger the pupils' negative freedom or public order as Lautsi's children remained free to believe in any religion: however, Dahlab's veil, another 'passive symbol' as she did not carry out any proselytising activities, was considered a symbol that could endanger the *inner state* of pupils as well as the public order of the school. The distinction the ECtHR made between the veil and the crucifix shows that the Court acted as a theologian in defining which religious symbol could interfere with the *forum internum* of others.

What is worth noting in these comparisons is not only the reiteration of western binary oppositions through the division between the *forum internum* and *forum externum*, beliefs and action, but different notions of religion: one locates religious beliefs in the private sphere, while the other understands religion as a discursive tradition that informs the subject's interiority (Mahmood, 2015). This difference between the veil as linking the interiority and the exteriority of the subject, and the crucifix as related exclusively to the subject's *forum internum*, is based on a prior normative understanding of religion applied by the Court, which entails a prescriptive notion of the self and collectivity and has important implications for how individual and collective religious life is lived and performed in secular Europe (Mahmood, 2015). The confusion about the *forum internum* is linked to the paradox of the *forum externum*: while the *forum internum* (a category of exception from state intervention) is linked to the *forum externum* (the right to manifest a religious belief), the limitation of the *forum externum* is based on an exception itself (public order). This paradox, in turn, creates two different notions of public order which, in the case of the headscarf ban in Europe, is translated into the ambiguity about whether the state of exception is applied to the *forum internum* or to the *forum externum*.

Western and Human Rights law, then, have the power to essentialise a specific idea of religion and the religious subject that is protected by the (western) right to religious liberty. However, as Asad (2001) argues, the

> "problem with universal definitions of religion is that by insisting on an essential singularity, they divert us from asking questions about what the definition includes and what it excludes – how, by whom, for what purpose, and so on. And in what historical context a particular definition of religion makes good sense" (p. 220).

Hence, the concept of religion is discursively constructed "not [as] a neutral descriptor of a reality that is simply out there in the world", but as a category that is inseparable from western history and goes hand in hand with its "siamese twin secularism" (Asad, 2001, p. 205 and 221). As I have argued, the modern western notion of secularism is not only intertwined with, but is also constitutive of the notion of religion in such a way that it is impossible to track the history of secularism without tracking the history of religion, and *vice-versa* (Agrama, 2010; Asad, 2003; Keane, 2007). The western/secular/liberal understanding of faith presupposes a specific modern liberal perception of society which is at the foundation of western positive and Human Rights law (Ingvill Thorson Plesner, 2008). Western law, then, emerges as part of a modern project which seeks to institutionalize specific principles and subjectivities in the public secular sphere: in other words, "modernity is not primarily a matter of cognizing the real but of living-in-the-world" (Asad, 2003, p. 14).

By giving a specific definition of religion and the religious subject, secularism, which has become synonymous with 'modernity', defines specific forms of knowledge and (religious and non-religious) practices and it becomes the framework through which to read and understand the religious, political and ethical spheres of the Christian/secular/liberal subject (Hirschkind, 2011). Secularism, then, is a concept that "brings together certain behaviors, knowledge, and sensibilities in modern life" (Asad, 2003, p. 25): it follows that "a secular person is someone whose affective-gestural repertoires express a negative relation to forms of embodiment historically associated with (but not limited to) theistic religion" (Hirschkind, 2011, p. 638). The secular subject is formed by an internal truth which is represented by (but not generative of) its outward life, re-establishing in this way a split subject, always oscillating between opposite categories. In light of this, the separation between private and public, secular and religious, creates not only an understanding of how private and public life should be lived and experienced, but also a specific imagination which mediates people's identity in the 'modern' world (Asad, 2003). Therefore, secularism is not a neutral position but, rather, it is a "normatively prescriptive model that favours certain forms of modern religion at the expense of others that are equally legitimate" (Denli, 2004, pp. 497–511).

Thus, what the legal decisions over the headscarf reveal is that, by defining religion as a private belief, secularism tries to define and re-define the place of religion and religious practices in the public sphere: in other words, by giving a specific definition of religion and the religious subject, secularism hierarchizes different religions and different manifestations of religious beliefs (Mahmood, 2015), raising problems in the area of equality. By giving a fixed Christian/secular definition of religion and the religious subject, secularism, as embedded in western and Human Rights law, emerges not as the separation between private and public, religious and secular, but as the re-configuration of religious sensitivities and religious practices in the secular sphere (Mahmood, 2009). Hence, more than the mere separation between religion and the state, secularism emerges as a continual management of religious subjectivities which establishes a specific form of knowledge and embodied sensitivities that are produced and reproduced in western culture.

The definition of what is religion and who is the proper religious subject to be protected by the law discloses the prerogative of the secular state to guard the individual private sphere to which religious sentiments are assigned. The prerogative of western and Human Rights law to define and regulate religious symbols in the public sphere and so to blur the line between secular and religious, is made evident by the obsession of European judges in defining whether veiling is a religious or a political symbol: once veiling has been defined as a practice indifferent to (proper) religious doctrine, it was easy to bring it under the state's regulation without perceiving the ban as an infringement of the right of religious liberty (Mahmood, 2013). In fact, the headscarf ban has not been seen as a limitation of the individual freedom of religion, as veiled women could (supposedly) continue to have their beliefs in the private sphere. Hence, while the law has tried to justify the banning of the veil as a matter of public order, the conceptualization of religion as something private has allowed judges and politicians to perceive the limitation of the practice of veiling not as an attack on Muslim women's freedoms (Fernando, 2012), but as a normative practice that regulates the simple manifestation of an inner state. However, if European democracies are founded on the principle of pluralism, as stated in the analysed cases, then they should consider that religion is not always essentially the same and, as I will argue in the next chapter, its definition very much depends on different cultures and historical periods (Asad, 2001).

The blindness of European Courts concerning different understandings of religion and religious practices indicates that western positive and Human Rights law protects an individual who complies with the principle of secularism and with a secular mode of experiencing religion based on the requirements and sensibilities of liberal governance (Agrama, 2010): in this view, "the political solution that secularism proffers […] lies not so much in tolerating difference and diversity but in remaking certain kinds of religious subjectivities (even if this requires the use of violence) so as to render them compliant with liberal political rule" (Mahmood, 2006, p. 328). In other words, what transpires from these decisions is the imposition of a new universal law that in principle 'saves' the part of humanity which has yet to be allowed to enter into the arrangement of liberal law but, in reality, it reinforces its own absolute power and, as a metaphysical Christian God did before, it controls and guides individuals in their existence: thus, although western liberal law is centred upon a liberal concept of the individual, it increasingly aims at state control of human conduct and the individual's physical being, the body, even though it calls for the protection of minorities. This is the paradox of the secular, that while it divides among spheres of influence, among different categories of people and among different individuals' spheres, it also defines and regulates the individual life accordingly (Fernando, 2014).

Hence, European decisions over the practice of veiling emerge as the mirror of liberal paradoxes: if, on the one hand, the individual has rights, then on the other, those rights can be threatened, according to how the society and the nation-state want them to be regulated. It follows that positive and Human Rights law conceives the individual as free and, at the same time, compelled. Put differently, in the west, the subject of law has the autonomy to express her/his identity only when those identities can be assimilated into secular liberal sensitivities. In this sense, the 'salvation' project of positive and Human Rights law in reality means assimilation into Christian/secular/liberal understandings of law and politics. Failing to assimilate into a new law's subject, as veiled women did when they refused to remove the veil, means the disappearance of the individual from the public space because it represents the failure of the western/liberal secular system to be the best (universal) system able to accommodate differences. More than secular/liberal toleration, then, the matter of the veil seems to be linked to the European idea of 'assimilation' where prohibitionist laws are justified as mechanisms to ensure that 'outsiders' can be adjusted into secular, democratic western society, as I will further argue in the next chapter. In the case of the headscarf ban, the Court has broadened the definition of the *forum internum*, instituting specific criteria of inclusion and exclusion through article 9. This line of inclusion/exclusion, which is embedded in western law from its inception, institutes the double structure of the right of religion, at the same time private and privative, protective and detrimental (Weil, 1986).

4.4 Excluding Through Law: Freedom of Religion, and the Public/Private Divide

Locke's *Letter Concerning Toleration* (1689) is considered one of the most important texts to have led to the conceptualisation of religious liberty in the west. He (2003) writes that "all the life and power of true religion consists in the inward and full persuasion of the mind; and faith is not faith without believing" (p. 219). As the sphere of beliefs is inviolable, it cannot be compelled by "outward forces," which makes "penalties [...] absolutely impertinent; because they are not proper to convince the mind" (pp. 219–220). Since its inception, the notion of religious liberty was split between two different spheres: one inviolable (the *forum internum*) and the other regulated by the state (*forum externum*). Hence, the western notion of religious freedom is not neutral, as it is constituted and constitutive of a specific form of sovereignty and, along with it, of a specific relation between law, the (internal) individual's sphere, and the sovereign power. This understanding, in turn, is linked to the western historical development of the right of freedom of religion. Scholars (Bhuta, 2014; Danchin & Mahmood, 2014) have observed that two historical understandings of religious freedom are prominent in western contemporary debate on the right to religious liberty: the first is linked to the early western preoccupation with religious plurality and its danger in relation to public order, while the second is associated to the post-war Christian attempt to equate Christianity with western civilization and reformulate European culture on human dignity, which had important implications in east-west relations. This understanding is exemplified by the paradoxes surrounding the legal decisions concerning the practice of veiling, where the secular draws and re-draws the line between public and private, *forum internum* and *forum externum*, re-establishing specific historical relations between the Christian/west and the Muslim/'other'. The analysis of the western notion of religious freedom, then, poses another dichotomy; that between public and private, also at the centre of the European decisions to ban the veil.

Historically, the Peace of Westphalia (1648), which put an end to the religious wars in Europe, has represented the establishment of the modern western form of sovereignty and, along with it, a new formulation of the concept of religious liberty.[16] The Peace resulted in the signing of various treaties that established a protocol to handle religious dissidents (or what today we call 'religious minorities') (Mahmood, 2015): under different secular settings, religious minorities that were previously penalised started to be regulated by the state in the name of societal peace and public order. Notably, with the Peace of Westphalia, the notion of freedom of conscience, associated with the idea of toleration, started to be linked to the act of the sovereign state (Dunn, 1996), as only the state could interfere and limit the individual's religious liberty when this represented a danger for the freedom of others or for reasons of public order. Hence, toleration towards other religious creeds was based on the notion of *public order* and not on the basis of an individual's right. In this sense, the notion of freedom of conscience and religion did not render the *forum internum* immune from the state's intrusion, nor did it give special value to the importance of religious plurality (often seen as potentially dangerous) (Geuss, 2001). Rather, it was the (exceptional) notion of public order that assured the sovereign's right to expand its power and to limit the individual's private sphere (Mahmood, 2015). Hence, the seventeenth-century distinction between civil and religious domains, private and public, state and religion, has given to the state the legitimacy of regulating any visible practices in the civil domain in the name of the civil interests of 'this-world'.

The Treaty of Versailles (1919), with the consolidation of nation-states in Europe, saw the emergence of new nationalist ideas with the promise of popular sovereignty and equality between citizens (Mahmood, 2012). Along with it, minority rights were established by law to distinguish between those who could claim minority rights and those who could not (such as refugees, migrant workers etc.) (Preece, 1998). As in the nation-state's ideology religious minorities represented a threat to the nation's (imagined) unity and shared culture and traditions, by giving minorities a specific legal and political place, the nation-state aimed to solve (or hierarchize) differences that the nation-state's ideology aimed to eliminate (Mahmood, 2015); with the promise of equality, the nation-state standardizes the individual's beliefs in such a way as to render the citizen loyal to the state (Asad, 1992).

[16] For Scott (2017), the association between Christianity and Western democracies is a legacy inherited from the Westphalia Treaty of 1648 whereas state sovereignty and Christian practices become linked.

The western notion of religious liberty as a fundamental universal individual right was strengthened in the aftermath of WWII, which had witnessed the persecution of minorities, and an unprecedented need for the cultural and ethical restoration of the old continent (Moyn, 2010). This is why, probably, Maritain's philosophy was so well received in Europe. Maritain's Christian personalism focuses on the person as the locus of a restored humanity responding to a universal natural law and presupposing pre-political human rights. With Maritain's personalism, Christianity operated a shift from a rejection of western bourgeois individualism to a private/personalist notion of the universal value of the human being (Maritain, 1994). Maritain created a Christian political theology of democracy in which secularity could be limited thanks to a form of governance that was committed to the dignity of the person- a notion understood to be of Christian inheritance. With the conversion of the Church to Maritain's Christian personalism and its active political participation in post-war Europe, along with the need for a new order, Christian democracy was increasingly seen as a model of stabilization of the old continent after the horrors of WWII (Kaiser, 2007; Papini, 1981). Slowly, Christianity started to be linked with the emergence of western democracy as both were (supposedly) based on a political order that preserves the value of the human being (Vinen, 2002).

Maritain's personalism also influenced the activities of Christian missionaries in the twentieth century who, with the support of colonial powers, introduced the public/private divide to undermine Ottoman sovereignty and favour their proselytising activities (Mahmood, 2015): this, in turn, determined a detachment of the colonial subject from communal forms of religious life and rituals (Leiter, 2014).[17] In trying to disseminate the western notion of religious liberty, in 1940, the Joint Mission Council for Religious Liberty affirmed its willingness to work for a Human Rights Charter which would include a "satisfactory place for the protection of religion and conscience" within it (Lindkvist, 2013, p. 440). Influenced by Searle Bates and Jacques Martain's personalist thought, religious missionaries aimed to contrast Russian secularism and Fascist ideologies as well as Orthodox Islam, seen as "the contrary of religious liberty [because it] finds no room for the concept as developed in Western lands" (Bates, 1945, p. 9).

The influence of missionary thought is particularly evident in the Universal Declaration of Human Rights (UDHR) and the ECHR which reveals a specific personalist notion of the individual as expressed by Maritain in his writing on the philosophical grounding of human rights for UNESCO (Maritain, 1955; Maritain & UNESCO, 1949):

---

[17] In the name of a defence of the eastern Christian minority under the Ottoman Empire, western Christian missionaries were particularly active from the sixteenth century thanks to the Ottoman's 'capitulations' which granted to western traders special privileges, providing them with a certain autonomy on matters of criminal and civil law, as well as freedom of religion and worship (Mahmood, 2015). The 'capitulations' were part of the wider Millet system which gave a certain freedom to different religious communities in juridical matters concerning personal and religious affairs. This autonomy, granted to different religious communities, is what distinguished the modern western notion of religious liberty (based on the individual) and the Ottoman one (based on community rights) (Mahmood, 2012).

> "the human person possesses rights because of the very fact that it is a person, a whole, master of itself and of its acts, and which consequently is not merely a means to an end, but an end, an end which must be treated as such. The dignity of the human person? The expression means nothing if it does not signify that by virtue of nature the human person has the right to be respected, is the subject of rights, and possesses rights" (Maritain, 1955, p. 65).

Maritain's association between the person and human rights is based on the universal/liberal/western principle of self-determination owned by any human being, regardless of their race, gender or religion. This notion is not in contraposition with God's sovereignty: rather, it derives from it since humans have received their sovereignty rights from God, because they are created in the image of their creator (Esposito, 2012b). This view was shared by Charles Malik, the Lebanese Christian who drafted the UDHR. He argued that "in Christianity, the individual human person possesses an absolute value […]. The ultimate ground of all our freedom is the Christian doctrine of the absolute inviolability of the human person" (as cited in Moyn, 2015, p. 92).

The inviolability of the conscience of the individual is clear in article 9 of the ECHR and article 18 of the UDHR. Article 18 protects a person's freedom of religion 'either alone or in community with others and in public or private, to manifest his religion or belief in teaching, practice, worship and observance', while article 9 protects a person's 'right to freedom of thought, conscience and religion; [which] includes *freedom to change his religion or belief* and freedom, either alone or in community with others and in public or private, to manifest his religion or belief, in worship, teaching, practice and observance'.[18] Mahmood (2015) points out that the conceptualization of freedom of religion as protecting only the individual's private sphere and not the condition for the flourishing of religious communities is of particular importance when considering religious minorities which, without a specific protection of their communal life, risks exposing their vulnerability, obliging them to assimilate to the majoritarian religion. Clearly, this conceptualization of religion and the right to religious liberty cannot equally accommodate every notion of religion, but only a privatist/Christian one (Lindkvist, 2014).

Western historical understanding of the notion of freedom of religion is mirrored in the European juridical decisions concerning the practice of veiling. Firstly, the notion of freedom of religion as linked to the concept of public order resonates with the medieval preoccupation for religious plurality in relation to the danger of different religious affiliations; secondly, the juridical decisions that have banned veil clearly apply a Christian/Protestant understanding of religious freedom as covering the *forum internum* while limiting the *forum externum,* establishing a specific relation between the individual and the sovereign power; thirdly, those decisions are based on the assumption that Christianity is synonymous with tolerance and democratic principles, which mirrors Maritain's philosophy (Bhuta, 2014). It is not only the separation made by article 9 between *forum internum* and *forum externum*, faith and its manifestation, private and public divide, that follows this pattern: the whole juridical construction of the veil reinforces these concepts.

---

[18] *Italics added.*

The notion that the veil endangers public order is clear in all the ECtHR's decisions. Most of the ECtHR decisions were based on the idea that "the measure pursued the legitimate aims of protecting the rights and freedoms of others and of protecting public order" (*Sahin v Turkey*, 2005, para. 99). However, no reference is given to how the veil could represent a danger to the freedom of others or to public order, nor to whether the limitation of the claimants' right to freedom of religion could be a necessary means to achieve the state's objective. In *Dahlab* (2001), no evidence were found to indicate that her veil had upset a number of children or that she had carried out proselytising activities, and in *Dogru* (2009) no justification was found of the danger of the veil (or hat) during gym classes, while in the *Sahin* case (2005) it is unclear how the claimant could endanger the peace and public order of the university. What is clear in the cases is that the conflict is not between the claimants' right to freedom of religion and the others' freedom of conscience, but between her right to religious liberty and public order (Danchin & Mahmood, 2014). The test of proportionality and necessity was never applied to the supposed risk the veil posed for public order, as clearly not all religious symbols are seen as a threat to public order.

This is evident in the comparison with the *Lautsi* case (2011) decided at the ECtHR. In the case, the Court stated that

> "there is no evidence […] that the display of a religious symbol on classroom walls may have an influence on pupils and so it cannot be asserted that it does or does not have an effect on young persons whose convictions are still in the process of being formed" (para. 66).

In contrast, in cases concerning the wearing of the veil, the Court was preoccupied to balance abstract concepts (religion v secularism, democracy v the veil's symbology etc.), rather than concrete conflicting rights and interests. Based on the ECHR legislation, the ECtHR should apply the doctrine of the margin of appreciation in order to balance national authority and the individual's rights: however, in cases concerning the wearing of the veil, the ECtHR goes further by blindly accepting that the veil would create religious conflict. Clearly, the matter of public order has been used and abused by the courts. In cases concerning the manifestation of religious symbols, the ECtHR has taken a quite inconsistent approach in the application of the doctrine of the margin of appreciation, redefining the notion of 'necessity' as a subjective notion which is no longer required to assess whether it could be proved that a specific symbol is a danger to public order and the common good. In the analysed cases, it seems that for the Court the problem was not the public expression of religious liberty, but the headscarf *per se*. By defining the veil as a dangerous threat to the peace of a society and the crucifix as a cultural symbol which represents values of tolerance, the Court has distorted (or excessively expanded) the notion of public order, rendering necessary a sovereign intervention to ban the veil, as I will further argue in the next chapter.

The identification of the veil as the symbol of the 'other' and the crucifix as the symbol of western secular values, also discloses Maritain's equation between Christian and western civilization. Rather than universally embracing all humanity, however, this conceptualization has led to a different treatment of different religious creeds, privileging Christianity over any other religion, in particular Islam. This is clear in the *Lautsi* case (2011) in which the Veneto Administrative Court established that the crucifix did not contradict the principle of secularism.[19] Echoing the decision of many German *Länders* to ban the veil while allowing the display of Christian religious symbols, the Italian Supreme Administrative Court linked the crucifix with the secular democratic values of

> "tolerance, mutual respect, valorization of the person, affirmation of one's rights, consideration for one's freedom, the autonomy of one's moral conscience vis-à-vis authority, human solidarity and the refusal of any form of discrimination" (*Lautsi v Italy*, 2011, para. 15).

Hence, while the veil is automatically linked to a danger for European public order, no doubt has been raised about the meaning of the crucifix that emerges from the *Lautsi* case and from the legal decisions of many German *Länders*. Notably, the banning of the veil and the display of Christian symbols in the European public sphere has been applied by shifting the meaning of the veil (from religious to political symbol) and the crucifix (from religious to secular symbol). Here it is possible to detect the emergence of a political theology of Christian democracy in which the culture, tradition and identity of western democratic values are intrinsically linked to Christianity, which emerges as a civilization marker. The difference made by European judges between Christian and Islamic religious symbols demonstrates western anxiety in regulating (alien) religions. This anxiety is, in turn, linked to the western concept of freedom of conscience and religion which is deeply rooted in western colonial and religious missionary history, and so to specific historical power relations.

The double structure of the right of religion, at the same time private and privative, protective and detrimental, reveals the embeddedness of Christian/secular values in western law and all its potentiality for exclusion. It is through the semiotic-architectural structure of western law as expressed in article 9 of the ECHR and in the western conceptualisation of the notion of freedom of religion that the law establishes specific dichotomous criteria of inclusion/exclusion, public/private, veil/un-veil. The establishment of these dichotomies has two main implications. Firstly, it creates a specific law and religious subject – one who is split between inward and outward, *zoe* and *bios*, human and in-humane, public and private sphere: a Christian/secular/liberal subject who acquires its being and humanity only through its inscription in western and Human Rights law. By

[19] This was upheld by the ECtHR and the Supreme Administrative Court, which interpreted the crucifix as a symbol of the religious origins of secular values such as tolerance, freedom, human rights etc. The Veneto Administrative court stated that: "Looking beyond appearances it is possible to discern a thread linking the Christian revolution of 2000 years ago to the affirmation in Europe of the right to liberty of the person and to the key elements of the Enlightenment […] namely, the liberty and freedom of every person, the declarations of the rights of man, and ultimately the modern secular state […]. It can therefore be contended that in the present-day social reality the crucifix should be regarded not only as a symbol of a historical and cultural development, and therefore of the identity of our people, but also as a symbol of a value system: liberty, equality, human dignity and religious toleration, and accordingly also of the secular nature of the state" (Veneto Administrative Court's judgment, quoted in *Lauts v Italy*, 2011, para. 15).

defining religion and the religious subject through art 9 and through the lenses of western/Christian/secular notions of freedom of religion, western law has unveiled Muslim women to re-veil them with the mask of the abstract western/secular/liberal individual: one who is defined and constituted *by* and *through* the force of the law and is split and oscillating between opposite categories such as public/private, freedom/un-freedom, humanization/de-humanization, veil/un-veil, inside/outside the protection of the law. In this view, Human Rights and western secular law do not signal the inclusion of all humans within the protective pale of the law; rather, it reiterates the dipositive of inclusion/exclusion typical of Roman law (Esposito, 2012b). Hence, it is exactly through the western/liberal/secular notion of the person and the dissociation between life and rights that it is possible to understand western law's exclusionary forces (Esposito, 2015). In the case of the headscarf ban, those forces have worked to exclude (certain) religious sensitivities from the public sphere, contrary to western and Human Rights law's claim to safeguard the plurality of European societies.

This exclusion, as I will further argue in the next chapter, is linked to the establishment of a specific form of western sovereignty, where "the inclusion of bare life in the political realm constitutes the original – if concealed – nucleus of power" (Agamben, 1998, p. 6). 'Bare life', for Agamben, is a juridical-politico construction which indicates a life included in the legal/political realm through its exclusion by an act of sovereign power. In light of this, the logic of power is a logic of exclusion decided by a sovereign act that defines the value of the human being. In the case of the headscarf ban in Europe, through the abuse of the notion of public order, the sovereign expands its power into the private life of the individual, redefining the line between the secular and religious spheres. Hence, while on the one hand the secular state claims a separation between private and public, then on the other the sovereign power intervenes in the private life of the individual, re-drawing the line between public and private on which is based.

This paradox should not surprise western eyes as the ambiguity and the continuous re-definition of the public/private divide is internal to the western notion of freedom of religion which "serves to generate the distinctive antinomies and contradictions that arise in struggles over its meaning, justification, and realization" (Danchin & Mahmood, 2014, p. 4). It is exactly through the western notion of freedom of religion and the definition of religion and the religious subject that the sovereign guards the individual's private sphere to which religious sentiments are assigned. More importantly, by defining religion and the religious subject, secularism defines specific forms of knowledge and (religious and non-religious) practices, and it becomes the framework through which to read and understand the religious, political and ethical spheres of the Christian/secular/liberal subject (Hirschkind, 2011).

For Agrama (2010), this paradox discloses a fundamental characteristic of secularism, namely its indeterminacy and instability. He asserts that this instability is ensured by the impossibility of drawing a clear-cut dividing line between the secular and the religious. This is not to be seen as a paradox, but as the condition for the exercise of secularism:

"for the peculiar intractability of secularism lies not only in the normativity of its categories, but significantly, in the indeterminacies it provokes. Indeterminacies that powerfully contribute to the continually felt gap between the ideals secularism promotes and the realities that it establishes" (Agrama, 2010, p. 500).

In other words, secularism itself continuously blurs and blends the line between secular and religious, rendering precarious the same categories that it establishes. In the case of the headscarf ban, through the notion of public order the law blurs the lines between public and private, re-fashioning the public sphere and protecting the sensibility of the majority in a way that undermines the western abstract notion of equality but also the public/private division on which is based (Agrama, 2010). More than pursuing equality, tolerance, and democratic values, the notion of public order has assured the secular state to define what is public and private, secular and religious; this, in turn, requires an abstract articulation of what religion is. By defining religion, the secular state also defines the appropriate religious practices of the secular subjects, authorising specific sensibilities while disciplining different traditions to conform to the abstract western/secular/liberal notion of religion and the religious/secular subject (Agrama, 2010). However, by defining religion, the secular/liberal collapses politics into religion, limiting individual liberal rights (Agrama, 2010) by excluding different subjectivities.

References

Agamben, G. (1998). *Homo sacer: Sovereign power and bare life*. Stanford University Press.

Agamben, G. (2005). *State of exception*. University of Chicago Press.

Agrama, H. A. (2010). Secularism, sovereignty, indeterminacy: Is Egypt a secular or a religious state? *Comparative Studies in Society and History, 52*(3), 495–523.

Ahmed, L. (1992). *Women and gender in Islam: Historical roots of a modern debate*. Yale University Press.

Amin, Q. (2000). *The liberation of women*. Cairo American University Press.

Anghie, A. (2005). *Imperialism, sovereignty and the making of international law*. Cambridge University Press.

Arendt, H. (1967). *The origins of totalitarianism* (3rd ed.). Allen & Unwin.

Asad, T. (1992). Religion and politics: An introduction. *Social Research*, 3–16.

Asad, T. (2001). Reading a modern classic: WC Smith's "the meaning and end of religion". *History of Religions, 40*(3), 205–222.

Asad, T. (2003). *Formations of the secular: Christianity, Islam, modernity*. Stanford University Press.

Augustine, S. (1998). *Augustine: The city of god against the pagans*. Cambridge University Press.

Baldi, G. (2018). Re-conceptualizing equality in the work place: A reading of the latest CJEU's opinions over the practice of veiling. *Oxford Journal of Law and Religion, 7*(2), 296–312.

Baring, E. (2010). *Frontmatter. Political and literary essays, 1908–1913*. Cambridge University Press.

Bates, M. S. (1945). *Religious liberty: An inquiry*. Studies in the world mission of Christianity.

Bhuta, N. (2014). Two concepts of religious freedom in the European court of human rights. *South Atlantic Quarterly, 113*(1), 9–35.

Brown, W. (2008). *Regulating aversion tolerance in the age of identity and empire*. Princeton University Press.

Calvin, J. (2008). *Institutes of the Christian religion*. Hendrickson Publishers.

Cavanaugh, M. W. T. (1995). “A fire strong enough to consume the house:” the wars of religion and the rise of the state. *Modern Theology, 11*(4), 397–420.
Cavanaugh, W. T. (2009). *The myth of religious violence: Secular ideology and the roots of modern conflict*. Oxford University Press.
Cumper, P., & Lewis, T. (2008). “Taking religion seriously”? Human rights and Hijab in Europe—Some problems of adjudication. *Journal of Law and Religion, 24*(02), 599–627.
Danchin, P. G., & Mahmood, S. (2014). Politics of religious freedom: Contested genealogies. *South Atlantic Quarterly, 113*(1). https://doi.org/10.1215/00382876-2390401
Davary, B. (2009). Miss Elsa and the veil: Honor, shame, and identity negotiations. *Journal of Feminist Studies in Religion, 25*(2), 47–66.
Denli, O. (2004). Between Laicist state ideology and modern public religion: The head-cover controversy in contemporary Turkey. In T. Lindholm, W. Cole Durham Jr., & B. G. Tahzib-Lie (Eds.), *Facilitating freedom of religion or belief: A Deskbook*. Martinus Nijhoff Publishers.
Diamantides, M. (2014). On and out of revolution: Between public law and religion. *Law, Culture and the Humanities, 10*(3), 336–366.
Douzinas, C. (2000). *The end of human rights: Critical thought at the turn of the century*. Bloomsbury Publishing.
Dunn, J. (1996). *The history of political theory and other essays*. Cambridge University Press.
Durkheim, É. (1972). *Selected writings*. Cambridge University Press.
Esmeir, S. (2006). On making dehumanization possible. *PMLA, 121*(5), 1544–1551.
Esmeir, S. (2012). *Juridical humanity: A colonial history*. Stanford University Press.
Esposito, R. (2012a). The dispositif of the person. *Law, Culture and the Humanities, 8*(1), 17–30.
Esposito, R. (2012b). *The third person*. Polity.
Esposito, R. (2015). *Persons and things: From the body's point of view*. John Wiley & Sons.
Evans, C. (2001). *Freedom of religion under the European convention on human rights* (Vol. 1). Oxford University Press.
Fanon, F. (1967). *The wretched of the earth*. Penguin.
Fernando, M. L. (2012). Belief and/in the law. *Method & Theory in the Study of Religion, 24*(1), 71–80.
Fernando, M. L. (2014). Intimacy surveilled: Religion, sex, and secular cunning. *Signs: Journal of Women in Culture and Society, 39*(3), 685–708.
Festa, L. M. (2006). *Sentimental figures of empire in eighteenth-century Britain and France*. Johns Hopkins University Press.
Foucault, M. (1981). *The history of sexuality*. Penguin Books.
Foucault, M. (2012). *Discipline and punish: The birth of the prison*. Vintage.
Foucault, M. (1991). *The Foucault effect: Studies in governmentality : With two lectures by and an interview with Michel Foucault*. Harvester Wheatsheaf.
Gauchet, M. (1997). *The disenchantment of the world: A political history of religion*. Princeton University Press.
Geuss, R. (2001). *History and illusion in politics*. Cambridge University Press.
Gilligan, C. (1982). *In a different voice: Psychological theory and women's development*. Harvard University Press.
Haefeli, E. (2015). The problem with the history of toleration. In W. F. Sullivan, E. S. Hurd, S. Mahmood, & P. G. Danchin (Eds.), *Politics od religious freedom* (pp. 105–114). Chicago University Press.
Hallaq, W. B. (2009). *An introduction to Islamic law*. Cambridge University Press.
Hart, H. L. A. 1907-1992. (1997). *The concept of law* (2nd ed.). Oxford University Press.
Hegel, G. W. F. (1991). *The philosophy of history*. Prometheus Books.
Hirschkind, C. (2011). Is there a secular body? *Cultural Anthropology, 26*(4), 633–647.
Hobbes, T. (1991). *Leviathan*. Cambridge University Press.
Hunter, F. R. (1984). *Egypt under the Khedives*. Cambridge University Press. http://journals.cambridge.org/production/action/cjoGetFulltext?fulltextid=3007488
Inayatullah, S., & Boxwell, G. (2003). *Islam, postmodernism and other futures: A Ziauddin Sardar reader*. Pluto Press.

Kaiser, W. (2007). *Christian democracy and the origins of European Union*. Cambridge University Press.

Kantorowicz, E. H. (1957). *The King's two bodies: A study in mediaeval political theology*. Princeton University Press.

Keane, W. (2007). *Christian moderns: Freedom and fetish in the Mission encounter*. University of California Press.

Keane, W. (2015). What is Religiou freedom supposed to free? In W. F. Sullivan, E. S. Hurd, S. Mahmood, & P. G. Danchin (Eds.), *Politics of religious freedom* (pp. 57–65). University of Chicago Press.

Kennedy, D. (1999). Images of religion in international legal theory. In M. W. Janis & C. Evans (Eds.), *Religion and international law*. Martinus Nijhoff Publishers.

Khalid, M. (2011). Gender, orientalism and representations of the 'Other'in the war on terror. *Global Change, Peace & Security, 23*(1), 15–29.

Kotef, H. (2009). On abstractness: First wave liberal feminism and the construction of the abstract woman. *Feminist Studies, 35*(3), 495–522.

Kymlicka, W. (1995). *Multicultural citizenship: A liberal theory of minority rights*. Clarendon.

Leiter, B. (2014). *Why tolerate religion?* Princeton University Press.

Lévinas, E. (1993). *Outside the subject*. Athlone.

Lindkvist, L. (2013). The politics of article 18: Religious liberty in the universal declaration of human rights. *Humanity: An International Journal of Human Rights, Humanitarianism, and Development, 4*(3), 429–447.

Lindkvist, L. (2014). *Shrines and souls: The reinvention of religious liberty and the genesis of the universal declaration of human rights*. Bokbox förlag.

Locke, J. (1960). *Two treatises of government: A critical edition*. Cambridge University Press.

Locke, J. (2003). A letter concerning toleration. In I. Shapiro (Ed.), *Two treatises of government and a Letter concerning toleration*. Yale University Press.

Luther, M. (1962). Temporal authority: To what extent it should be obeyed. *Luther's Works, 45*, 81–129.

MaAdams, C. (2006). Charles Taylor, multiculturalism and the "politics of recognition.". *Vera Lex, 7*(1–2), 127–139.

Macdonald, M. (2006). Muslim women and the veil: Problems of image and voice in media representations. *Feminist Media Studies, 6*(1), 7–23.

Mahmood, S. (2006). Secularism, hermeneutics, and empire: The politics of Islamic reformation. *Public Culture, 18*(2), 323.

Mahmood, S. (2009). Religious reason and secular affect: An incommen-surable divide? *Critical Inquiry, 35*(4), 836–862.

Mahmood, S. (2012). Religious freedom, the minority question, and geopolitics in the Middle East. *Comparative Studies in Society and History, 54*(02), 418–446.

Mahmood, S. (2013). Sexuality and secularism. In L. E. Cady & T. Fessenden (Eds.), *Religion, the secular, and the politics of sexual difference*. Columbia University Press.

Mahmood, S. (2015). *Religious difference in a secular age*. Princeton University Press.

Mahmood, S., & Danchin, P. G. (2014). Immunity or regulation? Antinomies of religious freedom. *South Atlantic Quarterly, 113*(1), 129–159.

Maritain, J. (1955). The range of reason (New York, 1952), chs. 14–15; see also True humanism (New York, 1938) and Man and the state (Chicago, 1951). *Maritain's Prophetic Thought Is conveniently anthologized by Joseph W. Evans and Leo R. ward in their social and political philosophy of Jacques Maritain: Selected readings* (New York, 1955). See in Particular Chs, 18–19.

Maritain, J. (1994). *The person and the common good*. University of Notre Dame Pess.

Maritain, J., & Unesco. (1949). *Human rights: Comments and interpretations; a symposium*. Columbia University Press.

Massad, J. A. (2012). *Colonial effects: The making of national identity in Jordan*. Columbia University Press.

McCrea, R. (2016). Singing from the same hymn sheet? What the differences between the Strasbourg and Luxembourg courts tell us about religious freedom, non-discrimination, and the secular state. *Oxford Journal of Law and Religion, 5*(2), 183–210.

McNay, L. (2013). *Gender and agency: Reconfiguring the subject in feminist and social theory*. John Wiley & Sons.

Mervat, H. (2004). The nineteenth century Discoursive roots of the continuing debate on the social-sexual contract in Today's Egypt. *Hawwa, 1*(2), 64–88.

Milner, A. (1892). *England in Egypt*. Edward Arnold Publisher.

Mohanty, C. T. (1988). Under Western eyes: Feminist scholarship and colonial discourses. *Feminist Review*, 61–88.

Moyn, S. (2010). Personalism, community and the origins of human rights. In S.-L. Hoffman (Ed.), *Human rights in the twentieth century*. Cambridge University Press.

Moyn, S. (2015). *Christian human rights*. University of Pennsylvania Press.

Olsen, F. (1992). Statutory rape: A feminist critique of rights analysis. In K. T. Bartlett & R. Kennedy (Eds.), *Feminist legal theory: Reading in law and gender* (pp. 305–317). Westview Press.

Osborne, S. (2016, August 14). *Not in my courtroom—Judge throws out case after woman refuses to remove headscarf*. Express.co.uk. http://www.express.co.uk/news/world/699607/burka-hijab-court-ban-judge-montreal-quebec-canada

Otto, D. (1997). Rethinking the universality of human rights law. *Columbia Human Rights Law Review, 29*, 1.

Pagden, A. (1986). *The fall of natural man: The American Indian and the origins of comparative ethnology*. Cambridge University Press.

Papini, R. (1981). *L'apporto del personalismo alla costruzione dell'Europa* (pp. 49–78). Massimo.

Plesner, I. T. (2008). *Freedom of religion and belief- a quest for state neutrality?* University of Oslo.

Preece, J. J. (1998). *National minorities and the European nation-states system*. Oxford University Press.

Renucci, J.-F. (2005). *Introduction to the European convention on human rights. The rights guaranteed and the protection mechanism*. Council of Europe Publishing.

Said, E. W. (2003). *Orientalism* (25th anniversary Ed with 1995 Afterword Ed edition). Penguin Books.

Salecl, R. (1994). *The spoils of freedom: Psychoanalysis and feminism after the fall of socialism*. Routledge.

Scott, J. W. (2017). *Sex and secularism*. Princeton University Press.

Serafini, L. (2017). Beyond the person: Roberto Esposito and the body as 'common good.'. *Theory, Culture & Society, 34*(7–8), 215–228.

Skinner, Q. (1978). *The foundations of modern political thought: Volume 2, the age of reformation* (Vol. 2). Cambridge University Press.

Supiot, A. (2007). *Homo Juridicus: On the anthropological function of the law*. Verso.

Taylor, C. (1998). Modes of secularism. In *Secularism and its critics (Bhargava, Rajeev)*. Oxford University Press.

van Hoecke, M. (2016). Islamic jurisprudence and Western legal history. In J. S. Nielsen & L. Christoffersen (Eds.), *Shari'a as discourse: Legal traditions and the encounter with Europe*. Routledge.

Vinen, R. (2002). *Bourgeois politics in France, 1945–1951*. Cambridge University Press.

Volpp, L. (2007). The culture of citizenship. *Theoretical Inquiries in Law, 8*(2), 571–602.

Weil, S. (1986). Human personality. In S. Miles (Ed.), *Simone Weil: An anthology* (pp. 49–78). Weidenfeld & Nicolson.

Yegenoglu, M. (1998). *Colonial fantasies: Towards a feminist reading of orientalism*. Cambridge University Press.

Zaki, L. (2004). Laïcité: Le bon choix de Chirac. In *La laïcité dévoilée: Quinze années de débat en quarante 'Rebonds'* (Jean-Michel Helvig, pp. 156–162). Les dossier de Liberation.

Legal References

Arrowsmith v the United Kingdom App. N. 7050/75 (ECtHR 1978).

Case C-157/15 *Achbita, Centrum voor geliijkheid van kansen en voor racismebestrijding v G4S Secure* [2017] EU:C:203.
Case C-188/15 *Bougnaoui and Association de defense des droits de l'homme (ADDH) v Micropole SA* [2017] EU:C:204.
Case C-303/06 *Coleman S. v Attridge Law and Steve* [2008] EU.
Dahlav V Switzerland, (ECHR, 2001) Application 42393/98 (ECHR, 2001).
Dogru v France (ECHR 2008 and 2009) 27058/05, ECHR 1579, [2009] ELR 77, (2009) 49 EHRR 8.
Karaduman vs Turkey, 1993, ECmHR, App. No. 16278/90, D&R 74/93.
Kokkinakis v Greece, Application 14307/88 (ECHR 25 May 1993).
Lautsi v Italy [2011] ECHR Application no. 30814/06.
Otto-Preminger-Institut v Austria 19 EHRR 34 (1995) ECtHR; 19 EHRR.
Sahin *v. Turkey*, (ECHR 10 Nov. 2005) Application No. 44774/98.

Chapter 5
Revealing Paradoxes: Muslim Women in Secular Europe

In July 2019, the Nobel laureate Malala Yousafzai, a symbol of women's rights for her struggle for girls' education in Pakistan, was photographed with Quebec's education minister, Mr Jean-François Roberge (*Why this photo with Malala is being criticised*, 2019). After the photo, a journalist asked Mr Roberge whether Ms Yousafzai could ever teach in the francophone province, given the latest law forbidding public servants to wear conspicuous religious symbols. The minister answered that he would be honoured to have Ms Yousafzai to teach in Quebec once she removed her veil. His statement sparked a passionate debate, as Malala is not an ordinary person: she started her struggle for girls' education in Pakistan when she was only 10 years old, after the Taliban took the power in her village and closed many female schools, forbidding girls' public education in the area. In 2012 Malala was shot by the Taliban (*Why this photo with Malala is being criticised*, 2019), but this did not stop her struggle and in 2014 she won the Nobel Peace Prize, becoming the youngest person to receive such an important honour (*The Nobel Peace Prize 2014*, n.d.). Malala, a young, veiled Muslim girl, seems at odd with the representation of veiled women: while she symbolises the courage to struggle against women's oppression, the discourse concerning the veil in the west has constructed veiled women as oppressed by their patriarchal culture or as a threat to secular values of gender equality; the headscarf has been understood as a provocation, a 'mobile prison' (Fadil, 2018), and a symbol of terrorism (Hamid, 2015). This representation has been widely used by politicians to create a specific narrative in which Muslim women's body emerges as the symbolic nexus through which a specific reality is established. The assumptions this reality carries are mirrored in the European legal decisions to ban the veil and in the excessive focus on the regulation of Muslim women's body which works to reinforce secular/liberal dichotomies at the expense of the plurality of subjectivities that inhabit contemporary Europe. In fact, as I have argued in the previous chapter, western secular oppositional categories embedded in western and Human Rights law are problematic when dealing with different subjectivities, excluding those who do not conform to western/secular image of the legal and the religious subject.

G. Baldi, *Un-Veiling Dichotomies*, Boundaries of Religious Freedom: Regulating Religion in Diverse Societies,
https://doi.org/10.1007/978-3-030-79297-8_5

In this chapter, I try to think about veiling beyond western/secular dichotomous categories through the analysis of Muslim and Christian techniques of the body, in order to challenge the universality of liberal/secular notions embedded in western and Human Rights law and to understand what the debate on the female headscarf discloses about secularism. I focus on the body because, as Esposito (2015) argues, while western legal, political, and philosophical thought has understood the human as shaped between soul and body, internal and external, the body is the place of "rejection of the dichotomous order that has always organized the relationship" (pp. 143–144) between person and things. Since the body is neither a 'person' nor a 'thing', it is neither a subject nor an object, because it cannot be ascribed to any category; rather, it connects the human to things and, for this reason, it acquires a special place.

In my analys is, the body, and its performative practices, emerges as a key element to understand the exclusionary power of western and Human Rights law because it challenges western dichotomous categories on which the European decisions to ban the veil are based (such as women's freedom v women's oppression, faith v manifestation, internal v external etc.), un-masking the limits of the secular polity, and showing that secular oppositional categories have worked, in the discourse on the veil, to reinforce gender and civilizational differences at the expense of Muslim women's freedom. Contrary to the liberal/secular claim to be the best system to advance freedom, tolerance, and gender equality in western heterogeneous societies, secular universalist notions embedded in the law work to highlight social conflicts and to maintain western/secular forms of gender inequality, while advancing a new notion of women's emancipation, now linked to a specific way of dressing and behaving in the modern world.

I employ Agamben's notion of 'form of life' (2013) which is based on a non-dichotomous understanding of the relation between life, norms and the body, disclosing a notion of religion, semiotics, agency and freedom that escapes that of liberal polity. His study of the techniques of the body used by Franciscans to achieve a specific form of life is mirrored in Asad's (2009a, b) and Mahmood's analyses (2005) of Muslim religiosity. Both Franciscans and the women of the piety movement in Egypt that Mahmood (2005) worked with understand their body as a tool to achieve a specific kind of ethical subjectivity (Asad, 2009b; Mahmood, 2001): this, in turn, is linked to a way of life, an inhabitation of the model. Agamben (2013) recounts that in the Cenoby, the life of monks was not regulated by rules, but by their *habits* and *habitus,* which transformed their lives into the living soul of the gospel, in which their clothes represented an *habitus* that was able to change the interiority of the subject and to create a specific 'form of life' (that is, a life inseparable from its form) (Agamben, 2013). Similarly, for many women of the piety movement with whom Mahmood (2005) worked, habitual bodily acts, such as veiling, become indispensable to achieve specific values able to change the interiority of the subject. This affective/emotional/non-communicative understanding of religion and religious practices does not depend upon a specific discursive tradition because it aims at the self-cultivation of the subject (Keane, 2015). Hence, in contrast with seculars who conceive religion as simple personal belief located in the consciousness of the individual, my analysis attests that religious practices can also be seen as an integral part of the individual's ethical formation; through veiling, Muslim women perform a specific emotional/non-cognitive relation between norms, their veiled body, and life which has been rendered possible thanks to a notion of religion that embodies a 'form of life' beyond the western/secular/liberal dichotomous categories on which western law is based. In fact, if, on the one hand, secular rationality defines religion (and religious signs/practices) as a personal belief located in the consciousness of the individual and separated from its manifestation (as per art. 9 of the ECHR), then on the other, many Muslim women disclose a performative/affective understanding of (religious) bodily practices that goes beyond the internal/external western/secular division, revealing that the external practices of the individual cannot be separated from its internal being. In other words, while article 9 of the ECHR discloses a subject split between *forum internum* and *forum externum*, beliefs and manifestation, form of life goes beyond those dichotomous categories exactly because the body emerges as a tool to achieve a specific form of subjectivity and therefore it cannot be separated from the subject's interiority (Agamben, 2013).

The 'form of life' lived and performed by many veiled Muslim women indicates a shift in thinking human actions from the "level of practice and acting to that of form of life and living" (Agamben, 2013, p. 61). For secular/liberals, autonomy means freedom from traditions and irrational beliefs that have constrained the human for centuries: based on this reasoning, because the religious individual is subjected to transcendental rules and not to its own, it cannot be free, or act based on its own inner desires (Keane, 2015). While the 'moral narrative of modernity' (Keane, 2015, p. 62) is based on the notion of self-mastery and human emancipation from false and irrational beliefs, posing freedom and religion as opposing poles of a binary, my analysis discloses that many Muslim women understand the practice of veiling as a modality of freedom which allows them to achieve a specific self, linking in this way self-realization to religious authority, and problematising the secular/liberal dichotomies on which the notion of autonomy and women's freedom is understood in liberal secular thought. In fact, for many Muslims, agency resides in the will and is linked to performativity and to the work of the individual in shaping specific internal dispositions within heterogeneous discursive traditions. Since 'form of life' is located in the will to implement a way of life in order to achieve a specific subjectivity, agency is understood as an attribute of the subject, and not as an innate property of the abstract individual, as in liberal/secular thought. This, in turn, challenges the liberal dichotomy between freedom and authority, faith and reason, as many Muslim women understand freedom as a way to inhabit and serve authority (Brown, 2015) (which is often understood by Muslims as freedom from enslavement by worldly desires) (Rosenthal, 1960), whereas the 'true self' is cultivated through religious authority and not against it (Fernando, 2010). Hence, unlike liberals who see freedom and agency in opposition to religion, my analysis attests that a different understanding of religion does not negate freedom and agency: rather, it shapes a specific (non-binary) form of agency, along with a different notion of freedom that escapes western eyes. By universalising the western notion of freedom and possibility of agency, European judges overlook the fact that many Muslim women freely choose to wear the veil and that this is often understood as a mark of agency, or as a tool to acquire a specific subjectivity. Thus, "what is seldom problematized in [western] analysis is the universality of the desire – central for liberal and progressive thought – to be free from relations of subordination" (Mahmood, 2001, p. 206).

The universalization of women's desire in the European decisions to ban the veil has important implications: firstly, it traps Muslim women inside the paradoxes of the liberal system to the point that for them it becomes impossible to conceptualise their practice as freely chosen because the veil is blindly understood as a religious obligation and therefore as a limitation of women's autonomy, and not as fundamental tool for their ethical subject formation (Fernando, 2017). In fact, the western conceptualization of religion encourages a strict interpretation of religious dogma and symbolic manifestations by drawing on "a normative wedge between two kinds of meaning-giving commitments, those that are inflexible and conscientious and those that are habitual and embodied. This has the effect of singling out individual conscience -as opposed to cultural or community membership- as especially worthy of protection" (Laborde, 2015, p. 276).

Secondly, by understanding Muslim women's practice within western dichotomous categories, European judges have objectified veiled Muslim women and created an imaginary fixed religious subject along with a monolithic notion of womanhood. In fact, the construction of oppositional categories in the discourse concerning the veil has the power to naturalise a specific idea of womanhood to which Muslim women in Europe are blindly asked to conform. They are asked to display a specific form of western/secular/liberal heterosexual femininity in which hair is not covered: a form of femininity that draws attention to women's sexuality through an excessive focus on the visibility of their bodies as the locus of wider civilizational struggles. It is through the contraposition between covered and un-covered body that European decisions to ban the veil have elevated western women to a higher standard of civilization by establishing a specific law and religious subject, along with a fixed notion of womanhood and the form of sexuality to be displayed in the public sphere, revealing in this way the inadequacy of western/secular/liberal universal(ist) discourse in advancing women's freedom and possibility of agency within pluralistic contexts. For Scott (2013), it is exactly through the hyper-regulation of religion and sexuality that secularism surveys and manages gender and national differences, creating new understandings of the human, women's freedom and gender equality as linked to an empty, dichotomous contraposition between the west and the east. Through the objectification of Muslim women's body, a new notion of gender equality, emancipation and women's sexuality is advanced, now linked to a specific way of living and behaving in the modern world: emancipation, in light of this, is not anymore synonymous with freedom, but is based on specific forms of prescribed behaviour (Scott, 2017). Contrary to its claim to be the best system to deal with cultural/religious differences and to advance women's freedom, the secular state intensifies gender and religious inequalities. In fact, while all the legal cases that have banned the veil in Europe are based on the idea that banning the veil is a necessary means to advance the secular/liberal notion of gender equality, it is difficult to understand how gender equality can be advanced through punitive measures or through a totalizing understanding of Islam and women's freedom. Hence, while on the one hand, secularism claims to free women from religious constraint, then on the other, it imposes a specific transcendental notion of womanhood and the modern secular/religious subject, overcoming the public/private divide on which is based and disclosing a form of reverse fundamentalism aimed at regulating the internal and the external world of the individual.

This, I argue, is attained thanks to a specific western/secular/semiotic understanding of symbols that has been applied by European judges. I employ Goodrich's (1995) work on the power of images, Mahmood's analysis (2001, 2005) of Muslim performative practices, and Asad's study (2006) of the secular, in order to move away from common western/secular semiotic assumptions about the symbolic meaning of religious rituals. In fact, while in western semiotic ideology, symbols are understood through the binary distinction between signifier and signified (Keane, 2007) which, in turn, maintains secular binary dichotomies, my analysis discloses that rituals should not be seen as a mere text carrying a specific meaning; rather, they shape and are shaped by the individual within specific discursive traditions. This suggests that the fixed symbology attached to the practice of veiling by western judges and politicians is not neutral, because it does not take into consideration the "affective and embodied practices through which a subject comes to relate to a particular sign" (Mahmood, 2009a, pp. 841–842) and naturalizes and defines the religious subject as an individual who simply submits him/herself to a set of recommendations based on general beliefs; one who can choose to separate its internal from its external being. This understanding is strictly linked to the place of religion within the secular state and to the role of the law in regulating 'visible' religious practices, such as veiling, in the public sphere: in fact, the western/secular/liberal "tradition of defining religion in terms of beliefs [...] tends to privilege individual interiority and its sincere expression – thus implying a local semiotics by which externals are or are not taken to reveal inner states" (Keane, 2015, p. 60).

However, the understanding of veiling as a fixed religious symbol in contrast with secular values not only ignores the social, political, psychological and legal dimensions of the practice, but it also reinforces a strict division of the private/public spheres (Vakulenko, 2007a, b, 2012) which depends upon a prior normative understanding of what religion is and how the secular law subject should experience its religious life: this understanding is today embedded in (and imposed by) western positive and Human Rights law, where the definition of veiling as a 'sign', a 'symbol' of something intrinsically 'other', allows and encourages the emergence of certain kinds of (homogeneous) subjectivities, namely the (abstract) Christian/secular/liberal autonomous individual, at the expense of other plural subjectivities, namely the 'diversity of the other' represented in the image of a veiled woman: as such, veiled Muslim women have been un-unveiled to be re-veiled with the veil, the mask, of the western 'liberated' and 're-humanised' western/secular/Christian law's female subject. By so doing, however, European courts 'naturalize' women's desires as something 'neutral' to be defined by the state through an 'act of sovereignty' that decides which symbols are to be regarded as 'religious' and gives to religious practices their proper place within western secularized democracies, bringing, in this way, religious practices into the civil domain. It is exactly through the employment of a specific western semiotic ideology that it is possible to comprehend the sovereign's prerogative to shape, through the force of the law, the internal and the external world of the subject.

Drawing on Mancini (2014a, b), I argue that this 'act of sovereign power' (Asad, 2006, p. 101), in defining the appropriate symbol to be displayed in the public sphere, aims at defending a specific kind of democracy, as described by Schmitt. He (1985) argues that democracy is based on a form of 'substantial homogeneity' which, in turn, forms the unity of a people. This unity and homogeneity are artificially constructed through the creation of a fundamental dichotomy between 'self' and 'other', 'friend' and 'enemy', 'insider' and 'outsider' which underlines every democracy. In the name of an artificially constructed homogeneity, the 'other', the 'different', the 'outsider' (the presence of other subjectivities) has to be excluded by an exceptional act of sovereign power in order to 'save' the (imagined) unity and homogeneity of western democracies. It is exactly in this context that the *hijab* emerges as a symbol, a 'sign', a dividing line, between 'insider' and 'outsider', 'friend' and 'enemy' where the 'Muslim woman' is the 'enemy', disloyal to a secularized transcendental power that wants only to rescue her by un-veiling her.

For Mancini (2012), the contraposition between friend and enemy in the discourse concerning the veil is nothing more than a 'false projection', a way for majority cultures to project on to minorities some of their rejected features. In this projection, "the receiving liberal society—projects one of its structural features (patriarchy) onto an object—a cultural minority" (Mancini, 2012, p. 423). By projecting patriarchy (rejected in western thought) towards the other, western society "symbolically destroys the intolerable within itself" (Mancini, 2012, p. 423) and creates an 'imagined community'(Anderson, 1991) in which Christianity and post-Christianity emerge as a useful tool to strengthen social cohesion and build a unified European identity. In this way, veiled Muslim women in Europe emerge as the enemy exactly because of the way they live, expressing a different relation between the individual and the sovereign that goes beyond dichotomous categories: since a form of life is based on the use of the body (which is a use of the self) (Agamben, 2014) Muslim women escape the logic of western sovereignty and of the law because their form of life is not based on precepts and norms, but on the living soul of the gospel, changing the relation between life, body and norms. In other words, exactly because their form of life represents a use of the body beyond western dichotomous categories, it escapes the authority of the law because it presupposes the existence of singularities without identities (Agamben, 1993). For this reason, the sovereign power needs to intervene and establish a state of exception able to exclude 'bare life' (Agamben, 1998) in order to sustain itself, creating in this way specific legal boundaries between inside and outside the protection of western and Human Rights law. As a prince and supreme legislator, the sovereign act creates a (necessary) exception, a 'disturbance' symbolized in the veil, which must be rendered invisible by 'exceptional' rules of law. In this way, the unity and homogeneity of a people "are easily attained when the basic difficulty is emphatically ignored and when, for formal reasons, everything that contradicts the system is excluded as impure" (Schmitt, 1985, p. 21).

This can be ascribed to what Agamben (1998) calls the logic of sovereign exception, which is based on the creation of 'bare life' (that is the inclusive exclusion of *zoe* into the political life): through the state of exception, the sovereign draws the borders between outside and inside, assigning different rights to different individuals, from which veiled Muslim women are excluded because they perform a form of life (that is a novel understanding of the relationship between life, norms, and body), that breaks the relation of exception established by the sovereign: since 'form of life' reveals a different notion of religion, it brings a different relation between life and norms and how the body inhabits norms in different contexts. The form of life lived and experienced by many veiled Muslim women un-masks all the limits of secular polity and allows us to understand the human beyond western/liberal categories and to think about the coexistence of different singularities without identities.

5.1 On Women's Agency: Habitus, Habit and Habits

In Pakistan a popular new animated television series, 'Burqa Avenger', offers a different understanding of veiled Muslim women by challenging the western universal(ist) understanding of the relation between the (gendered) body and norms. In the series, Jiya, an unveiled teacher in a female primary school in Pakistan, struggles in defence of women's rights by 'transforming' herself into her alter ego, 'Burka Avenger': a super heroine who wears the *burqa* to conceal her identity while using 'Takht Kanaddi', a special martial art involving books and pens, to struggle against the enemy (Zeeshan Mukhtar, 2015). Through her *burqa*, which she wears just when she needs, the main character acquires the possibility of agency as she can hide her identity and fly. 'Burqa Avenger' is an interesting character because she escapes from the western monolithic view of Muslim women and offers a different understanding of Muslim women's agency and performativity. She represents a different way to use her own body through the practice of veiling, where what is at stake is not a simple opposition with the western image of Muslim women as subjugated to chauvinist/religious norms and principles, but a different way of life based on a non-dichotomous relation between life and norms. This understanding of the practice could be ascribed to what Agamben (2013) calls 'form of life' which is defined as "a human life entirely removed from the grasp of the law and a use of bodies and of the world that would never be substantiated into an appropriation… [a] life […] which is never given as property but only as a common use" (Agamben, 2013, p. xiii). In Agamben's work, the notion of form of life (which is a life that is inseparable from its form) represents the possibility of thinking a non-relation between *zoe* and *bios* which would allow an understanding of politics and ethics beyond the law and western secular dichotomous categories. Likewise, I argue, by using their body as a means to achieve specific values, many Muslim women disclose a form of life able to change the relationship between life, body and norms. In my analysis, veiling emerges as a practice at the intersection of *habit, habitus* and *habits*: *habit* indicates a technique of the body which is based on a series of repetitions of acts; *habitus*, on the contrary, refers to the way in which specific repeated acts leave a sign in the soul of the individual; while *habits* refers to law and norms. The relation between *habit, habitus* and *habits* mirrors a specific relationship between body, life and norms which is in contrast with western conceptualizations of religion and religious practices as well as western/liberal/secular notions of agency and individual autonomy that emerge from the European decisions to ban the veil. The analysis of Muslim performative practices allows us to problematise and challenge the western/secular binary categories that have framed the headscarf debate (secular v religious, internal v external, women's freedom v women's oppression). Here, I focus on the first dichotomy that emerges from the European decisions to ban the veil: that between women's freedom and oppression, which translates into the dichotomy covered/un-covered body and is linked to the notion of women's agency and autonomy. By challenging western liberal assumptions about women's freedom and agency through the analysis of Muslim and Christian religious practices, I argue that religion does not negate agency; rather, it establishes a specific form of agency based on a non-dichotomous understanding of internal/external, resistance/subjugation, form/substance etc., where norms comes into life as vital, not legal, precepts. This understanding discloses the limits of western thought when western/secular notions of women's freedom and agency are legally applied in reading Muslim religious practices: in the case of the headscarf ban, this has led to the exclusion of many veiled Muslim women from the European public sphere, and the consequent negation of their freedom and possibility of agency.

Agamben's (2013) understanding of 'form of life' is based on analysis of the monks' lives in the Cenoby. For Agamben (2013), the Cenoby's project was to transform life into liturgy and liturgy into life, where life emerges as an *officium*, a place of indifference between norms, being and practice. In the Cenoby, Christian monks learned the art of obedience, which was seen as a virtue developed through discipline (Asad, 1987); a notion that has the power to shape the soul through the body "in ways of dressing (*in habitu*), in posture and movement (*in gestu*), in speech (*in locutione*), and in table manners (*in mensa*)" (Asad, 1987, p. 170). In this view, gesture is not only a mere technique of the body linked to specific cultures, as Mauss (1979) claims, but it is subjected to discipline and is aimed at transforming the soul, feelings and emotions of the performer (Asad, 1987). Through the life in the monastic community, monks learned the virtue of developing and forming a particular self, where emotions express particular dispositions which are independent of cognition and, at the same time, integral to it (Asad, 1987). Hence, the point of monastic rule was not the life itself, but "the ways, norms, and techniques by means of which one succeeded in regulating it in all its aspects" (Agamben, 2013, pp. 93–94). Hence, what is central in monasticism is not the rule, but the life or the ability to live based on a specific religious (but not normative) model. In other words, monks claimed the existence of a life as a rule, a *forma vitae*: not subjection to a series of textual commandments to be interpreted, but living the gospel. In fact, monks lived an ascetic life by "reproducing the model that Christ was… [which] is neither the object of a religious obligation, nor the consequence of a determinate juridical situation…it seems that what is in question here is only the ascetic on the removal of clothes and the assumption of the monastic *habit*" (Agamben, 2013, p. 39). Drawing on the Roman term *form*, which signifies *imago*, exemplar, model, *forma vitae*, Agamben (2013) identifies a form of life as a life constituted as an example, a life that cannot be separated from its form.

This understanding resonates with different anthropological studies of Muslim religiosity (Asad, 2003; Hirschkind, 2006; Mahmood, 2005) which show that for many Muslim believers, Islam is not simply a series of religious precepts to be followed, but a way of life, an inhabitation of the model. Mahmood (2009a) explains that Muslims' love for the Prophet is mirrored in their wish to imitate his behaviour and way of life, "not as a commandment but as virtues where one wants to ingest, as it were, the Prophet's personal into oneself" (p. 75). Thus, Muslims' performative practices lie "not so much upon a communicative or representational model as on an assimilative one" (Mahmood, 2009b, p. 76). The Aristotelian term *schesis*, which is defined as the way in which something relates to something else, can capture this sense of pluralistic embodiment and inhabitation (or intimacy) which is experienced differently by Muslim believers throughout the world: "such an inhabitation of the model (as the term *schesis* suggests) is the result of a labor of love in which one is bound to the authorial figure through a sense of intimacy and desire" (Mahmood, 2009a, p. 848). Hence, in both Christian and Islamic religion, it is possible to find an understanding of religious practices which is more related to a way of living according to a model and to a form of life that cannot be understood as a simple rule (Agamben, 2013). At stake is not the degree of obligation or whether a rule should be understood as a precept or advice, but the re-conceptualization of the very relation between life and law (Agamben, 2013). For the monks, for instance, the vow did not represent an obligation but the fulfilment of a way of life which is attained through an habitual and permanent bond produced in the will (Agamben, 2013).

This bond is created by *habitus*: a central notion in Islam and Christianity. *Habitus,* which derives from the verb *habitare* and "designate[s] not only a factual situation but a way of life […] [and] originally signified 'a way of being or acting'" (Agamben, 2013, p. 13), is understood as the product of a specific totalizing religious tradition in which the individual's acts are judged based on its ability to live and inhabit Islam (Asad, 1993; Mahmood, 2005). Asad (2001) notes that the Arabic term *Iman* (faith)

> is not a singular act that one performs naked before God. It is the virtue of faithfulness toward God, an unquestioning habit of obedience that God requires of those faithful to him, a disposition that has to be cultivated like any other, and which links one through mutual responsibility and trust to others who are faithful (pp. 218–219).

Hence, *habitus* is a disposition, a form of life aimed at transforming life into an *officium*: *habitus,* therefore, resides in the will and it is expressed in the will of embracing a specific form of life. Aristotle (1941) defines *habitus* as the ethics formulated through bodily practices: hence, *habitus* is a quality acquired by doing and repeating certain actions until those actions become an integral part of the subject. This understanding is mirrored in both the Christian theology of Aquinas (Davies, 2005) and in medieval Islamic thought (such as in the work of Abu Hamid al-Ghazali, al-Miskawayh, Ibn Rush and Ibn Khaltum) who analyse the importance of instituting a specific (pious) form of life (Mahmood, 2005): the Latin term *habitus,* translated into the Arabic term *malaka,* is defined as the repetition of a specific performance which has the power to discipline and to shape the internal feelings and emotions of the individual (Lapidus, 1984). As Mahmood (2005) argues, "it is *through* repeated bodily acts that one trains one's memory, desire, and intellect to behave according to established standards of conduct" (p. 157).[1] Hence, *habitus* is a means through which the subject acquires a moral virtue and is linked to the discipline of the body. Since *habitus* aims at ordering the soul, it is implemented for the sake of the performer, not of the audience (Asad, 1987). However, as Asad (1987) emphasises, the acquisition of specific dispositions is not achieved through the mere repetition of specific practices: discipline is "a complex learning process in which discourse, emotion, desire, and the body are involved in different combinations and sequences" (p. 193). Using the Greek term 'paideia' which indicates a "physical, intellectual, and moral cultivation of the person" (Asad, 1987, p. 168), and drawing on the Aristotelian understanding of *habitus* as a repeated performance that creates in the individual a particular disposition, a way of life, as a result of an habituation (Joachim & Rees, 1952), Asad (2009a) defines *habitus* as a means of structuring the subject through technique of the body aimed at inculcating specific virtues and values. This approach emphasises the permanence of the link between outward behaviour and inward disposition (Mahmood, 2005) so *habitus* refers to the way in which certain acts leave a mark upon the interiority of the subject (unlike *habit* which refers to the repetition of specific acts). *Habitus*, then, is a way of shaping one's own interiority through embodied worldly practices that direct one to a particular form of life: it is an habituation through which the subject directs its feelings and desires in order to acquire moral characteristics (Asad, 1993, 2009b; Mahmood, 2005).

The Muslim cassette listeners Hirschkind (2011) has worked with, for instance, understand listening to Islamic religious cassettes as an *habitus* able to change the interiority of the subject in order to achieve excellence. Similarly, for women of the piety movement Mahmood worked with, repeated bodily acts such as praying or wearing the veil become indispensable for acquiring specific values considered necessary attributes of the self. In fact, for most of the women of the piety movement, the veil not only expresses the value of modesty, but it is also the means *through* which this value is acquired (Mahmood, 2005). While women of the piety movement understand veiling as a means through which achieving a specific moral self, Franciscans have invested dressing with similar meanings (Agamben, 2013). Dressing emerges as a technique of the body through which Franciscans achieve a specific being, a *forma vitae* where garments are not linked to appearance, but are constituent of a way to conduct oneself, a form of life based on the repetition of

[1] *Italics added.*

specific practices. Agamben (2013) explains that the term *habitus cinguli* used by Franciscans indicated a repeated practice which constituted a sacrament, a sacred sign which is more than a holy cloth: dressing in a specific way, for the monks, was not a rule, but an inhabitation of the model, a *morum formula*. It was a *habitus*, a form of life that expressed the form of life that the monks symbolized. For the monks, a form of life meant to share not only a space (the Cenoby) or to wear the same clothes, but to share a *habitus*, which itself is a form of life: "life is a habit of living, and a kind of form generated by living" (Agamben, 2014, p. 221). Hence, by wearing specific clothes, monks inhabit a specific form of life, in which life and *habitus*, life and dress, coincide.[2] As clothes are used to achieve a specific form of life, dresses are made of life; they are a form of liturgy which is itself a form of life. In this view, things are not to be considered in their commercial understanding as 'objects of exchange' but they form a relation with the people who use them. What is at stake in the establishment of the practice of dressing as a *habitus* through which to reach specific values is not the item itself, but the use that people make of items (Esposito, 2015). Through items, individuals monitor and regulate their own lives in order to attain specific values deemed important to form the internal world of the religious subject. Similarly, by establishing the practice of veiling as a *habitus*, women of the piety movement create a specific relation between the body and things where objects acquire a meaning that cannot be reduced to rational/cognitive terms. It is an affective meaning which forms and shapes the life of the body and the subject (Esposito, 2015; Pasolini & Hood, 1983). In fact, it is *through* the shape that specific ethical practices take that it is possible to analyse ethical subject formation;

> the importance of these practices does not reside in the meanings they signify to their practitioners, but in the work they do in constituting individuals: similarly, the body is not a medium of signification but the substance and the necessary tool through which the embodied subject is formed (Mahmood, 2005, p. 29).

Form of life discloses a different understanding of bodily practices, ethics, and agency from that of the liberal polity. Agency, in this light, emerges as the "capacity for action that historically specific relations of subordination enable and create" (Mahmood, 2001, p. 203). This understanding helps us to "move beyond the teleology of emancipation underwriting many accounts of women's agency," (Mahmood, 2001, p. 210) and to analyse the relationship between body and subject formation within non-liberal discourses, by challenging the idea of agency central to the liberal concept of autonomy.

Butler (1997) breaks with a long feminist tradition which presumes that all humans are "endowed with a will, a freedom, and an intentionality". Drawing from Derrida's interpretation of Austin's concept of the 'performative', she formulates the idea of a subject performatively constituted through the repetition of heterosexual norms which retroactively produce the appearance of gender: in other words, norms are the necessary ground in which the subject can enact her agency in terms

---

[2] Notably, the monastic rules are the first texts in Christianity in which to clothes is given a moral meaning (Agamben, 2013).

of repetition and/or subversion of identities and subjectivities.[3] Hence, for Butler, while on the one hand the reiteration of structures of norms consolidates particular discourses, then on the other, it is the very structure of norms that provides the subject with the means for its destabilization, where agency emerges as located *within* a productive reiterability and is related to the work of re-signification of norms.

In contrast with Butler, who reduces agency to a binary and antagonistic framework in which norms are reiterated and/or re-signified, Mahmood (2005) intends agency "not simply [as] a synonym for resistance to social norms but [as] a modality of action" (p. 157). In fact, women of the piety movement's understanding of the body as a means to achieve specific values, shows that it is one's performative practice that determines one's desires and not the opposite: for the pietist women, "action does not issue forth from natural feelings but creates them" (Mahmood, 2009, p. 35) and a repeated bodily act such as veiling is an indispensable attribute of the self. Imagine, Mahmood (2001) argues, a pianist who submits herself to a strict disciplinary regime to gain the ability, 'the requisite agency', to play the piano virtuously: in this case, her ability to play the piano is compounded with her ability to be taught. 'Docility', a term associated with the absence of agency, "literally implies the malleability required of someone to be instructed in a particular skill or knowledge – a meaning that carries less a sense of passivity and more that of struggle, effort, exertion, and achievements" (Mahmood, 2001, p. 216). Desire, in this context, is not repressed, but is linked to discipline and emerges as an essential means to become virtuous: "the critical distinction here is therefore not simply between 'love for God' and 'human love', but between desire which is measured by an authoritative law, and desire as the motive for exercising virtue" (Asad, 1987, p. 173). Hence, agency is linked with performativity and emerges as "the specific ways in which one performs a certain number of operations on one's thoughts, body conduct, and ways of being", in order to "attain a certain kind of state of happiness, purity, wisdom, perfection, or immortality in accord with a particular discursive tradition" (Mahmood, 2001, p. 210). If agency is seen as the capacity to undertake moral actions, then this capacity "is entailed not only in those acts that resist norms but also in the multiple ways in which one inhabits norms" (Mahmood, 2005, p. 15). For the women of the piety movement, for instance, piety "rises from practice, is perfected by practice, and then governs all actions and practices" (Mahmood, 2001, pp. 215–216). By considering the possibility that norms can actually structure the interiority of the subject, Mahmood (2005) eludes Butler's antagonistic and dualistic framework: norms can be confirmed or subverted, but they can also be *inhabited*, aspired to and consumed. Hence, agency is not 'resistance to power', but the capacity for action which is understood as the ability to take specific kinds of performative action, just one of which is resistance/reiteration. Agency is thus located *within* specific discourses which, in turn, form the subject who, performatively, reiterates/subverts/inhabits norms (Mahmood, 2001).

This mirrors Foucault's (1997) understanding of ethics as a series of practical performances that are relevant to a specific way of life. For Foucault (1997), ethics

[3] Butler (Butler & others, 2011) calls this process the 'constitutive outside of the subject' (p. 3). This term is used to mark the realm of what is unspeakable and unintelligible but remains necessary for the subject's self-understanding.

refers to a particular set of procedures and techniques through which the subject comes to be formed in a particular (localized) context. In this view, subjectivity is an effect of the modality of a specific structure of power in which the subject is formed through the re-enactment of practices delimited in advance. However, Foucault (1981) also recognizes another kind of subject formation, namely 'moral subjectification', which refers to the available model "for setting up and developing [a] relationship with the self, for self-reflection, self-knowledge, self-examination, for the decipherment of the self by oneself, for the transformations that one seeks to accomplish with oneself as object" (p. 29). Hence, if on the one hand the subject resists or complies with moral codes, then on the other, Foucault (1981) recognizes that the subject has many different ways of forming a relationship with a 'moral code' which, in turn, establishes a relationship between the inner self (will, desires, actions etc.) and norms within a particular discourse. Foucault's analysis of ethical formation helps us to understand agency, firstly as a capacity required to take specific moral action and, secondly, as bound to cultural and historical discourses through which the subject is formed, where what is at stake is not what a certain ethic *means* but what it *does*. Women of the piety movement, as well as monks in the Cenoby, learn how to analyse body and soul movements in order to acquire a specific selfhood. Thus, what is at stake is not the capacity of women to subvert or re-enact the norm of modesty, but rather the relationship between the body, the norm, and how the body inhabits norms in different contexts. For the women of the piety movement Mahmood (2005) worked with, the veil is an *habitus* that shapes the interiority of the wearing subject into a more pious religious subject, where the acts of the body are transformative of the subject's interiority. Hence, while on the one hand, the subject dictates external behaviour, then on the other, external behaviour forms the subject's interiority: what is important to understand is "the complex relationships between the immanent form of a normative act, the model of subject it presupposes, and the type of authority on which it is based" (Mahmood, 2005, p. 23).

The relationship between the body and norms established by Franciscans and women of the piety movement operates a re-conceptualization of law, ethics and politics. Form of life calls into question the idea that rule and life are separated, proposing the establishment of a form of life in which norms and life cannot be distinguished. In fact, as Agamben (2013) points out, it is not the form of life that derives from the rule, but the opposite: form of life makes the rule. This has important implications: "a norm that does not refer to single acts and events, but to the entire existence of an individual, to his *forma vivendi*, is no longer easily recognizable as a law, just as a life that is found in its totality in the form of a rule is no longer truly life" (Agamben, 2013, p. 26). Hence, for Agamben (2013), what is at stake in form of life is the abdication of law, or the subtraction of life from law. In the case of Franciscans, this was made possible through their understanding of *use*, which Agamben (2013) links to the notion of form of life, and which characterises the relationship between norm and life. Drawing on Paul's notion of *chrésis* (use) and the Franciscan concept of *usus pauper*, which is a form of use of goods and of the self beyond the law, Agamben (2013) shows how poverty, for the monks, was a *habit*, a form of life based on the use, and not ownership, of anything needed for life (including the use of their own bodies). However, the adoption of a specific form of life, mirrored in the *de facto* simple use of things, constituted a phenomenon alien to the Church and the property logic of Roman law. Franciscans maintained that the life of the apostles was guided by the notion of use and not by the notion of ownership; the Curia however insisted on differentiating between *ius* and *licentia* (right and permission) and between life and liturgy (which culminated in the Christian doctrine of the *opus operatum*) (Agamben, 2013). To Roman law's notion of ownership, Franciscans opposed the notion of *usus facti*, which is the *de facto* use of something, claiming the possibility to separate the notion of *usus* from that of ownership: in other words, through the notion of *usus* as *usus facti*, which indicates the simple act of using something beyond the relation of property typical of Roman law (Agamben, 2013), Franciscans juxtapose *de facto* and *de jure* use, opening the door to the possibility of abdicate the law in order to pursue a form of life based on use without any form of ownership (Agamben, 2013). For Franciscans, it was not a rule, but a form of life that implied the renunciation of property and rights: hence, the highest form of poverty and the simple *de facto* use of things is "the right to have no rights" (Agamben, 2013, p. 124). It is exactly Franciscans' renunciation of all rights that allowed them to think life beyond the law (Agamben, 2013). A life outside the law is a life in a permanent state of necessity, which is the notion through which Franciscans try to neutralize the law and, at the same time, to create a new relationship with it. Although use and state of necessity (defined, in Roman law, as a state of exception) are the two extremes that define monastic rules, neither rule nor state of exception could be said to be part of a juridical apparatus, as Franciscans refer to a form of life, and not to specific acts or events related to an abstract juridical subject (Agamben, 2013). Hence, on the one hand, life seems to disappear when everything is a rule, while on the other, norms comes into life as vital (and not legal) precepts so that law seems to be abolished or fall into an indetermination in which life and law are in a sphere of indistinction.

Likewise, the way in which women of the piety movement *use* their bodies has opened conflicts with religious and secular authorities. Mahmood (2005) recounts that although many liberal feminists see subjects in search of piety as being outside the 'modern-civilized' 'first world' trajectory, what seems to unite women from different social classes in this movement is the open conflict with several structures of (patriarchal) authority such as Islamic orthodoxy, liberal or secular/nationalist discourse, family relations, state institutions, etc. In fact, their understanding of the use of their own body has deeply challenged nationalist as well as Islamist movements because of the role that the body acquires within nationalist imaginary, be it secular or Islamist. Women of the piety movement are quite critical towards nationalist-identitarian interpretations of religiosity, understood as an abstract system of beliefs without any connection to the way in which those beliefs are lived, performed, experienced, and inhabited: based on their point of view, this understanding of the body treats performative acts primarily as a 'sign of' the self rather than as a 'means to' its formation (Mahmood, 2005). By using their body as a tool to achieve specific values, women of the piety movement re-appropriate their body, revealing a specific form of life. In other words, by giving a different conceptualization of their own bodies, Muslim women avoid being re-scribed as a fixed subject of the nation-state and they manoeuvre their agency through the different *use of their body* within a community and a plurality of normative choices. It is exactly their elusive form of life, along with the plurality of uses of their bodies, that threaten western forms of sovereignty, exactly because a body without property, a body that is simply used by the individual to perform a specific form of life, is a body that escapes the authority of the law.

This is why 'Burqa Avenger' is such an interesting character: in her plurality of performative acts, she escapes the logic of the singular state sovereignty that needs to sustain a fixed identitarian subject. By using the veil based on her own needs, Burqa Avenger discloses a form of use of things and of her body beyond the normative (secular and/or religious) prescriptions of veiling, establishing an affective non-cognitive relation between her body and the veil, which transforms her into a super hero and gives her an exceptional possibility of agency. Not only does she embody a different concept of freedom and agency beyond western oppositional categories, but also, more importantly, she represents an 'intimacy', what Agamben (2014) calls a *use of the body* or a *use of the self* which is defined as "a relation to an inappropriable and un-representable zone of un-known" (p. 128).[4] As my analysis discloses, this relation between subject and object, internal and external, cannot be captured through the secular division of spheres but should be understood through a pluralistic/non-binary understanding of the religious and legal subject. The relation that many Muslims establish between internal and external, form and substance, signifier and signified, shows that is impossible to analyse the matter of veiling through western oppositional categories. In light of this, a secular conceptualization of (Muslim) religiosity as backward because it is unable to separate internal from external, secular from religious, does not take into consideration the many ways in which the individual uses its body and experiences religion, imposing a very specific secular/Christian understanding of religious practices and ignoring the plurality of subjectivities that inhabit contemporary Europe.

My analysis discloses how specific body performances can be understood in non-secular terms, operating a shift from a centred human subject to its 'condition of possibility' *within* specific discourses which, in turn, determine those conditions: agency comes from "within sematic and institutional networks that define and make possible particular ways of relating to people, things, and one self" (Asad, 2003, p. 78). This notion presupposes that there does not exist a homogeneous idea of personhood, but that different subjectivities cohabit in a specific pluralistic cultural and historical space and that each of those configurations of personhood is the product of different discourses. This plurality of normative choices is embedded in the very structure of classical Islamic law, which reveals a certain flexibility, as witnessed by Muslim scholars as well as illiterate Muslims, towards different Islamic schools and Islamic sources (Mahmood, 2005). In fact, as I have argued, the essence of classic Islamic jurisprudence, based on the comprehension of the past for a reformulation of practices in the present, creates a link between the past and the present, practitioners and scholars, and between theory and how, praxiologically, norms are lived, experienced, performed and inhabited (Asad, 2009a): as Roy (1999)

[4] *My translation.*

points out, it is exactly the lack of a religious authority and a fixed juridical and cultural system that has rendered Islam an individual experience. In fact, the engagement of ordinary Muslims with Islamic founding texts depends on the context through which those texts acquire a specific meaning for the believer (Asad, 2003, 2009b). Hence, the interpretation of a particular norm depends not only on classical Islamic sources but also, more importantly, on the practical context in which these norms are performed, inhabited, and experienced.

In this sense, the veil can also be seen as a 'possibility of action', a tool for women to negotiate certain norms and/or inhabit pluralistic non-liberal patriarchal traditions. The full-face-veil worn by 'Burqa Avenger', for instance, is not only a tool through which she achieves her goals, but it is also an element that empowers her by giving her an exceptional possibility of agency, exactly like the mask worn by 'western super-heroes'. It is the plurality of her performative acts that gives her the freedom to perform and manoeuvre her agency within particular discourses. In this view, religious beliefs do not negate agency, but they shape a specific form of agency that is historically and discursively constructed (Scott, 2013). In fact, as I have argued, if agency resides in the will to implement a specific form of life, then it should not be seen as an innate property of the abstract secular individual, but as an attribute of the subject. Therefore, the donning of the veil should not be confused with lack of agency, but should be intended within particular discourses that form not only the subject but also its desires (Abu-Lughod, 2002). This theoretical framework allows for an analysis of the discourse concerning the veil beyond western/secular dichotomies, which leads to a re-conceptualization of women's freedom and agency as well as a deeper understanding of the limits of western/liberal/secular thought in advancing Muslim women's rights in contemporary Europe.

5.2 'Measuring Freedom': An East/West Perspective

My analysis of form of life, a notion linked with desire and agency, allows us to rethink the liberal/secular understanding of women's freedom that lies at the centre of the European decisions to ban the veil. I want to introduce the topic with something that happened in the middle of the 'headscarf turmoil'. In 2015, a group of French girls were expelled from school because their skirts were considered 'too long' and thus a 'provocation, and potential act of protest' (Tahroor, 2015). The decision, made by the Head of School, was taken after the banning of religious symbols from public schools in the context that the 'long-skirt' was considered 'Muslim clothing' and thus a 'religious symbol'. Immediately after, a campaign with the hashtag 'I wear my skirt as I like' filled many pages of social media, along with images of VIPs, such as Nicole Kidman, wearing long dresses on the red carpet at Cannes. The slogan is reminiscent of western women's struggle for the miniskirt, but in 2015 it seemed to acquire a new meaning related to the dichotomy between the 'naked-liberated' body and the 'covered-constrained' one where the length of women's skirt becomes the measurement of women's freedom. Western women are deemed to be autonomous individuals able to pursue their desires, in contrast with Muslim women who, by hiding their beauty, signal their subordination to men. In other words, 'less covered women' are supposedly free to realise their desires, while covered women are seen as unable to choose.

As I shall argue, this dichotomy, which is mirrored in western legal decisions over women's clothes where the 'naked body', symbolized in the miniskirt, is considered a 'sign of' women's liberation associated with the possibility of agency while the 'long-skirt' (along with the *hijab*) is regarded as a 'conspicuous religious symbol' incompatible with Christian/secular values of tolerance and gender equality, endorses problematic assumptions about western notions of freedom, autonomy and sexuality, especially when violently imposed on other cultures and discursive traditions. In fact, while my analysis discloses that religion shapes a specific form of agency and a specific notion of freedom, European legal decisions to ban the practice of veiling clearly apply a very liberal/secular understanding of women's freedom and autonomy, reducing Muslim women to a single subjectivity, and negating, in this way, any other understanding of women's freedom and agency, while imposing a specific notion of womanhood and emancipation. In light of this, secular assumptions about individual autonomy, freedom and agency, which are based on dichotomous contrapositions (personal autonomy v religious authority, external constraints v self-realization, etc.) and are embedded in western law, render the kind of religiosity experienced by many Muslim women intelligible. In fact, my analysis shows that many Muslim women conceptualize the practice of veiling both as a modality of freedom and as a necessary act to achieve a specific ethnic/religious subjectivity. This conceptualization of their practices challenges secular/liberal dichotomous categories based on the idea that freedom and religion are opposite poles of a binary, and discloses a different understanding of freedom. On the contrary, by imposing a specific notion of women's freedom and agency, European judges objectify Muslim women's body and shape a specific notion of womanhood as well as a new understanding of gender equality and women's emancipation.

In liberal/secular thought, freedom is intended as the mere possibility of the subject to choose autonomously, based on its own desires. In fact, since in western/secular thought modernity is understood as the long human struggle against irrational beliefs (Keane, 2015), freedom is conceived as freedom from transcendental and irrational beliefs that have constrained the individual, especially women, for a long time. Hence, in liberal/secular thought, individual autonomy defines the 'human' and emerges through the distinction between positive and negative freedom, which has deeply informed liberal and feminist analyses of women's freedom and women's rights.[5] Negative freedom is defined by the absence of external obstacles, while

[5] From 'natural freedom', associated with the emergence of 'natural rights', to a new concept of freedom linked to a specific concept of humanity, as emerges in human rights law, ideas such as self-determination, autonomous will and (abstract) 'equality' come to define Christian/secular/liberal culture and polity: the social contract, for instance, is based on a specific (individualist) western concept of freedom, choice, and consent. The spread of the western concept of freedom, conceptualized in individualistic terms, and strictly related to the idea of women's rights, was a focal point in the 1995 Beijing UN conference on women, CEDAW, and the 1985 Nairobi Forward-Looking Strategies for the Advancement of women. It is clear that, if on the one hand such language supports a universalistic idea of 'natural freedom' intrinsically related to the concept of 'humanity', then on the other, echoing Esmeir's (2012) work on the stop of temporality operated by colonizers, it confirms the hegemonic power of the west (Hirschmann, 1997; Mill, 1998).

positive freedom is understood as the capacity to realize an autonomous will: thus, in western liberal thought, autonomy "is a procedural principle, and not an ontological or substantive feature of the subject, it delimits the necessary condition for the enactment of the ethics of freedom" (Mahmood, 2005, p. 11).

Based on Berlin (1971), negative freedom is defined as something external, alien, 'other' to the self; it means "not being interfered with by others. The wider the area of non-interference, the wider my freedom" (p. 123). Negative freedom draws a clear distinction between 'subject' and 'object', the 'self' and what is 'other', 'external' to the subject while, at the same time, it relies on a very strict notion of individual responsibility (Taylor, 1988). Thus, freedom is understood as something 'measurable' because 'the less external constraints we have, the more we are supposed to be free' (Hirschmann, 1997, pp. 46–47): hence, in liberal thought, freedom is an 'objective', and not a 'subjective' principle. Negative freedom's individualism is revealed in the distinction between the 'self' and the 'other', while constraints "contain an inherently conflictual character, because individuals' desires and interests inevitably collide with them" (Hirschmann, 2009, p. 5). The difficulty in this approach is revealed in the complexity of drawing a clear line between an internal self, with its own particular desires, and the external world, in which the subject exists: "without such specificity of context, the individual too is unspecified, an abstraction" (Hirschmann, 2009, p. 10). This understanding is linked to the ontological idea behind the modern legal subject, which is the very abstract notion of the individual: Hegel (1991) named it the 'hypothetical self of modernity' and pointed out that "as this person, I know myself to be free in myself. I can abstract from everything, since nothing confronts me save pure personality and free ego" (p. 235). The abstract notion of the western subject is possible only if the individual is free from all cultural and social constraints: to become an 'abstract individual', "we have to completely forget the relationships (e.g. ethical, juridical, amorous etc.) we are used to thinking about" (Hegel, 1991, p. 235). Thus, the external world, traditions, sentiments etc. are seen as deformations of the natural individual who is (abstractly) free only once s/he is free from external oppressive structures of power (Rahbari, 2000). Since the western/Christian/secular individual emerges as a mask, an abstraction, the western approach does not help us to understand how will and desires are formed. If, as many liberal scholars argue, we have conflicting internal desires and interests, then how can we understand our true will (Hirschmann, 2009)? As argued, in order to understand how desires and interests come to be formed, it is essential to understand them within specific historical and cultural contexts which, in turn, form the subject, her choices, will, and desires: in fact,

> in ordinary life the wish to do one thing rather than another is rooted in dominant conventions, in loyalties and habits one has acquired over time, as well as in the anxieties and pleasures experienced in interaction with lovers and friends, with relatives, teachers, and other authority figures (Asad, 2006, p. 99).

If, echoing Foucault (1981), the subject emerges as the product of a particular form of social formation and as such is not only 'constrained' but also formed by it, then we need to interrogate the liberal assumption of a 'rational-self-master' who knows exactly what his/her true desires are. In fact, if the 'choosing subject' exists within a specific discourse, then "the ideal of the naturalized and unified subject utilized by most freedom theories is [...] deeply problematic and simplistically overdrawn" (Hirschmann, 2009, p. 13) because our desires and interests come to be shaped by what the general discourse renders 'available' (Elster, 1983). Hence, it is difficult to apply this distinction to analyse how people, in the 'East' as well as in the 'West', live and experience life and to think that this opposition between the individual and the society is universally valid.

Positive freedom, in contrast, focuses on the analysis of political and social conditions which emerge as limits to individual freedom and it tries to find positive actions in order to overcome those constraints. The paradox of this approach is that while the individual is supposed to be a self-master who knows what its true desires are, the state intervenes to regulate individual's desires. In other words, individual 'will' or 'desires' come to be determined by 'others', the state and its law: "since the law embodies the true will, then by forcing me to obey the law the state is only 'forcing me to be free' that is, to follow my true will, whether I know it or not" (Hirschmann, 2009, p. 8). The western idea of (positive) freedom is embedded in modern western positive law and it is revealed by the fact that many European states feel the need to legislate on women's bodies. In the context of western legal decisions over the veil, the main concern of the judges was to 'rescue' Muslim women from religious fundamentalist groups, whether they wanted it or not: by implying that they knew the true 'will' and 'desire' of Muslim women (which, surely, is not 'wearing a veil'), European judges acted as 'rescuers' for those women, supposedly unable to make a choice based on their true interests and desires. However, if the freedom of the western individual is based on her ability to choose, then Muslim women, who choose to wear the veil as autonomous individuals, should be free to dress as they please; paradoxically, the law that is founded on the concept of freedom and individual autonomy is the same one that limits women's agency by normatively regulating their attire. This paradox is well expressed by the dissenting opinion of Judge Tulken in the *Sahin* case (2005):

> The applicant, a young adult university student, said -and there is nothing to suggest that she was not telling the truth- that she wore the headscarf of her own free will. In this connection, I fail to see how the principle of sexual equality can justify prohibiting a woman from following a practice which in the absence of proof of the contrary, she must be taken to have freely adopted. Equality and non-discrimination are subjective rights which must remain under the control of those who are entitled to benefit from them. 'Paternalism' of this sort runs counter to the case law of the Court, which has developed a real right to personal autonomy. Finally, if wearing the headscarf really was contrary to the principle of equality of men and women in any event, the state would have a positive obligation to prohibit it in all places, whether public or private (para 12).

While Judge Tulken discloses liberal/secular paradoxes of the notion of women's freedom, the 'autonomous individual' that emerges from the juridical decisions to ban the veil is a secular/liberal/individual whose actions and desires come to be 'universalized', 'naturalized' and properly measured and regulated by the positive action of the law. Those decisions reveal a specific concept of women's freedom (that of the 'liberated' western woman) and show that the immanent and multi-layered pluralistic practice of veiling escapes western eyes.

This indicates that liberal concepts of women's freedom and agency are not just part of a philosophical tradition, but have become a normative feature of the modern liberal/secular state which serves to reinforce a sense of the superiority of western liberal thought (Abu-Lughod, 2002). The European decisions to ban the veil are based on a very western/liberal understanding of freedom and individual autonomy that is fundamentally paradoxical and problematic when dealing with different cultures in a globalised world. They mirror liberal ideas that freedom and religion are opposite spheres: "reason, agency, choice, and responsibility in one part, and faith, authority, submission, and fate in another" (Brown, 2015, p. 325).

My anthropological study of Muslim bodily practices challenges the liberal/western dichotomy between freedom and authority (mirrored in the binary faith/reason) by considering freedom as a way to inhabit, negotiate, and also serve, authority. Brown (2015) argues that for many religious individuals (including Muslims, Christians and Jews) everyday practices link freedom to a transcendental authority which often submits the individual to practices that apparently contradict its freedom. In fact, many religious people derive their freedom from obedience to a transcendent authority, where "religious freedom inheres in realizing God's authority, vitalizing it, publicly enacting it" (Brown, 2015, p. 331). Rosenthal (1960) observes that for many Muslims freedom means liberty from the enslavement of worldly desires, which allows the believer to attain a virtuous and modest self. This resonates with Abu-Lughod's study (2000) of Bedouin women: she argues that, in Bedouin society, a practice such as veiling, understood as a symbol of women's oppression by western judges and politicians, is considered a source of honour and so of freedom; it attests to a certain independence from men because it "serves as a statement that the wearer is intent on preserving herself as separate from others, emotionally and psychologically as well as physically; it is a tangible marker of separateness and independence" (Hirschmann, 1997, p. 474). If, for many women of the piety movement the veil is a tool to achieve specific abilities and internal dispositions, for the Bedouin women Abu-Lughod (2000) worked with, the veil indicates esteem and autonomy because it 'covers' not only the body but also "the natural needs and passions" (p. 115), helping them to control their emotions and thus to be free. In this view, being sovereign and master of one's own desires is the condition for freedom: "freedom lies in becoming slave to the Prophet rather than to one's own soul and has as its prerequisite mastery (enslavement) of bodily and worldly cares" (Brown, 2015, p. 331). In essence, freedom is conceived as subordination to a divine order able to replace the worldly order with one that is divine. This understanding of freedom is also evident in Mahmood's analysis of the women of the piety movement and their understanding of *habitus* as residing in the will and expressed in a specific form of life. In the case, submission emerges as a free choice which highlights the difference between autonomy and self-governance: a distinction that is embedded in the idea of Islamic *umma* where "the *sharia* system of practical reason morally binding on each faithful individual, exists independently of him, or her. At the same time, every Muslim has the psychological ability to discover rules and to conform to them" (Asad, 2003, p. 197). Hence, Muslim understandings of bodily practices challenge the secular/liberal opposition between the self and forms of authority and between norms and personal freedom

> by conceptualizing self-realization as the realization of the transcendent will—the enactment of which requires submission to certain religious obligations—...reimagin[ing] the relationship between norms and the self, such that the "true self" is cultivated and realized not against social and religious authority but, rather, through it (Fernando, 2010, pp. 23–24).

By linking self-realization and religious normativity (Fernando, 2010) and overcoming the secular/liberal division between personal autonomy and religious authority, Muslim veiled women problematize the secular/liberal understanding of women's freedom and personal autonomy, revealing a specific relation between authority, women's body and freedom. The studies I have taken into consideration hypothesise a possible separation between self-realization and autonomous will and between agency and discursive infrastructures, where agency is an attribute of the subject who is defined by a discourse in which, at times, the individual freely chooses to subordinate itself. In light of this, contemporary western/secular/liberal emphasis on women's freedom in the discourse on the veil helps to sustain liberal/secular notion of personal autonomy, showing the anxiety produced by the link drawn by those women between autonomy and religious authority (Fernando, 2010). My analysis of Muslim women's performative practices reveals the possibility of thinking about freedom and agency in ways that are different from liberal/Christian/secular thought: while liberal secularism understands freedom and religion as opposing poles of a binary, my exploration discloses that religion forms a specific notion of freedom and agency.

Knowing the context within which some choices are made possible helps us to understand concepts of freedom and agency as being located *within* a community, structures of power, and relationships (Hirschmann, 1997). For many women, the veil is not the symbol of a chauvinist religious imposition that obliges them to cover their heads, as implied by European judges, but a tool through which they negotiate their preferences. The veil helps them to express their agency *within* their community: through this, they achieve specific concepts of freedom, agency and ethics (Hirschmann, 2009). Hence, when analysing concepts of women's freedom and agency, it is essential to understand the local context in which certain bodily acts are performed and certain desires formed. Therefore, the analysis of the practice of veiling should take into consideration "not just [...] whether the choosing subject can act on her choice but how that subject and her choices are constructed in the first place" (Hirschmann, 2009, pp. 46–47). In this sense, when studying the practice of veiling, the liberal opposition between those who defend the 'free will' of Muslim women and those who see veiling as a backward cultural imposition is a fake one. '*The paradox of liberalism lay exactly in the formulation of choice as measurement offreedom*' (the more choices I have, the more I am supposed to be free) (Hirschmann, 1997, pp. 46–7). Clearly, a study of veiling cannot be mapped from the western binary distinction between more and fewer choices, as the way in which we experience our daily life is far more complicated. In fact, if, on the one hand, women manoeuvre their agency within structures of power, often re-enacting patriarchal norms, then on the other, those norms gave them the framework within which they negotiate their choices through intervention in customary practices, despite those practices being affected by specific power relations. Hence, if on the one hand, every human is confronted with choices, then on the other, those choices are formed by the discourse people live in because it is the

> general ethical dimension that not only gives sense to the self in relation to others but also forms a notion of freedom that can only unfold itself in a specific cultural narrative. A cultural narrative does not imply a restriction against which a will would have to be formulated; rather, it defines a person and his or her will as a bent toward the world (Alvi, 2013, p. 182).

In other words, the western universalist model of "human action presupposes [...] a natural disjuncture between a 'person's true desire' and those that are socially prescribed [...]. Identify[ing] moment and places where conventional norms impede the realization of an individual's real desires, or at least obfuscate the distinction between what is truly one's own and what is socially required" (Mahmood, 2005, p. 149). My analysis shows that the liberal distinction between a subject's own desires and social conventions cannot be easily presumed since "socially prescribed forms of behaviour constitute the conditions for the emergence of the self as such and are integral to its realization" (Mahmood, 2005, p. 149).

In the debate about banning the veil, Muslim women have strategically tried to use the liberal argument of personal choice to justify their practice, challenging liberal discourse by associating choice with submission and not emancipation[6] where, in liberal/secular thought, "emancipation and equality are traits presumed to inhere in individuals, establishing their agency- their very humanity – and so their eligibility for membership in the community of the nation" (Scott, 2017, p. 169). However, the strategy of Muslim women to use the liberal language of choice has further constrained them: in fact, on the one hand, presenting veiling as a religious obligation transforms those women into radicals (as the veil is not compulsory in Islam), while on the other, by posing the practice of veiling as a personal choice, they lose the possibility of expressing their moral values, which are integral to individual subject formation (Fernando, 2017). This is well expressed by Mrs. Isabelle Charest, the Quebec Minister of Women's Affairs, who stated that "when a religion dictates clothing or something, for me, this is not freedom of choice. When someone doesn't have freedom of choice, for me it's a sign of oppression [...]. The hijab does

[6] Scott (2017) argues that, historically, emancipation has not always been associated to the notion of equality. In Roman law, for instance, emancipation indicated the liberation of women and children from the patria potestas: hence, emancipation was not a synonymous of equality, given that their liberation did not provide them equal status with the husband or father. In fact, as Marx (1978) argues, emancipation of minority groups did not alter power relations; rather it naturalises inequalities. With the liberal/secular idea of the abstract individual, the notion of emancipation and equality started to conflate (Scott, 2017). Scott (2017) argues that in liberalism desire is at the centre of individual's freedom, whereas the state just facilitates the interaction of desiring individuals, leaving equality at the doorstep.

not correspond to my values. My values are that a woman should be freed to wear what she wants to wear or not to wear" (Authier, 2019). This shows that exactly because the dominant western understanding, which links conscience and choice as opposing poles of a binary, relies on the dichotomy between personal and religious authority, Muslim women are given no space to conceptualise veiling as essential to their religious/ethical subject formation, which "entails a very different relationship between desire and social and religious authority" (Fernando, 2010, p. 29). In light of this, within the liberal/secular framework, it becomes impossible for Muslim women to conceptualise their practices as a personal commitment to the creation of a specific ethical/religious self.

The rhetoric of women's freedom and their possibility of agency in the legal discourse that has banned the veil has important implications: through the objectification of Muslim women's body, European judges have shaped a fixed notion of womanhood and the female religious subject to which Muslim women are blindly asked to conform, reducing the 'woman question' to a single piece of cloth. This, in turn, has the power to shape a different understanding of the notion of gender equality and emancipation, now linked to a mere contraposition between western and Muslim women.

In the western narrative concerning the veil, which "serves as a provocation to sexual discourse in ways that are parallel to the overt display of women's body"(Mahmood, 2013, p. 57), the focus "is not about women exercising their independent sexual agency but about advertising their sexual availability, and so appealing to long standing gender asymmetries" (Scott, 2017, p. 158). This is exemplified by a passage of the Stasi Commission report which states that "young men force [girls] to wear clothes that are concealing and *asexual*, and to lower their eyes on seeing a man; and if they do not conform with such rules, they are stigmatized as 'whores'" (*Commission De Reflexion,* 2003, p. 46).[7] This passage implies that women, in order to be 'free' and 'equal' to men in liberal societies, should underline their sexuality. European judges have elevated western women's body to a standard of civilization, and they have implicitly drawn a link between the veil and women's sexuality: it is supposed that because Muslim women's body is covered, they cannot be as free as an un-covered body is. In the European decisions to ban the veil, the 'covered body' emerges as un-natural or as a violation of women's autonomy, and the 'liberated' and 'sexualized' western woman is seen as the natural condition for women's freedom. However, women should not even discover too much: comparing the 'Affaire du Foulard' with other bans (such as the banning of 'too tight' trousers, or short skirts from schools) (Fletcher, 2013; Brown, 2009), a specific form of femininity and womanhood emerges, which is delimited by the western secular imaginary, disclosing the power of the secular to establish specific boundaries of gender and sexuality. This is clear in the European decisions to ban the veil, which reveal a very specific idea of 'womanhood' and what constitutes the (female) body, where hair is visible. Fernando (2017) argues that the association between veiling and

[7] *Italic added.*

women's sexuality inevitably collapses sex into gender because being a woman comes to be associated with heterosexual western notions of femininity and normative sexuality that necessitate women being uncovered. In light of this, Muslim women in Europe are asked to display a specific form of secular religiosity and a 'normalised' sexual life through the display and sexualisation of their bodies (Fernando, 2017), publicly rejecting 'aberrant' norms such as veiling and polygamy: in other words, veiled Muslim women are asked to perform a self-calculating secular self (Scott, 2017) able to visibly display the (gendered) division between public and private:

> the secular self means a set of bodily practices to be learned, rehearsed, and performed, ranging from ways of dressing (and undressing), talking and socializing with men to acting in public. The habitations of the secular are not transmitted 'naturally' and implicitly, but on the contrary become part of a project of modernity and politics of self (Göle, 2010, p. 48).

Hence, "the 'power of the secular' seems [...] to reside in its capacity to naturalize such a distinctive perspective on the female body, and to represent and grasp the non-veiled body as the natural and 'free' body" (Fadil, 2011, pp. 96–97), disclosing a kind of reverse (secular) fundamentalism which is at work in the European legal decision to ban the veil. In fact, while secularism claims to free women from religious constraints, it also imposes a transcendental notion of what is natural, establishing specific boundaries of gender and sexuality, and transcending the public/private divide on which is based by rendering public and visible what is considered private. In essence, by imposing a specific public and private standard of behaviour, the secular state emerges as a theological state far from the neutrality it supposedly defends (Brown, 2015): "although modern secularism is often presented as the answer to the problem of gender and sexual regulation by religious forces [...] secular modernity produces a normative discourse of sexuality that is the driving force behind making sexual politics so central" (Jakobsen, 2010, p. 47). The privatisation of religion and sexuality has been interiorised by the modern secular subject who is constructed through the legal category of sex and religion and in an unprecedented way regulated and normalised in its private sphere by the secular state (Mahmood, 2013), revealing the power of western and Human Rights law to define not only its subject, but also, more importantly, the image that the subject has of itself: only in this way does the power of the law enable the Christian/secular/liberal subject to become part of a 'universal humanity'. In this way, however, secularism negates the freedom and agency of the women it claims to protect by elevating western women as the universal standard of a civilized humanity (Scott, 2017), disclosing a form of femininity that draws attention on the body and its visibility as the locus for wider civilizational struggles.

Since the discourse on the veil focuses on whether Muslim women are sufficiently emancipated and sexualised to become active members of European secular societies (Scott, 2017), emancipation is not anymore synonymous with freedom, but it is dependent on how the individual understands itself and behaves in the modern (secular) world. This indicates that the rhetoric of gender equality and emancipation in the discourse on the veil discloses a new way for secularism to represent the human, especially women, where the contraposition between eastern and western women has defined the very notion of womanhood and gender equality. This, however, is not translated into the advancement of Muslim women's freedom: rather, Muslim women are expected to conform to a specific notion of womanhood and a particular (secular) form of gender inequality which reinforces gender and racial stereotypes.

Göle (2010) argues that "the Islamic veil, when it is not enforced on women by state power or communitarian pressure, and expresses the personal trajectories of women and their self-fashioning piety, presents a critique of the secular interpretation of women's emancipation" (pp. 49–50) by showing the limits of the liberal/secular system. These limits are expressed in European decisions to ban the veil whereas veiled Muslim women represent secularism's failure to emancipate women from religious and irrational beliefs that have oppressed them for so long. In fact, the 'moral narrative of modernity'(Keane, 2015, p. 62) is based on the assumption that the treatment of women is the criterion for judging the modernity of a nation. For this reason, western secular law should save Muslim women from unreal and backward beliefs by bringing their private sphere into the public, re-veiling them with the mask of the liberated western woman.

However, by trying to save Muslim women from their (supposedly) backward religion, European judges violate women's understanding of their own practices, and they reduce the 'woman question' to a single piece of cloth which takes different forms, lengths, colours, and meanings in different cultural and historical contexts. In fact, in the legal decisions on the practice of veiling, Muslim women are portrayed as a unified category whose oppression is simply a variation of a basic theme (Hirschmann, 1997). This is clear in the French parliamentary report on the wearing of the burqa which defines it as an "assault on women's dignity and on the affirmation of femininity" (Rapport d'information no. 2262, 2010, p. 14). The report takes into consideration the position of Élizabeth Badinter, one of the most famous French philosophers, who wrote that:

> It would be wrong to compare fully veiled women to cloistered nuns, because the latter were cloistered and invisible to others, whereas fully veiled women are often married, sometimes mothers, and they aim at imposing themselves in the public space without identity, without body, skin, in short, erasing all signs of their humanity. I cannot help seeing in their attitude an expression of a pathological contradiction: on the one hand, they refuse to show their face under the pretext that they do not want to be the subject of un-pure looks … on the other hand, they indulge in a true exhibition of themselves, with everyone staring at these unidentified objects. By arousing curiosity, these women attract glances that they would probably not attract had their faces been uncovered—in short, they become the objects of a fantasy. Being looked at without being seen and being able to watch the other without being watched, satisfies a triple perverse pleasure: the pleasure that derives from exercising a sort of omnipotence on the other, an exhibitionist pleasure and a voyeuristic one. So when I hear women explaining that the full veil makes them feel good and protected—but protected from what?—I believe that what they say is true, but I think these women are very sick and I do not think we may have to determine ourselves according to their pathology (as cited in *Rapport d'information* no. 2262, 2010, p. 335).

Clearly, to understand the veil as a simple item that covers women's body is extremely reductive. In fact, as I have argued, the simple wearing of a specific garment cannot be linked to women's oppression, and Islam cannot be seen as incompatible with democracy, because it is a religion open to interpretation and not a political movement that threatens western democracy. Indeed, "to assume that the mere practice of veiling women in a number of Muslim countries indicates the universal oppression of women through sexual segregation not only is analytically reductive, but also proves quite useless when it comes to the elaboration of oppositional political strategy" (Mohanty, 1988, p. 67). Failing to recognize that all humans are 'multiple-layered' and that the practice of veiling represents a plurality of norms, ethics and bodily practices reduces the subject to a singular and fixed identity. It is exactly for this reason that the veil is seen as a 'clash of civilizations': if we reduce the human to a singular and fixed identity, then this identity can be *measurable* only through allegiances to a specific power which, in turn, forms identities, subjectivities and desires. It is in this way that the plural subjectivities and identities of Muslim women have been reduced to a static and monolithic law's subject. This 'reductionism' is not only theoretical but is part of a wider neo-colonial and paternalistic political context in which the juridical regulation of women's body becomes a useful tool to control the public sphere. Thus, what the headscarf ban really unfolds are particular power relations: in the case of the headscarf ban, the power of western discourse lies exactly in the homogenised representation of covering practices which allows the continuation of an epistemic violence against Muslim women (Husain & Ayotte, 2005). In fact, the Muslim women's body has also been a useful tool to justify western imperialist warfare in Afghanistan and Iraq, as well as Islamists' struggles for the establishment of a territorial nation-state under a singular and fixed *sharia* law: "arguably, in neither case do women take part in constructing the framework within which decisions about dress take place, but rather, are forced to respond in conflicting directions to frameworks constructed by men" (Shaheed, 1994, p. 1003). The mandatory de-veiling operated by the Shah in pre-revolutionary Iran, for instance, was no less oppressive than the compulsory re-veiling ordered by the Islamic revolutionaries in the aftermath of the 1979 Iranian revolution (Chehabi, 1993; Homa Hoodfar, 1997): both (patriarchal) regimes aim at legally regulating and controlling women's attire by inscribing women's bodies as fixed symbols of cultural belonging and not as subjects of history. This indicates that it is not the veil that renders women free or unfree, but the means that patriarchy allocates to a specific article of clothing in order to control and limit women's agency. More than a universal truth about the necessity to liberate Muslim women from the burden of the veil, western decisions to ban the headscarf show the limits of secular/liberal tolerance. Brown (2008) argues that the discourse of liberal tolerance is also a discourse of power: in the case of the banning of the veil, the power of the secular resides exactly in the homogenised representation of Muslim women, which has been inimical to Muslim women, who have become the objectified symbol of an imaginary other: a useful tool to bolster and maintain a specific form of gender inequality, masked as freedom.

5.3 On Signified and Signifier: Western Semiotics and Muslim Women's Body

In 2016, several mayors of the French Riviera forbade the *burkini*, a type of swimwear used by some Muslim women which covers the whole body except for the face, hands and feet, on all public beaches. The ban came into force after the July 2016 attack in Nice, where 86 people died. The mayors' decision was based on the assumption that the veil is 'a sign of' the proliferation of radical Islam in opposition to French liberal/secular/democratic values (Ganley, 2016). The '*burkini* ban' sparked passionate debates on various social media, especially after the publication of a video in which four male French police asked a Muslim woman to undress on the beach in front of everybody (*France warns of Muslim stigmatisation amid burkini ban*, 2016). After the fact, social networks started to be filled with photos showing veiled Catholic nuns having fun on the beach along with images comparing women wearing *burkini* with divers, until France's highest administrative court overturned the mayors' decision to ban the *burkini* because it was considered in violation of French laws on civil liberties, freedom of movement, and religious freedom (Breeden & Blaise, 2016). The '*burkini* ban' poses a significant challenge to the western/liberal/secular understanding of the semiotic of symbols and signs in the public sphere: in fact, from a purely aesthetic point of view, there is no difference between a *burkini* and swimwear worn by divers. Moreover, plenty of people cover up on the beach to protect themselves from the sun or for a variety of other reasons (Chemaly, 2016). This indicates that the danger attached to the *burkini* does not lie in the mere image of a covered body, which is widely accepted in western societies, but in the symbology attached to a specific article of clothing. Hence, attention should be paid to the semiotic of signs and how it works in modern western/secular/liberal public space. As I shall argue, western semiotic ideology, which gives to images and signs a fixed meaning arbitrarily defined by social conventions or by law, does not take into consideration the "affective and embodied practices through which a subject comes to relate to a particular sign" (Mahmood, 2009a, pp. 841–842) and naturalizes and defines the religious subject as an individual who simply submits him/herself to a set of recommendations based on general beliefs. This understanding, which is strictly linked to the place of religion within the secular state and to the role of the law in regulating 'visible' religious practices in the public sphere, reveals the imposition of a specific western/secular semiotic ideology through which law acquires the power to shape the internal and external world of the individual, blurring in this way the line between public and private, and disclosing a specific relation between the individual and the sovereign power.

Modern anthropologists have interpreted religious rituals as symbols to which a specific meaning is attached, and not as instrumental to subject formation, as in the studies that I have taken into consideration (Asad, 1987; Hirschkind, 2006; Mahmood, 2005). Leach (2004), for instance, argues that symbols have the power to evoke in the participants a specific social structure that guides their activities and practices: in this view, signs are understood through their symbolic form and so are in need of interpretation. Similarly, Douglas (2002) understands rituals as a "pre-eminently form of communication" (p. 20) linked to social functions. While these anthropologists do not deny that rituals shape the individual's interiority, they nevertheless assume that the meaning of the ritual cannot be shaped by the individual's intention (Asad, 1987). Hence, rituals are read as a text and reduced to their symbolic meaning (Asad, 1987). This semiotic approach, which follows Austin's analysis of the speech-act (1962) and the division between locutionary, illocutionary and perlocutionary acts, mirrors western/secular dichotomies by inevitably separating the "(public) meanings of ritual from the (private) feelings and intentions of its performers" (Asad, 1987, p. 163). This understanding of rituals is linked to the western/Christian/secular binary division between signifier and signified in the reading of symbols and images.

In 'Christian Moderns', Keane (2007) reveals how the western semiotic distinction between signifier and signified, object and subject, form and essence, mirrors Calvinist and Protestant concerns to institute a separation between the transcendent world and the reality of this world. This distinction was imposed on other cultures by western missionaries and has become embedded in the secular idea of what it means to be modern and how images work in the liberal/secular world. As, in western semiotic ideology, clothes are conceived as images (Goodrich, 1998), they are intended as a vehicle for meanings: they signify structures behind what is represented, irrespective of the modality of the subject/object relation. Hence, images, symbols and metaphors do not only 'differentiate' and shape the public space, they also allow people to give a meaning free from any context:

> [t]he process of signification is both rational and clear. It is assumed that a given sign signifies something that is clearly 'religious'. What is set aside in this assumption, however, is the entire realm of ongoing discourses and practices that provide authoritative meanings. The precision and fixity accorded to the relationship of signification is always an arbitrary act and often a spurious one where embodied language is concerned. What is signified by the headscarf is not some historical reality (the evolving Islamic tradition) but another sign (the eternally fixed 'Islamic religion') which, despite its overflowing character, is used to give the 'Islamic veil' a stable meaning (Asad, 2006, p. 97).

Hence, if the power of symbols lies in their capacity to evoke a static belonging, then the veil has the power to evoke the 'Islamic veil', so "more than an image, the veil is an imaginary – a shrouded difference waiting to be unveiled, to be brought into the light of reason, and made indifferent" (Asad, 2006, p. 100). In essence, in the western/Christian/secular imaginary, the veil "can only symbolize the world of authority and tradition that already stands in a false relation to history and requisite progress: its proper meaning is decided by a prior verdict, namely, that this tradition (often glossed as literalist) must be destroyed in order for reason, culture, and the free spirit to grasp the true meaning of religion" (Mahmood, 2006, pp. 343–344).

By contrast, although the veil as a cultural/religious symbol has been "constructed by and through various and conflicting discourses surrounding ideas of nation, culture, personhood, and power as well as gender" (Hirschmann, 2009, p. 177), what I have tried to show is that the veiled woman, intended as a 'cultural/religious other', should be distinguished from the 'veiled' woman as a subject of culture and history within historical heterogeneous non-liberal discourses (Mohanty, 2003). In light of this, the western semiotic division between signifier and signified "fail[s] to realize that signs and symbols are only arbitrarily linked to the abstractions that humans have come to revere and regard as sacred" (Mahmood, 2009b, p. 73). In fact, my analysis suggests that many Muslim women who wear the veil as an act of piety do not want to communicate something; rather, for them, the veil is a tool to achieve a specific selfhood, hence rituals should not be understood only through their merely symbolic meaning (as the revelation of a written text), but as instrumental in shaping the interiority of the individual. Monastic life as exposed by Agamben (2013) and Asad (1987) shows that specific daily rituals were used as a tool to form moral dispositions (in particular the virtue of obedience) that constitute the virtuous religious subject. This understanding is mirrored in Mahmood's study (2005) of the piety women in Egypt, where the practice of veiling is understood as a tool to acquire the value of modesty and therefore to shape the subject's interiority. This comprehension of the relation between the body and clothes by both Franciscans and women of the piety movement is not new: according to Plutarch (1924), Romans would cover their heads when worshipping, but not in front of respectful and honourable men. Recalling Dionysius of Halicarnassus, he hypothesized that the Romans' use of the veil was not a 'sign of' respect or modesty, but a 'means to' protect the worshipper from the gaze of the enemy, considered a bad omen. Hence, by veiling during sacrifices to the gods, Romans did not aim to protect their body from the enemy's gaze, but to hide the gaze of the worshipper from any alien body: "the veil was not meant to divert the attention of alien spectators, but to create a prestigious, sacral curtain around the worshipper" (Leone, 2012, p. 4). Hence, veiling was a device to establish a relation with the deity, where bodies gave life to things, and vice-versa (Esposito, 2015). In this process, the meaning of a specific performance cannot be separated from that of the intention and emotions of the performer: rather, it is exactly the interrelation between meaning, intentions and emotions that is central. As Asad (1987) argues,

> although the formation of moral sentiments is dependent on a signifying medium, we cannot read off that formation from the system of significations that may be authoritatively identified and isolated as a distinctive semiotic phenomenon. The reading is a product of social discipline, and 'the text', the symbol, the rite, is the product of (varyingly) disciplined performers who discourse with one another in historically determinate ways (p. 165).

In other words, rituals are not to be seen as a symbolic text to be interpreted, but as processes of the individual's formation (Asad, 1987). In light of this, what is at stake in the European decisions to ban the headscarf is the (western/secular) implied duality between signifier and signified, and the association between the wearing of particular attire and specific 'desires' as it is presumed that "the wearer's act of displaying the sign [...] incorporates the actor's will to display it – and therefore becomes part of what the headscarf meant" (Asad, 2006, p. 97). In the case of the headscarf ban, the Muslim gendered identity becomes central in the meaning attributed to the headscarf to display 'that' particular identity, namely a fixed and monolithic, backward Muslim tradition. By giving a fixed definition to the practice of veiling, western judges have eluded the gender dimension of the problem, so not only does the 'veil' emerge as a 'fantasy', but also the (Muslim) 'woman' becomes an 'imaginary objectified body', a mere carrier of specific cultural values. It is through the definition of veiling as a 'symbol', a 'sign of', that the 'covered body' becomes something static, a symbol of a specific cultural belonging, an 'object'.

The victimization and objectification of Muslim women operated by European judges has become a weapon to disempower, rather than empower them. Studies have found out that the objectification experienced by women contributes disproportionally to the rise of mental problems (such as depression and eating disorders) (Fredrickson & Roberts, 1997; Swim et al., 2001). Indeed, women internalise objectification experiences, changing their perspectives on their own bodies by excessively focusing on the evaluation of their appearance, and producing bodily shame and anxiety (which results from measuring oneself against an interiorised standard) (Fredrickson & Roberts, 1997). For Mackinnon (1989), "women's intimate experience of sexual objectification [...] is definitive of and synonymous with women's lives as gender female" because women "can grasp self only as thing" (p. 124). Since women's body emerges as an object, women are forbidden their full expression. Nussbaum (1995) identifies seven major implications of women's objectification which, I believe, are evident in the representation of the veil as intrinsically other: 'instrumentality' (as Muslim women are treated as a useful tool to strengthen the political antagonism between the east and the west); 'denial of autonomy' (as Muslim women have been seen as incapable of freely choosing to veil); 'inertness' (as Muslim women have been seen as subjects without agency); 'fungibility' (as Muslim women are seen through their function in their community and not as independent subjects); 'violability' (as Muslim women have been seen as subjects lacking integrity and so as enemies); 'ownership' (because Muslim women have been treated as belonging to something, denying their plural subjectivities and independence); and 'denial of subjectivity' (as the feelings and voices of Muslim women have not been taken into account). In this process of objectification, women's body is 'naturalized', and their 'desires' turn into something 'neutral' to be defined by the appropriate authority. In fact, by defining the veil as a 'religious' symbol, European courts operated a detachment of the subject from its 'object': desire, in this context, becomes something neutral to be defined by the state, so the object of the desire (the veil) can be defined as 'religious' or 'irreligious' and not any more through a socio-psychological approach (Asad, 2006, p. 94).

For Asad (2006), the definition of veiling as a symbol of something intrinsically other can be seen as an *exercise of sovereign power* as it is the sovereign that decides which symbol is to be regarded as 'religious' and, consequently, it acquires the power to shape the public sphere. Since the definition of 'religious symbols' becomes a juridical matter, the sovereign gains the teleological and transcendental power to impose those definitions on its subjects. The necessity for a sovereign power to decide upon exceptions is made clear in the Stasi Commission's report, which points out that the donning of the veil overloads teachers and public officers who "are often left isolated, in a difficult environment" (*Commission De Reflexion*, 2003, p. 31) to define which 'religious symbol' can be legitimate in a public school.

Thus, if it is the sovereign power that decides exceptions and defines symbols, then "all modern concepts of the state are secularized theological concepts" (Kelly, 2004, p. 128) as the state assumes the teleological duty of defining images and metaphors in the public sphere. As Hobbes (1991) argued,

> we are not everyone to make our own private reason or conscience, but the public reason, that is the reason of God's supreme lieutenant, judge; and indeed we have made him judge already, if we have given him a sovereign power to do all that is necessary for our peace and defence (Ch. XXXVII).

If the sovereign has the absolute power to decide on everything, it also has the authority to decide on religious symbols in the public sphere: therefore, the 'exercise of sovereignty' becomes a necessary act to maintain 'peace and order' where "public order refers not merely to security or the absence of material disorder, but also to all the conditions of life in a well ordered society" (Troper, 2014, pp. 151–2). In other words, the state, the *Leviathan*, which embodies an absolute transcendental and abstract power, also defines symbols and their place in the public sphere. As religion directs people to other loyalties and other 'worldly-powers', the state has to define its place in the worldly care of its population in order to assure the loyalty of the Christian/secular law's subject to a transcendental absolute power embodied in the sovereign. In this sense, the separation between spiritual and temporal power is blurred, as it is the state that regulates not only the public but also the private lives of its subjects. As Mahmood (2006) puts it,

> the ongoing regulation of religious life through juridical and legislative means suggests a far more porous relationship than the doctrine of secularism suggests [...] [it] shows how a self-avowed secular state has come to define what religious and nonreligious attire is in the public domain (something normatively considered a matter of personal choice within liberalism) (p. 325).

This is clear in the analysis of the '*hijab* cases' where, on the one hand, liberal polity tries to operate a separation between private and public, spiritual and temporal, while on the other, the state takes the responsibility for creating 'Christian/secular' citizens by regulating their private lives, ethics and sentiments. In light of this, citizenship emerges not as a natural right, but as something constructed by an act of sovereignty through the force of the rules of law, where the Christian/secular/liberal citizen emerges as "a particular kind of contradictory individual – one who is morally sovereign and yet obedient to the laws of the secular republic, flexible and tolerant yet fiercely principled" (Asad, 2006, p. 104); a 'citizen' able to take part in the 'game of the signs' and show his/her loyalty to an absolute sovereign power through an exercise of sovereignty and the inclusion of the individual *within* the pale of the law (Esmeir, 2012). Secular/liberalism defines its subjects and forms a specific Christian/secular citizen loyal to a centralized transcendental sovereign power: paradoxically, the sovereign state "realizes its universal character through a particular (female Muslim) identity, that is, a particular psychological internality" (Asad, 2006, p. 98).

By defining what the appropriate attire is for Muslim women, not only did the sovereign state remove many Muslim women in Europe from the public sphere, but it also brought private sentiments into the public scrutiny of the secular polity and, by so doing, it operates a re-configuration of religious practices in the public sphere (Mahmood, 2009a). Through the juridical regulation of women's attire, western judges tried to regulate specific kinds of sociability and to bring private sentiments into the public sphere. However, by so doing, European judges not only exclude different concepts of freedom and agency and different forms of 'humanities' (Esmeir, 2006, 2012), but they also operate a re-configuration of religious practices and sentiments in the 'modern/secular world' (Mahmood, 2015). Hence, more than a crusade against a visible/invisible evil, the juridical decisions over the veil reveal not only the contradictions inherent to the human rights discourse which claims to safeguard dignity for all (Lisbet Christoffersen, 2010, p. 65), but also the inadequacy of western/secular universal(ist) discourse within pluralistic contexts. They disclose the fragility, vulnerability and paradoxes of the implicit assumptions of a liberal universalist thought in search of a universal and abstract identity. This, however, has resulted in the exclusion of Muslim veiled women from the secular public sphere: this exclusion, operated by and through law, has been made possible through the application of a specific semiotic ideology which has objectified Muslim women by rendering them the 'other', and by trapping them in a fundamental dichotomy between 'us' and 'them', 'Islamic' and Christian' religious symbols, gender equality and women's oppression.

5.4 Excluding the 'Racialised Other'

In *Orientalism*, Said (1994) begins with an epigram from Karl Marx: '[t]hey cannot represent themselves; they must be represented' (p. xiii). He argues that Marx's statement highlights the reality about western representations of oriental societies, which often rests on a pattern of cultural hegemony. For Said (1994), the dominance of European colonial powers, primarily Great Britain and France, over subjugated populations is what allowed the colonised to be depicted in a way that reinforces "the idea of European [superiority] in comparison with [...] non-European peoples and cultures" (p. 7). His words capture a fundamental point of today's western discourse concerning the veil: that the definition and re-definition of western/secular/liberal notions is dependent on a dichotomous relation established with the 'oriental other'. This relation constructs Muslim veiled women as a monolithic other, disclosing a western/secular/liberal form of sovereignty that is at odds with the plurality of contemporary European societies.

For Mancini (2014a), the construction of Muslim women as the 'other' could be inscribed in Schmitt's analysis of western democracies. For Schmitt (1976), what is important in a democracy is the unity of a people, which is based on some sort of 'substantial homogeneity' and is symbolized in the figure of the sovereign. For Schmitt (1985), the homogeneity and unity of a people is based on a false illusion, a 'fabrication', a 'false consciousness' constructed in order to maintain a homogeneous 'imagined' unity; as Anderson (1991) argues, communities "are to be distinguished, not by their falsity/genuineness, but by the style in which they are imagined" (p. 6). Thus, the unity and homogeneity of a community is established through a certain form of 'affective identity' which is attained through shared memories as well as a present will to live together (Renan, 1947): on the one hand, the will to live together and the defence of this 'togetherness' enables the principle of 'unity' to become the normative principle of legitimacy expressed in the 'right of belonging', while on the other, 'shared memory' provides for the need of affective source of national consent by binding people together in a unified fashion. Goodrich's work (1995) reveals how this 'affective attachment' is formed through the control and juridical regulation of symbols and metaphors in the public sphere. As a matter of fact, historically, the appropriation of images and icons was compounded with the implementation of rules related to clothes (Goodrich, 1998; Hunt, 1996). For Schmitt (1976), in order to create a unified homogeneity, politics needs to create a contrast, a differentiation, between homogeneity and plurality because pluralism is the enemy of democracy, threatening the sovereignty of the state and, at the same time, the existence of a (valuable) concept of politics.

The battle between 'homogeneity' and 'plurality' is particularly evident in the *Sahin* case (2005) in which the court repeatedly emphasized the impossibility of reconciling Turkey's secular-liberal and democratic values with extremist (Islamic) religious movements by referring to the Refah Party that, based on the court reasoning, attempted to introduce *sharia* law which "would oblige individuals to obey static rules of law imposed by the religion" (*Refah v Turkey*, 2003, para 70). However, the court confused Refah neo-Ottomanism, which calls for a plurality of legal systems based on personal status, with Islamist fundamentalists who call for the establishment of an Islamic empire where jurisdiction is territorial. Indeed, with regard to the distinction between personal/communitarian Islamic law and territorial/individualistic western law, it is clear that the ECtHR's decision to dismantle Refah was partly based on the ground that the party was planning to set up a plurality of legal systems. In the case, the court's ignorance of the plurality of Islamic traditions regarding the veil was compounded by its rejection of a plurality of legal systems within the same territory *qua* political unit. It is clear, therefore, that in seeking to forcibly expose Turkish women's bodies to their natural rights, the ECtHR was also seeking to subjugate them under the logic of singular state sovereignty. This shows that what really threatens western societies is not a veiled woman, but the pluralism she represents. Islam is not only a pluralistic religion, as it is open to interpretation and is praxiologically lived and experienced differently in different cultural and historical contexts (Dupret, 2007), but also the practice of veiling itself takes different shapes, colours and meanings which mirror different normative choices (El Guindi, 1999; Mernissi, 2011).

The European construction of the veiled woman as the other from which western societies must be defended, mirrors Schmitt's (1985) conceptualisation of the contraposition between friends and enemies. According to Schmitt's analysis, political communities are bounded by a fundamental distinction between 'friend' and 'enemy', 'insider' and 'outsider': "'friend' and 'enemy', ultimately, have no content in themselves, they are oppositional positions capable of unifying the members of a group" (Mancini, 2014b, p. 128). In fact, a strong homogeneous and united community needs the identification and elimination or eradication of the 'other', the 'enemy': in light of this, the very idea of democracy is based on the concept of exclusion, of 'containing'/eliminating/hiding the differences and pluralities that ultimately threaten the monolithic character of liberal democracies by threatening their (imagined) homogeneity and unity (Schmitt, 2007). As a matter of fact, the people of a nation are bound by symbolic boundaries represented by the presence (as a negation) of the 'other' in the public sphere which challenges the national homogeneous identity of a people. Only in this way are territorial and personal boundaries secured by an exercise of sovereignty in defence of democracy.

Nowadays, Islam has become the 'other' and the female headscarf the symbol of 'otherness'. In fact, since the 1970s, sociologists (Barker, 1981) have noticed that racist discourses based on biological/ethnic claims have been replaced by different, and more subtle, forms of discrimination based on cultural belonging. As Balibar (1991) argues, it is not any more the category of race, but that of 'immigrant', understood as "the result of their belonging to historical cultures" (p. 22), which enables racist discourses: this, in turn,

> entails a superimposition of different dimensions of 'otherness' that exacerbates issues of boundaries, accommodation and incorporation. The immigrant, the religious, the racial, and the socio-economic dispriviledged 'other' all tend to coincide. Moreover, all those dimensions of 'otherness' now become superimposed upon Islam, so that Islam become utterly 'other' (Casanova, 2006, p. 242).

If Islam is the 'other', the veiled woman, who supposedly represents backward Islamic values incompatible with western democratic principles, is the symbol of this 'otherness': in this way, Muslim (veiled) women have been forcibly included in a symbolic and imaginary dichotomy between 'friend' and 'enemy', 'insider' and 'outsider'.

This dichotomy is clear in the analysis of the '*hijab* cases'. In the *Begum* case (2006), for instance, the dichotomy was between the *jilbab* (considered a symbol of radical Islam) and the *shalwar kameez* (considered the most appropriate uniform for Muslim women by three local *imams*). As Mancini (2008) argues, this is indicative of western binary perceptions of Muslims, as the court implied the existence of two kinds of Muslim: the one 'accommodated' in liberal/democratic societies, and Islamic fundamentalists from whom western democracy must be defended. My anthropological study reveals, however, that there are many kinds of Muslim and three local *imams* cannot decide what is the best attire for Muslim women (Mancini, 2008). The dichotomy between a 'tolerant' west and an 'intolerant' east is mirrored in a passage of the French resolution over the practice of veiling, which stresses the "power and the duty we have to oppose ideologies and ways of thinking that one can only qualify as 'barbarian', in the sense that they deny the idea of progress, of civilization, of democracy, of sex-based equality [...] it's our value system which is at issue [...] this is our Republic being tested in this way" (*Rapport d'information* no. 2262, 2010, 22f). This dichotomy is also visible in a bill supported by the right-wing party and the Christian Democrats in Holland which states that:

> The burqa […] is diametrically opposed to modernity. It expresses the rejection of essential Western values and norms, including the equality of men and women […]. The burqa, then, is a symbol of the oppression of women […]. Hence, wearing a burqa […] in the public space is contrary to the rule of law in a democracy […][t]he evidence gathered […] shows the difficulties and the deep unease felt by people who every day are in contact with the public […]. Barbarity is growing. Violence and threats are frequent […] conflicts degenerate particularly in the hospitals, as in the case of the women's hospital in Bron, where a man refused to have his wife attended by a male doctor during her child-delivery. This is not acceptable, and each time such an attack takes place, it is our living together based on the Spirit of the Enlightenment that is violated (cited in Moors, 2009, p. 402).

The statement is based on the dichotomy between 'modernity' and 'backwardness', 'barbarity' and 'Enlightenment', linking veiling with women's submission to men and lack of autonomy (Mancini, 2012). Similarly, in the *Begum* case, Lady Hale framed the veil through the dichotomy between freedom and patriarchy, advancing a very western/liberal model of women's emancipation; in fact, on the one hand she recognises that the *jilbab* worn by Shabina does not endanger gender equality, while on the other, she notes that the school should help children to 'choose' between 'their' and 'our' culture. Likewise, the German interior minister, Thomas de Maiziere, declared that the burqa "does not fit into our society … this is why we demand that you show your face" (Britton, 2019). In Germany, the idea that a veiled woman could play a role in the education of German children (Weber, 2012) has led to a different treatment of Christian and Islamic symbols. In fact, after the *Ludin* case, many German *Landers,* while allowing the display of Christian symbols, adopted laws that banned Islamic symbols in public schools. In fact, as I have argued, the legal language adopted by German courts has constructed Islam as the incarnation of un-democratic values and Christianity as the symbol of liberal democracy, although its relationship with the doctrine of secularism has not been seen to need examination.

Those legal decisions illustrate how the concept of 'radical otherness' (what Kristeva (1991) calls 'the abject') is established through the boundary expressed by the law: because veiling has been defined as a practice that contradicts secular values, Muslim women have become an imaginary enemy from which western/secular/liberal societies must be defended. Once the division is established between 'friend' and 'enemy', the 'abject', the 'stranger', must be excluded from civil liberties and civil rights as their plurality of cultures does not belong to liberal democracies. In order to maintain democracy, the boundary between 'insider' and 'outsider' becomes crucial and the identification, and expulsion of the 'other' from the public sphere necessary (Cash, 2004). As Fadil (2011) puts it in relation to the banning of the full-face veil in Belgium, "the exclusion of face-veiled women as 'abject other' enables a minimal sense of 'we-ness' in the fractured Belgium but also in other western-European countries where citizenship is increasingly cast in cultural terms" (p. 88). This is exemplified in the declaration of Sisco's mayor, Ange-Pierre Vivoni, during the '*burkini* affair' in France: he stated that the ban "has nothing to do with racism…I'm not against maghrebins (French word for people from Northwest Africa) or Arabs. I'm not an anti-Semite or anti-Arab, it is part of a battle for unity, for unity of people" (Britton, 2019).

These representations of sexed secular subjects indicate that symbols are constructed in order to create homogeneity in contraposition with an imaginary 'enemy', which is, at least, the 'plurality of the other'. In fact, it is exactly through the representation of veiling as incompatible with western secularity, and the veiled Muslim woman as the 'other' who endangers the principle of gender equality, that a 'pure' western secular identity is established and maintained because, as Benhabib argues (2002), it is through the symbology attached to women's body that ideas of the 'self' and the 'other' come to be constructed. Guénif-Souilamas (2013) shows wonderfully how the link between the conceptualization of the Muslim woman as the other and the protection of the French Republic works to protect France from its own multiculturalism. The mythology of a French essence is based on the idea that feminism and secularism are synonymous and that the liberation of western women from oppressive patriarchal norms has been reached thanks to secularism. This marriage has been constantly re-staged in French history, from the colonial period until today, in order to strengthen the unity of the Republic through women's body, where 'Frenchness' has become the test that minorities should pass in order to have the privilege of French citizenship (Guénif-Souilamas, 2013). This is exemplified by something that happened in 2008 when a Moroccan woman, mother of three children and married to a French citizen, was denied French citizenship because, based on the *Conseil D'Etat* reasoning, her full-face-veil did not fulfil the 'condition of assimilation', which is considered an essential requirement to gain French citizenship (Chrisafis, 2008). However, while the court did not grant her citizenship, the 'secular values' of her (Muslim) husband were not taken into consideration: hence, the link drawn by the court between secularism, the Republic and women's body indicates that only women should conform to the principle of secularism and gender equality (Weil, 2014), posing women's sexuality at the centre of western discourse concerning the veil. This reveals that the narrative on the veil in the west has been used as the framework through which to disempower Muslim women by blaming Islam, but also to survey and manage gender and national differences, where the visibility of women's body has "become the ground on which nation and citizens are established as civilized and modern, while Muslims and immigrants remain trapped in the pre-modern" (Razack, 2007, p. 150), represented by their covered bodies. It is exactly through these boundaries, expressed symbolically by the veil, that the (fixed) identity of the 'self' and the 'other' emerges, strengthening, through feminist rhetoric, imagined identitarian boundaries, and reinforcing western gender oppression through the political use of women's body (Mancini, 2012): the necessary exercise of sovereignty operated by the authority to bind Muslim women to a fixed subjectivity can be seen as an effort to maintain differences and, thus, a homogeneous and unified democracy.

In light of this, European legal decisions on the limitation of civil liberty and religious freedom show how 'defence mechanisms' tend, on the one hand, to belittle the image of the 'other', as 'veiled women' are seen as victims or brainwashed, while on the other, to assert a right of violence and aggressivity in limiting the personal sphere of the female legal subject. This is translated in the law's double movement of inclusion/exclusion, personalisation/de-personalisation (Esposito, 2015); in fact, as I have argued, by shaping and protecting a specific female subject, western secular and Human Rights law excludes the 'other' by 'de-humanising' it, while it 're-inscribes' the 'other' into a liberal trajectory by 're- humanising' it (Esmeir, 2006). The result of this 'law's double movement' is that

> religious freedom as a public, mainly collective, institution has been transformed into fragments of a diffuse 'right to identity' that blurs the line between the public and private domains. The public dimension of 'civil rights' shrinks and re-emerges as a diffuse 'right to recognition' of the freely chosen identity by public authorities and, finally, by every individual (Ladeur & Augsberg, 2007, p. 36).

Hence, on the one hand, by determining forms and languages in advance, the rules of law form a specific Christian/liberal/secular female subject and her being, her desires, while on the other, it takes significant steps in limiting the personal freedom of Muslim women by representing the constructed desires of a majority of European people in search of an abstract, unified, and universal identity.

In fact, if metaphors produce the necessary emotional attachment to legal obedience and political love, then the visible has to mirror a specific order of power and imagination and the legal subject should mirror a legitimate order of thought (Goodrich, 1995). Since democracy is based on the unity of an (imagined) community (Schmitt, 2007), then symbols and metaphors, which form and strengthen the unity and identity of a people (Goodrich, 1995), have to be regulated in order to save the homogeneity and unity of European democracy. For Schmitt (1985), to defend democracy, the rules of law are not enough as they are impotent to protect the homogeneity of the nation, so an act of sovereignty becomes necessary. The sovereign intervenes normatively exactly where the (procedural) law fails:

> if sovereignty as the 'highest legal power' sees itself as the need to exercise reflective judgement, then sovereignty as 'actual power' is concerned with survival and must be defined as the paradoxical self preservation of the law by extra-legal means, or rather, by the legal suspension of the law (Rasch, 2000, p. 9).

For Agamben (1998), the sovereign power establishes and reproduces itself exactly through the creation of a political system based on the exclusion of 'bare life' which is achieved through the continuous enactment of exceptions to the law. Through the state of exception, the sovereign traces the boundaries between inside and outside and defines which rights/rules could be assigned to different groups of individuals. In light of this, it is the exception that reproduces and sustains the juridico-political order (a biopolitical body) which is based on the inclusion of bare life through its exclusion (Agamben, 2005): as Agamben (2005) highlights, the relation between power and life is a 'relation of exception' or a 'relation of ban' from the political community and the law, which indicates exactly a relation of inclusion through exclusion. However, for Agamben (2005), the human that is located within this 'relation of banning' is not free from the law: through its own suspension in the state of exception, the "law encompasses living beings" (Agamben, 2005, p. 3) who are bound to the law and yet abandoned by it. In this way the human is included in the law through its exclusion, as in the case of veiled Muslim women in Europe who have been included within the pale of the law to be excluded from the public sphere.

Notably, "while the exception is an inclusive exclusion, [...] the example instead functions as an exclusive inclusion" (Agamben, 1998, p. 21). In light of this, form of life represents the only way to break the 'relation of banning' established by the sovereign exception. In fact, form of life shows the possibility of understanding and experiencing life as an example beyond oppositional categories: form of life does not mean the impossibility of transcending one's culture and tradition, nor of affirming the necessity to tolerate diverse forms of life (which is the logic of liberal/multicultural form of sovereignty based on the recognition and representation of various identities), but of the co-existence of a multitude of singularities without identities (Agamben, 1993). Form of life, then, does not deny the different forms within it, but contains all of them, overcoming western dichotomies between life and norm, public and private, veil and un-veil. For Agamben (2014), while, on the one hand, the politicization of life increasingly inscribes life into a political order, then to resist the sovereign ban the individual should establish itself in opposition to western dichotomies. By overcoming western dichotomies, the individual transforms itself into a form of life (intended as a practice of the self), freeing itself from the state (that is withdrawing from codified forms of belonging), and becoming an unfigurable singularity (Agamben, 1993). This is why the matter of the veil has attracted so much attention from legal and political authorities: in its plurality, veiling escapes the logic of western sovereignty that creates, names, defines, and hierarchizes different identities to be managed based on Christian/secular/liberal logic. Since veiled women disclose a new relation between humanity and rights, a relation free from the western dichotomous construction of the secular legal and religious subject, they represent what Agamben (2000) calls the possibility of thinking form and life as a unicity and therefore the possibility of bringing to an end a sovereign power which founded its legitimation in the separation of spheres, such as the separation of the sphere of naked life from the one of forms of life. More than that, form of life discloses the paradoxes of the western/liberal/secular system and its inability to deal with cultural and religious difference.

References

Abu-Lughod, L. (2000). *Veiled sentiments: Updated with a new preface: Honor and poetry in a Bedouin society* (2nd, Rev. ed.). University of California Press.

Abu-Lughod, L. (2002). Do Muslim women really need saving? Anthropological reflections on cultural relativism and its others. *American Anthropologist, 104*(3), 783–790.

Agamben, G. (1993). *The coming community* (Vol. 1). University of Minnesota Press.

Agamben, G. (1998). *Homo sacer: Sovereign power and bare life*. Stanford University Press.

Agamben, G. (2000). *Means without end: Notes on politics*. University of Minnesota Press.

Agamben, G. (2005). *State of exception*. University of Chicago Press.

Agamben, G. (2013). *The highest poverty: Monastic rules and form-of-life*. Stanford University Press.

Agamben, G. (2014). *L'Uso dei Corpi*. Neri Pozza.

Alvi, A. (2013). Concealment and revealment. *Current Anthropology, 54*(2), 177–199.

Anderson, B. (1991). *Imagined communities: Reflections on the origin and spread of nationalism*. Verso.

Aristotle. (1941). *The basic works of Aristotle*. Random House.
Asad, T. (1987). On ritual and discipline in medieval Christian monasticism. *Economic and Society, 16*(2), 159–203.
Asad, T. (1993). *Genealogies of religion*. Johns Hopkins University Press.
Asad, T. (2001). Reading a modern classic: WC Smith's "the meaning and end of religion". *History of Religions, 40*(3), 205–222.
Asad, T. (2003). *Formations of the secular: Christianity, Islam, modernity*. Stanford University Press.
Asad, T. (2006). French secularism and the "Islamic veil affair". *Hedgehog Review, 8*(1/2), 93.
Asad, T. (2009a). *Genealogies of religion: Discipline and reasons of power in Christianity and Islam*. JHU Press.
Asad, T. (2009b). The idea of an anthropology of Islam. *Qui Parle*, 1–30.
Authier, P., February 6, M. G. U., & 2019. (2019, February 7). Quebec minister for women stands by belief that hijabs are oppressive | Montreal Gazette. *Montreal Gazette*. https://montrealgazette.com/news/quebec/quebec-minister-for-women-stands-by-belief-that-hijabs-are-oppressive
Balibar, E. (1991). Is there a neo-racism? In E. Balibar & I. M. Wallerstein (Eds.), *Nation, class, ambiguous identities*. Verso.
Barker, M. (1981). *The new racism: Conservatives and the ideology of the tribe*. Junction Books.
Benhabib, S. (2002). *The claims of culture: Equality and diversity in the global era*. Princeton University Press.
Berlin, I. (1971). Two concepts of liberty. In I. Berlin (Ed.), *Four essays on liberty*. Oxford University Press.
Breeden, A., & Blaise, L. (2016, August 26). Court overturns 'burkini' ban in French Town. *The New York Times*. http://www.nytimes.com/2016/08/27/world/europe/france-burkini-ban.html
Britton, B. (2019, August). *What makes the burqa and burkini so controversial? – CNN*. CNN. https://edition.cnn.com/2016/08/19/europe/burqa-burkini-bans/index.html
Brown, W. (2008). *Regulating aversion: Tolerance in the age of identity and empire*. Princeton University Press.
Brown, M. (2009, October 7). *School bans "too tight" trousers*. Express.Co.Uk. https://www.express.co.uk/news/uk/132481/School-bans-too-tight-trousers
Brown, W. (2015). Religious freedom's oxymoronic edge. In W. F. Sullivan, E. S. Hurd, S. Mahmood, & P. G. Danchin (Eds.), *Politics of religious freedom* (pp. 324–334). Chicago University Press.
Butler, J. (1997). *Excitable speech: A politics of the performative*. Routledge.
Butler, J., & others. (2011). *Bodies that matter: On the discursive limits of sex*. Taylor & Francis.
Casanova, J. (2006). The long, difficult, and tortuous journey of Turkey into Europe and the dilemmas of European civilization. *Constellations, 13*(2), 234–247.
Cash, J. (2004). The political/cultural unconscious and the process of reconciliation. *Postcolonial Studies, 7*(2), 165–175.
Chehabi, H. E. (1993). Staging the emperor's new clothes: Dress codes and nation-building under Reza Shah. *Iranian Studies, 26*(3–4), 209–233.
Chemaly, S. (2016). France's burkini ban exposes how women are still violently oppressed in the name of nationalism. *Quartz*. http://qz.com/767796/frances-burkini-ban-has-exposed-the-way-women-are-oppressed-in-the-name-of-nationalism/
Chrisafis, A. (2008, July 12). France rejects Muslim woman over radical practice of Islam. *The Guardian*. https://www.theguardian.com/world/2008/jul/12/france.islam
Christoffersen, L. (2010). Is Shari'a law, religion or combination? European legal discourses on Shari'a. In J. S. Nielsen & L. Christoffersen (Eds.), *'Shari'a as discourse*. Ashgate Publishing Limited.
Davies, B. (2005). *Aquinas's summa theologiae*. Rowman & Littlefield Publishers.
Douglas, M. (2002). *Natural symbols*. Routledge.
Dupret, B. (2007). What is Islamic law? A praxiological answer and an Egyptian case study. *Theory, Culture & Society, 24*(2), 79–100.

El Guindi, F. (1999). *Veil: Modesty, privacy, and resistance*. Berg.
Elster, J. (1983). *Sour grapes: Studies in the subversion of rationality*. Cambridge University Press.
Esmeir, S. (2006). On making dehumanization possible. *PMLA*, 1544–1551.
Esmeir, S. (2012). *Juridical humanity: A colonial history*. Stanford University Press.
Esposito, R. (2015). *Persons and things: From the body's point of view*. Wiley.
Fadil, N. (2011). Not–/unveiling as an ethical practice. *Feminist Review, 98*(1), 83–109.
Fadil, N. (2018, May 24). *Taming the Muslim woman – The Immanent Frame*. The Immanent Frame. Secularism, Religion, and the Public Sphere. https://tif.ssrc.org/2018/05/24/taming-the-muslim-woman/
Fernando, M. L. (2010). Reconfiguring freedom: Muslim piety and the limits of secular law and public discourse in France. *American Ethnologist, 37*(1), 19–35.
Fernando, M. L. (2017). Intimacy surveilled: Religion, sex, and secular cunning. In D. L. Boisvert & C. Daniel-Hughes (Eds.), *The Bloomsbury reader in religion, sexuality, and gender*. Bloomsbury Academic.
Fletcher, D. (2013). *Jeremy Forrest's former school bans pupils from wearing short skirts and tight trousers—Mirror Online*. The Mirror. https://www.mirror.co.uk/news/uk-news/jeremy-forrests-former-school-bans-2138344
Foucault, M. (1981). *The history of sexuality*. Penguin Books.
Foucault, M. (1997). On the genealogy of ethics: An overview of work in progress. In M. Foucault & J. D. Faubion (Eds.), *Ethics: Subjectivity and truth* (Vol. 1). New York Press.
France warns of Muslim stigmatisation amid burkini ban. (2016). Al Jazeera. http://www.aljazeera.com/news/2016/08/france-warns-muslim-stigmatisation-burkini-ban-160824191045697.html
Fredrickson, B. L., & Roberts, T.-A. (1997). Objectification theory: Toward understanding women's lived experiences and mental health risks. *Psychology of Women Quarterly, 21*(2), 173–206.
Elaine Ganley. (2016). *Why France thinks the burkini is an attack on secularism | The Independent*. http://www.independent.co.uk/news/world/europe/burkini-ban-france-cannes-nice-muslim-islam-beach-french-secularism-a7206971.html
Göle, N. (2010). Manifestations of the religious-secular divide: Self, state, and the public sphere. In L. Cady & E. Hurd (Eds.), *Comparative secularisms in a global age* (pp. 41–53). Palgrave Macmillan.
Goodrich, P. (1995). *Oedipus lex: Psychoanalysis, history, law*. University of California Press.
Goodrich, P. (1998). Signs taken for wonders: Community, identity, and a history of sumptuary law. *Law & Social Inquiry, 23*(3), 707–728.
Guénif-Souilamas, N. (2013). On French religions and their renewed embodiments. In L. E. Cady & T. Fessenden (Eds.), *Religion, the secular, and the politics of sexual difference* (pp. 195–208). Columbia University Press.
Hamid, T. (2015). A strategic plan to defeat radical Islam. In L. Fenstermacher (Ed.), *Countering violent extremism scientific methods & strategies* (pp. 72–78). Air Force Research Laboratory.
Hegel, G. W. F. (1991). *The philosophy of history*. Prometheus Books.
Hirschkind, C. (2006). *The ethical soundscape: Cassette sermons and Islamic counterpublics*. Columbia University Press.
Hirschkind, C. (2011). Is there a secular body? *Cultural Anthropology, 26*(4), 633–647.
Hirschmann, N. J. (1997). Eastern veiling, Western freedom? *The Review of Politics, 59*(03), 461–488.
Hirschmann, N. J. (2009). *The subject of liberty: Toward a feminist theory of freedom*. Princeton University Press.
Hobbes, T. (1991). *Leviathan*. Cambridge University Press.
Hoodfar, H. (1997). The veil in their minds and on our heads: Veiling practices and Muslim women. In L. Lowe & D. Lloyd (Eds.), *The politics of culture in the shadow of capital*. Press.
Hunt, A. (1996). *Governance of the consuming passions: A history of sumptuary law*. Macmillan Press.
Husain, M. E., & Ayotte, K. J. (2005). Securing Afghan women: Neocolonialism, epistemic violence, and the rhetoric of the veil. *NWSA Journal, 17*(3), 112–133.

Jakobsen, J. (2010). Ethics after pluralism. In C. Bender & P. E. Klassen (Eds.), *After pluralism: Reimagining religious engagement*. Columbia University Press.
Joachim, H. H., & Rees, D. A. (1952). Aristotle: The Nicomachean ethics.
Keane, W. (2007). *Christian moderns: Freedom and fetish in the mission encounter*. University of California Press.
Keane, W. (2015). What is religious freedom supposed to free? In W. F. Sullivan, E. S. Hurd, S. Mahmood, & P. G. Danchin (Eds.), *Politics of religious freedom* (pp. 57–65). University of Chicago Press.
Kelly, D. (2004). Carl Schmitt's political theory of representation. *Journal of the History of Ideas, 65*(1), 113–134.
Kristeva, J. (1991). *Strangers to ourselves*. Harvester Wheatsheaf.
Laborde, C. (2015). Protecting Freedom of religion in the secular age. In W. F. Sullivan, E. S. Hurd, S. Mahmood, & P. G. Danchin (Eds.), *Politics of religious freedom* (pp. 269–279). Chicago University Press.
Ladeur, K.-H., & Augsberg, I. (2007). Myth of the neutral state: The relationship between state and religion in the face of new challenges. *The German Law Journal, 8*, 143.
Lapidus, I. M. (1984). Knowledge, virtue and action: The classical Muslim conception of Adab and the nature of religious fulfilment in Islam. In B. D. Metcalf (Ed.), *Moral conduct and authority: The place of Adab in south Asian Islam* (pp. 36–61). University of California Press.
Leach, E. R. (2004). *Political systems of highland Burma: A study of Kachin social structure*. Berg.
Leone, M. (2012). Cultures of invisibility: The semiotics of the veil in early Christianity. *Gramma: Journal of Theory & Criticism, 20*.
MacKinnon, C. A. (1989). *Toward a feminist theory of the state*. Harvard University Press.
Mahmood, S. (2001). Feminist theory, embodiment, and the docile agent: Some reflections on the Egyptian Islamic revival. *Cultural Anthropology, 16*(2), 202–236.
Mahmood, S. (2005). *Politics of piety: The Islamic revival and the feminist subject*. Princeton University Press.
Mahmood, S. (2006). Secularism, hermeneutics, and empire: The politics of Islamic reformation. *Public Culture, 18*(2), 323.
Mahmood, S. (2009). Agency, performativity, and the feminist subject. In L. Sjorup & H. R. Christensen (Eds.), *Pieties and gender*. Brill.
Mahmood, S. (2009a). Religious reason and secular affect: An incommensurable divide? *Critical Inquiry, 35*(4), 836–862.
Mahmood, S. (2009b). Religious reason and secular affect: An incommensurable divide? In T. Asad, W. Brown, J. Butler, & S. Mahmood (Eds.), *In critique secular? Blasphemy, injury, and free speech*. University of California Press.
Mahmood, S. (2013). Sexuality and secularism. In L. E. Cady & T. Fessenden (Eds.), *Religion, the secular, and the politics of sexual difference*. Columbia University Press.
Mahmood, S. (2015). *Religious difference in a secular age*. Princeton University Press.
Mancini, S. (2008). Power of symbols and symbols as power: Secularism and religion as guarantors of cultural convergence. *The Cardozo Law Review, 30*, 2629.
Mancini, S. (2012). Patriarchy as the exclusive domain of the other: The veil controversy, false projection and cultural racism. *International Journal of Constitutional Law, 10*(2), 411–428.
Mancini, S. (2014a). *The tempting of Europe, the political seduction of the cross: A Schmittian reading of Christianity and Islam in European constitutionalism*. Oxford University Press.
Mancini, S. (2014b). The tempting of Europe, the political seduction of the cross: A Schmittian reading of Christianity and Islam in European constitutionalism. In S. Mancini & M. Rosenfeld (Eds.), *Constitutional secularism in an age of religious revival*. Oxford University Press.
Marx, K. (1978). On the Jewish question. In R. Tucker (Ed.), *The Marx-Engels Reader*. Norton.
Mauss, M. (1979). Body techniques. In M. Mauss (Ed.), *Sociology and psychology: Essays* (pp. 95–123). Routledge.
Mernissi, F. (2011). *Beyond the veil: Male-female dynamics in modern Muslim society* (New ed.). Saqi.

Mill, J. S. (1998). *On liberty: And other essays*. Oxford University Press.
Mohanty, C. T. (1988). Under Western eyes: Feminist scholarship and colonial discourses. *Feminist Review*, 61–88.
Mohanty, C. T. (2003). *Feminism without borders: Decolonizing theory, practicing solidarity*. Duke University.
Moors, A. (2009). The Dutch and the face-veil: The politics of discomfort. *Social Anthropology, 17*(4), 393–408.
Nussbaum, M. C. (1995). Objectification. *Philosophy & Public Affairs, 24*(4), 249–291.
Pasolini, P. P., & Hood, S. (1983). *Lutheran letters*. Carcanet.
Weil, P. (2014). Headscarf versus burqa. In S. Mancini & M. Rosenfeld (Eds.), *Constitutional secularism in an age of religious revival*. Press.
Plutarch. (1924). *Αιτια ρομαικα*. Clarendon Press.
Rahbari, R. (2000). Unveiling Muslim women: A trajectory of post-colonial culture. *Dialectical Anthropology, 25*(3), 321–332.
Rasch, W. (2000). Conflict as a vocation Carl Schmitt and the possibility of politics. *Theory, Culture & Society, 17*(6), 1–32.
Razack, S. (2007). *Casting out: The eviction of Muslims from Western law and politics*. University of Toronto Press.
Renan, E. (1947). In H. Psichari (Ed.), *Qu'est-ce qu'une nation?', Oeuvres completes de Ernest Renan* (Vol. 1). Calmann-Levy.
Rosenthal, F. (1960). *The Muslim concept of freedom prior to the nineteenth century*. Brill.
Roy, O. (1999). *Vers un islam Européen*. Esprit.
Said, E. (1994). *Orientalism*. Vintage.
Schmitt, C. (1976). *The concept of the political*. Rutgers University Press.
Schmitt, C. (1985). *Political theology: Four chapters on the concept of sovereignty*. MIT Press.
Schmitt, C. (2007). *Constitutional theory*. University of Chicago Press.
Scott, J. W. (2013). Secularism and gender equality. In L. E. Cady & T. Fessenden (Eds.), *Religion, the secular, and the politics of sexual difference* (pp. 25–46). Columbia University Press.
Scott, J. W. (2017). *Sex and secularism*. Princeton University Press.
Shaheed, F. (1994). Controlled or autonomous: Identity and the experience of the network, women living under Muslim laws. *Signs*, 997–1019.
Swim, J. K., Hyers, L. L., Cohen, L. L., & Ferguson, M. J. (2001). Everyday sexism: Evidence for its incidence, nature, and psychological impact from three daily diary studies. *Journal of Social Issues, 57*(1), 31–53.
Tahroor, I. (2015). *After France, Muslim students in Belgium banned from school*. Europe News. http://en.europenews.dk/After-France-Muslim-students-in-Belgium-banned-from-school-77380.html
Taylor, C. (1988). What's wrong with negative liberty? In A. Rayan (Ed.), *The idea of freedom: Essay in honor of Isaiah Berlin*. Oxford University Press.
The Nobel Peace Prize 2014. (n.d.). NobelPrize.Org. Retrieved July 15, 2019, from https://www.nobelprize.org/prizes/peace/2014/yousafzai/biographical/
Troper, M. (2014). Sovereignty and Laicite. In S. Mancini & M. Rosenfeld (Eds.), *Constitutional secularism in an age of religious revival*. Press.
Vakulenko, A. (2007a). Islamic dress in human rights jurisprudence: A critique of current trends. *Human Rights Law Review, 7*(4), 717–739.
Vakulenko, A. (2007b). Islamic headscarves' and the European convention on human rights: An intersectional perspective. *Social & Legal Studies, 16*(2), 183–199.
Vakulenko, A. (2012). *Islamic veiling in legal discourse*. Routledge.
Weber, B. M. (2012). Hijab martyrdom, headscarf debates: Rethinking violence, secularism, and Islam in Germany. *Comparative Studies of South Asia, Africa and the Middle East, 32*(1), 102–115.
Why this photo with Malala is being criticised. (2019, July 5). https://www.bbc.com/news/world-us-canada-48794502

Zeeshan Mukhtar. (2015, April 30). *Pakistan's burqa-clad cartoon superhero makes foray into India | Global development | The Guardian*. http://www.theguardian.com/global-development/2015/apr/30/pakistan-burka-avenger-cartoon-superhero-india-women

Legal Cases and Document

Assemblée Nationale, Rapport d'information no. 2262, Au nom de la mission d'information sur la pratique du port du voile intégral sur le territoire national, 26 janvier 2010.

Commission De Reflexion sur l'application du principle de laicite dans la Republique, Rapport au President de La Republique. (2003). http://lesrapports.ladocumentationfrancaise.fr/BRP/034000725/0000.pdf. Accessed 15 Oct 2014.

R (Begum) v. Headteacher and Governors of Denbigh High School, [2004] EWHR 1389, [2005] EWCA Civ 199 2006 WL 690559, [2006] UKHL 15.

Refah Partisi (The Welfare Party) and others v. Turkey, Application nos. 41340/98, 42342/98 and 41344/98 (ECHR 31st July 2001).

Sahin v. Turkey, (ECHR 10 Nov. 2005) Application No. 44774/98.

Chapter 6
Conclusion

Recent debates concerning the veil show that in western public discourse, the veil is often seen as discharging a singular function: it 'hides' from the public sphere the female body, making transparent the symbolism of backward/'anti-modern'/anti-secular values. In my analysis, however, the veil does not conceal: it reveals. My exploration shows that the veil has been understood through western/secular dichotomies (faith/manifestation, internal/external, proper/improper, women's freedom/oppression etc.) which have been translated into the dichotomies of veiling/un-veiling, humanization/de-humanization inclusion/exclusion from the protective wing of the law. I have tried to unwrap the way in which the (supposed) tension between those oppositional categories is understood as an absolute polarization in order to explore what the discourse concerning the veil in Europe reveals about the secular/liberal system.

The first dichotomy I have taken into consideration is that between the plurality of meanings and uses of the veil and the singular and fixed meaning given to the practice of veiling for political goals. In fact, while my analysis discloses that the veil is not compulsory in Islam and is an ever-changing practice that acquires different meanings based on different social/political contexts (Ahmed, 1992; Mernissi, 1991), it is since the colonial period that the veil has been reduced to a footnote of the 'clash of civilizations', becoming the symbol of 'chauvinist' (Islamic) religion in contrast with liberal/secular/western values (Said, 1994). This view was crucial to the colonial project where the equation between un-veiling, 'civilization', and women's emancipation served to reinforce the idea of the backwardness of Muslims and the superiority of westerners. Regulation of the practice of veiling in the colonial period is linked to the use of symbols in nationalist discourse (Anthias & Yuval-Davis, 1989; Armstrong, 1982), which has been widely studied in critical legal theory (Goodrich, 1995); through symbols and images, it is possible to understand what cannot be said directly. For Lacan (1978), an idol "gives pleasure to other gods" (p. 113), as images remind us of ancestral myths still unattached to the symbols of institutional prose (Goodrich, 1995). Since symbols have the power to create

G. Baldi, *Un-Veiling Dichotomies*, Boundaries of Religious Freedom: Regulating Religion in Diverse Societies,
https://doi.org/10.1007/978-3-030-79297-8_6

an illusion of presence and attachment to what is 'un-representable', then images are the point of fracture that defines the boundaries between what is inside and outside the law. The 'veiled' woman, through her clothes, represents the boundaries of citizenship because it is through symbols and metaphors that it is possible to conceptualize nationality, geography and gender (Watt, 2013), and to shape the internal and the external world of the individual (Goodrich, 1998). Colonial rhetorical dichotomy – backward Islam/progressive west – is nowadays represented by and fabricated over the symbology of the veil, which has re-emerged as the metaphor of a 'clash of civilizations' between east and west.

In order to un-mask contemporary rhetoric on the 'clash of civilizations' (Huntington, 1998), symbolized in the battle over the headscarf, I have employed Diamantides' comparative analysis (2006, 2012, 2015) of sovereignty formation in the east and in the west. His analysis helps us to understand the link between women's dressed body and specific forms of sovereign power. He argues that both liberals and, ironically, Islamists try to create a fixed and static law's subject who is bound to a monolithic positivized and universal-ist law through the control and juridical regulation of images and symbols in the public sphere (Goodrich, 1995). In the case of headscarf regulation, the rhetorical construction of the veil as a symbol of something intrinsically other not only reproduces colonial discourses over women's body, but it also imposes a rhetorical truth which shapes a well-defined national identity (Vivian, 1999) mirrored in the dichotomy veiling/un-veiling: be it secular or Islamist. This reveals that the obsession over the veil, shared by both liberal/secular and Islamists, is not only related to the place of women's body as carrier of societal values within nationalist thought, but to the anxiety produced by the encounter between two dis-similar universal-ist and imperialist legal and political systems conjoined in modernity: European 'humane'/positive law and Islamist 'fixed codified *Sharia* law' (Diamantides, 2006). Both try to shape a national identity through Muslim women's bodies, which becomes the symbol of an 'imaginary' opposition between tolerant and backward values.

This dichotomy is mirrored in the European decisions to ban the veil: in fact, despite consistent differences between different forms of secularism(s), all European decisions to ban the veil are based on dichotomous oppositions which are embedded in western and human rights law: that between faith and manifestation encoded in article 9 of the ECHR, which discloses a specific notion of religion and the religious subject; that between humanization and de-humanization, which un-masks the paradoxes of Human Rights law; and that between public and private embedded in the western notion of the right to religious freedom, which is linked to a specific relation between the individual and the sovereign power.

Cavanaugh observes that

> "religion in modernity indicates a universal genus of which the various religions are species: each religion comes to be demarcated by a system of propositions; religion is identified with an essentially interior, private impulse; and religion comes to be seen as essentially distinct from secular pursuits such as politics, economics, and the like" (as cited in Asad, 2004, p. 286).

Since in liberal/secular thought 'religion' is understood as mere belief, an idea, a matter of personal choice, the secular subject is conceived as an autonomous abstract individual who is able to separate its internal from its external being, as revealed in the distinction made by art. 9 of the ECHR between faith and manifestation, which shows that the law protects a specific legal and religious subject. The notion of the legal subject as split between dichotomous categories (faith and manifestation, internal and external, etc.) derives from the western historical conceptualisation of the subject of law as split between freeman and slave, soul and body, internal and external (Esposito, 2015). Hobbes (1991) conceived the individual as split between its juridical, authoring/authorizing essence, and its 'outward appearance', its fictional representation, whereas the law's subject emerges as a *mask*, an 'appearance', and acquires its existence only through its inscription within the pale of a binding, fixed/positivized law which "establishes an indissoluble relation between the creation of a fictional representation, to which is attributed a Leviathan's power, and the juridical notions of the person in relation to authorship and authority" (Parsley, 2010, p. 15). In fact, as Esmeir's analysis (2012) points out, in positive and Human Rights law, the human comes out as a person *in* the law who enjoys specific juridical protection only when re-inscribed within the pale of a positive, 'humane' and universal-ist law. As Human Rights and positive law only protect a *mask*, an abstract secular individual, a 'human-yet-to-become' that needs the state law in order to be human (Esmeir, 2012), the individual oscillates between humanity and in-humanity, personalization and de-personalization (Esposito, 2012) which is translated into the dichotomy inside/outside the protection of the law. In light of this, it is exactly the western/secular/liberal understanding of the individual that allows the regulation of private (religious) sentiments in the public sphere, where the sovereign decides who is a person, and therefore who is recognised and protected by the law. This, in turn, discloses another troubling dichotomy to emerge from the European decisions banning the veil: the public/private dichotomy encoded in the western juridical notion of freedom of religion.

McClure (1990) shows how the 'modern'/universalist/liberal/secular definition of religion is linked to statecraft and authority. Through an analysis of Locke's work, grounded in a specific western epistemology that empowers the state, and a study of the concept of religion as developed from secular liberalism in the seventeenth century, she argues that the relegation of religion to the private domain allows the state to be the only rightful power to regulate the civil domain, and so to impose conformity or toleration towards different religious practices in the name of 'public order and security'. Locke's (2003) epistemology focuses on the distinction between 'this-world' (subject to civil regulations) and the 'other' (metaphysical) one: while religion concerns the individual's salvation in the 'other world', 'this-world' is regulated by civil authority. In essence, the seventeenth-century distinction between civil and religious domains, private and public, state and religion, has given to the state the legitimacy of regulating any visible practice in the civil domain in the name of the civil interests of 'this-world'. For McClure (1990), "the factual character of worldly effects [...] constitutes a standpoint from which all permitted practices of worship are rendered equal, independent and politically indifferent, a distinctly civil perspective that deploys empiricism as a mechanism for effectively converting religious 'difference' into religious 'diversity'" (p. 380). In other words, the emphasis on 'worldly effects' operated by western philosophers "foreclose[s] the use of coercion in religious matters even in the hands of those legitimately entitled to wield it in the domain of civil interests [...] it is precisely the civil criterion of worldly injury that operates to circumscribe the scope and limits of what might be advanced as an appropriate expression of religious belief and practice in the first place" (p. 378).

In this view, the rule of religious toleration established by western secular tradition is based not on a principle of 'personal conscience' or the individual right to manifest one's own religious belief, but on the notion of 'worldly harm', as evident in the analysis of the '*hijab* cases', in which the headscarf has been forbidden through the exceptions made by art. 9.2 of the ECHR, which limits the personal right of freedom of religion when it endangers the 'public order'. Although European judges have not presented any objective proof of the veil's danger to European democratic societies, they have constructed veiling as an element capable of 'disrupting societies', an ostentatious, un-necessary, and unacceptable manifestation of a religious internal belief, while defining what is perceived as a 'social harm' in modern western societies. In the case of the headscarf ban, the limitation of the *forum externum* is based on the notion of public order which, in turn, reflects majoritarian norms and so it suggests that the notion of religious liberty is used to control and discipline citizens who escape from the majoritarian norms (Danchin & Mahmood, 2014). The paradox is that while minority religious communities try to be recognised by legal and political institutions, those institutions marginalize and reorganize their religious life. Hence, "the conditions of their empowerment are also those of their vulnerability"(Mahmood, 2012, p. 446) as the right of religious freedom does not protect the individual from the state power; rather, it protects majoritarian religious sensitivity while shaping and re-organizing minority religious communities (Mahmood, 2015). In this view, secularism, which should not be intended as the gradual withdrawal of religion from the polity, but as the regulation of religion and religious sentiments in the modern Christian/liberal/secular world (Milbank, 1993), emerges as the force of sovereign power to manage and organise different religious sensitivities, assigning to them their proper space while encouraging a specific ethical sensitivity at the expenses of others through "a discursive operation of power that generates these very spheres [public and private], establish[ing] their boundaries, and suffus[ing] them with content, such that they come to acquire a natural quality for those living within its terms" (Mahmood, 2015, pp. 2–3). This shows that in western secularism it has become impossible to think about religious practices and communities without the mediation of the state. It is, indeed, a question that troubled the founder philosophers of secularism, from Hobbes to Rousseau: Is it possible to conceive the coexistence of different religions without the active interference of the state? Can state power escape its teleological dimension that allows it to limit the private and the public life of the individual? (Brown, 2015).

European decisions to ban the veil clearly show this paradox: that on the one hand, secularism claims a separation between the spiritual and the temporal, while on the other it legally defines the private life of the subject, disclosing the prerogative of the secular system to guard the public and private life of the individual. This difficulty in establishing a clear dividing line between the 'secular' and the 'religious' is not a contradiction, but the very condition for the exercise of secular power which continuously draws and re-draws the line between public and private on which the secular system is based (Hirschkind, 2011). In fact, as Fernando (2017) argues, "the reformation of immigrant subjects' sexual behaviour so as to reproduce the particular arrangement of public/private on which secular-republican sexuality depends requires the constant trespass of that boundary"(p. 695).

This is expressed in the European legal decisions to ban the veil, in which western/secular dichotomies reproduce the moving boundaries of the public/private divide and are constitutive of other oppositional categories through which the veil has been legally framed: the first is the dichotomy between women's freedom and un-freedom, which is translated into the opposition between covered and un-covered body/sexuality, western freedom/eastern oppression, faith/reason; while the second is between signifier and signified, which implies that a symbol carries a specific meaning where the veil has been seen as a fixed 'symbol of' something intrinsically other.

I have tried to problematise and challenge those oppositional categories through an analysis of religious techniques of the body (Agamben, 2013; Asad, 2003; Mahmood, 2005). The importance of exploring techniques of the body lies in the fact that in western legal and philosophical thought the body is neither a person nor a thing: for this reason, it has the power to go beyond western dichotomous categories, as it "is what the subject recognises inside itself, as different from itself" (Esposito, 2015, p. 108). Agamben's notion of form of life (2013), that is a life that is inseparable from its form, has allowed me to challenge the dichotomy between internal and external, faith and manifestation, women's freedom and women's oppression, signifier and signified, through which western and Human Rights law have discursively constructed the veil. My analysis shows that religious practices are not to be read as simple rituals that the individual performs, but as a way of life, an inhabitation of the model based on the achievement of a specific religious/ethical subjectivity (Mahmood, 2005). The Aristotelian (1941) notion of *habitus* has helped us to understand how specific bodily practices are intrinsically linked to the subject's interiority which, in turn, expresses a subject who "endows the self with particular capacities through which …[it] comes to enact the world"(Mahmood, 2005, p. 139). The comprehension of religious practices as linked to the construction of an ethical self, renders the understanding of veiling through western/secular dichotomous categories illogical and paradoxical.

As I have argued, European decisions to ban the veil are based on the liberal/secular contraposition between faith and reason, and between freedom and religion, where the secular/liberal individual is deemed autonomous once s/he is subjected to its own authority. The argument is that religion imposes norms and behaviours, rather than beliefs, giving rise to blind obedience to God's authority, which establishes what is right and wrong (Mancini, 2012). Since the 'moral narrative of modernity' (Keane, 2015, p. 62) is based on the myth that modernity is linked to human liberation from irrational and false beliefs that constrain the individual by limiting its agency to transcendental norms, Muslim women who persist on their religious view are seen in opposition to individual freedom: they "are not merely behind the times: by denying the agency that is properly theirs, they can even undermine the gains made by others over the course of that long struggle" (Keane, 2015, p. 5).

In contrast, my analysis of form of life reveals that religion does not negate agency; rather, it produces a specific form of agency along with a different understanding of women's freedom. In fact, form of life shows that agency resides in the will of the individual to shape a specific ethical self and is understood as an attribute of the subject (Mahmood, 2005; Scott, 2013). This, in turn, reveals a different notion of women's freedom: as form of life links self-realisation to religious authority, freedom is realised through God's authority and not against it, problematizing the western dichotomy between freedom and religion (Brown, 2015). Hence, exactly because European judges have applied a very secular/liberal understanding of women's freedom and their possibility of agency, for veiled Muslim women it has become impossible to conceptualise their practices as a free choice, as in Islam veiling is not compulsory (Fernando, 2017), nor is it a tool to achieve a specific religious subjectivity, as in western/secular thought the *forum internum* is separated from the *forum externum*. In light of this, European decisions to ban the veil reveal that the universalism of the western liberal concept of freedom and agency has been seen as the main way to read women's oppression and possibility of agency: however, by taking into consideration only the western notion of individual freedom, western/positive/universal(ist) law hides other forms of humanity and other concepts of freedom and agency.

The imposition of a western idea of women's freedom and possibility of agency has not only the power to exclude differences, but also, more importantly, to shape an imaginary, monolithic, fixed, and homogeneous female law's subject, as well as a naturalized and fixed idea of womanhood to which veiled women in Europe are asked to conform, thus inflicting upon them an epistemic violence through the objectification of their bodies and the fetishization of the 'un-veiling'. My analysis reveals that through the embeddedness of secular dichotomies in western and Human Rights law, secularism shapes a specific religious female law's subject, a gendered and sexualized liberal/Christian/secular individual who is (in the abstract) the holder of rights and the bearer of duties, but is at the same time free and compelled, creator and created – a subject bound to the force of a positivized law which shapes its 'internal desires' and its external world through the control of symbols and images in the public sphere (Goodrich, 1998). In the case of the headscarf ban, the imposition of a specific Christian/secular/liberal female subject has been rendered possible by article 9 of the ECHR, with its division between faith and manifestation which presupposes an individual split between its internal and its external world. In fact, while, on the one hand, article 9 is considered neutral thanks to its (supposed) ability to balance the right of the individual's freedom of religion with the notion of public order, then on the other, it encodes specific (western/liberal) assumptions about religion and the religious subject that particularly fit with the potentiality of exclusion intrinsic in western and Human Rights law.

In light of this, secularism emerges not only as a "constellation of institutions, ideas, and affective orientations that constitute an important dimension of what we call modernity, [but also as a] concept that brings together certain behaviours, knowledges, and sensibilities in modern life" (Asad, 2003, p. 25). In other words, secularism comes out as a prescriptive model which favours certain (religious and non-religious) sensitivities at the expense of others through a specific notion of religion and the religious subject, defining the limits of our imagination. This indicates that what is missed in the western debate over the women's headscarf is the way in which liberal secularism understands and defines the religious and legal gendered subject in the modern world, and how this understanding is encoded in and reproduced through the law. In the case of the headscarf ban, western law defines specific forms of knowledge and behaviour which are constituted by the forced introduction of a specific (Christian/secular) religious sensitivity. Thus, Muslim women have been un-veiled, only to be re-veiled with the mask of an abstractly free law's subject, where "(late) liberalism has become a form of life that decides the very way in which we imagine humanity" (Spanò, 2013, p. 195). In fact, as Asad (2003) argues,

> "secularism doesn't simply insist that religious practice and belief be confined to a space where they cannot threaten political stability or the liberties of 'free-thinking' citizens. Secularism builds on a particular conception of the world ('natural' and 'social') and of the problems generated by that world" (pp. 191–192).

This reveals that, in the liberal west, the subject of law, the citizen, has the autonomy to express her/his identity only when those identities can be assimilated into Christian/secular/liberal understandings of 'secular' and 'religious'. By imposing a specific notion of the female legal and religious subject, secularism has overlooked the ever-changing historical, social and religious meanings symbolized by the veil, giving to Muslim women the 'free' choice to be assimilated into western societies or to disappear from the public sphere. This shows that secularism and religion are not necessarily in opposition: rather, secularism and religion simply pose different problems regarding gender equality and sexual difference (Scott, 2013).

In light of this, the use of secular and feminist rhetoric in the discourse concerning the veil in Europe has served to reinforce gender roles and stereotypes, establishing a specific form of gender inequality through the objectification of veiled Muslim women. This is revealed by the excessive focus on the contraposition between (un-covered) western and (covered) Muslim women where "the Western subject (irrespective of the gender identity of the person who represents the Orient) occupies not only the position of the colonial, but also a masculine subject position" who reaches autonomy "through engagement in a process of differentiation with its non-Western (Oriental) Other" (Yegenoglu, 1998, p. 19 and 14). This highlights that in western/liberal/secular countries the 'woman question' has been a useful tool to create a dichotomy between two dis-similar imaginaries of womanhood; the 'constructed' western 'liberated' woman, and the 'imaginary' Islam-ist one, where sexual difference demarcates the line between a tolerant egalitarian west and a backward and patriarchal east (Mancini, 2014a). By elevating western women as the standard of civilization, European judges have drawn attention to the body as the locus of civilizational struggles, linking the notion of women's emancipation to a specific form of behaviour and knowledge in the modern world, and not to the notion of freedom, as in liberal thought (Scott, 2017); the case of the headscarf ban shows that emancipation and gender equality become linked to the dichotomous contraposition between Muslim and western women which, in turn, indicates the new way in which secularism represents and shapes the secular and religious female subject: "the extent of these representations [….] structure[s] the meanings of secularism, they feed into its normative expectations. Indeed, they contribute to the production of sexed secular subject" (Scott, 2013, p. 40). In other words, the narrative about gender equality in the debate concerning the veil serves to maintain religious and gender inequality (Mahmood, 2015), while shaping a new notion of gender equality and the proper display of women's sexuality, now understood as a relational notion between imaginary dichotomous worlds (Scott, 2017): this, in turn, has worked to reinforce gender roles constructed in western societies which highlight the importance of displaying a 'free sexuality', in contrast with covered Muslim women.

For Mancini (2012), the elevation of western women and degradation and devaluation of veiled women could be read as a 'false projection'(Horkheimer & Adorno, 2002), that is a way in which majority cultures project on minorities some of their own features, where patriarchy comes to be rejected in the west and projected into the 'other', establishing western and non-western identity: the equation between 'un-covered' and liberated woman "reflects […] the unconscious internalization by liberal feminists of Western gender roles and gender hierarchies, and, specifically, a major ambiguity having to do with the relationship between freedom, autonomy, and sexual openness" (Mancini, 2012, p. 413). It is therefore arguable whether the secular/liberal system, along with its assumptions embedded in western and Human Rights law, has actually protected and advanced Muslim women's rights in Europe: rather, secular assumptions have worked to reinforce western dichotomous categories and to bolster a specific form of sovereignty at the expense of the freedom and possibility of agency of many Muslim women in Europe, disclosing a form of reverse (secular) fundamentalism which entails the exclusion of many veiled Muslim women from the public sphere, as well as their disempowerment.

This exclusion has been rendered possible by a specific secular semiotic understanding of the practice of veiling. In fact, although there is a wide body of literature about the many uses and meanings of the veil (Ahmed, 1992; El Guindi, 1999; Stowasser, 1994), many western legal decisions on the practice of veiling have given to the headscarf a fixed and monolithic symbology which is defined through a particular liberal/secular discursive tradition. Following Saussure's distinction between signifier and signified, form and substance (Keane, 2007), the veil appears in law as carrying a single and fixed meaning, arbitrarily defined by law or social conventions, as in Christian/secular semiotics "there must be something that exists beyond the observed practices, the heard utterances, the written words, […] it is the function of religious theory to reach into, and to bring out, that background by giving them meaning" (Asad, 1993, p. 123).

In contrast, my analysis of form of life discloses that, for many Muslims, religious practices are not only the mere performance of a (fixed) internal self or the simple subjection to religious dogmatic norms, but an integral part of the individual (Mahmood, 2005), a way to inhabit, live, and experience life; in this view, religious practices cannot be understood simply as a text to be read. The Aristotelian term *schesis*, which is defined as the way in which something relates to something else, can capture this sense of pluralistic embodiment and inhabitation (or intimacy) which is experienced differently by Muslim believers throughout the world: "such an inhabitation of the model (as the term *schesis* suggests) is the result of a labor of love in which one is bound to the authorial figure through a sense of intimacy and desire" (Mahmood, 2009a, p. 848). Mahmood argues that Muslims' love for the Prophet is mirrored in their wish to imitate his behaviour and way of life, "not as a commandment but as virtues where one wants to ingest, as it were, the Prophet's personal into oneself" (Mahmood, 2009b, p. 75). Thus, Muslim performative practices lie "not so much upon a communicative or representational model as on an assimilative one" (Mahmood, 2009b, p. 76). In this view, symbols (in the form of religious performances) do not carry a specific meaning, but should be understood as a set of relations established between the 'object' and the person who performs a particular utterance: in other words, religious symbols and practices can also be understood as an emotional form of relationality that binds a subject to an object (Asad, 1993). In fact, symbols are not only intrinsically linked to the individual's social life (and, consequently, changing with it) but they are also a constitutive part of the individual self: as Asad (1993) argues,

> "different kinds of practice and discourse are intrinsic to the field in which religious representations (like any representation) acquire their identity and their truthfulness. From this it does not follow that the meanings of religious practices and utterances are to be sought in social phenomenon, but only that their possibility and their authoritative status are to be explained as products of historically distinctive disciplines and forces" (p. 129).

In other words, symbols and images are not to be read necessarily as mere representations which carry a fixed and monolithic meaning, but as a "cluster of meanings that might suggest a persona, an authoritative presence, or even a shared imagination. In this view, the power of an icon lies in its capacity to allow an individual (or a community) to find him- or herself in a structure that has bearing on how one conducts oneself in this world" (Mahmood, 2009a, p. 845). Since my analysis suggests that, for many Muslims, religion is not a simple idea and so a matter of personal choice, as in western/secular liberalism, but a way to live and inhabit the world bodily and ethically, it is impossible to analyse religious symbols through the dichotomy between signifier and signified because the analogy between words/text and religious practices, as presupposed in secular semiotic ideology and encoded in western/Christian/secular law, overlooks the 'form of life' (Agamben, 2014, p. 128) through which certain bodily practices are performed (Asad, 1993). The liberal/secular tendency to overlook the political dimension of specific bodily practices "is in part a product of the normative liberal conception of politics, one separate from the domain of ethics and moral conduct, and is in part a reflection of how the field of ethics has been conceptualized in the modern period" (Mahmood, 2005, p. 119) where religion emerges as an abstract system of regulatory norms, rather than something constitutive of the subject. In fact, the (western/Christian/secular) semiotic reading applied by western judges in the legal decisions to ban the veil (through the distinction between faith and manifestation made by art. 9.2), encodes a very specific liberal/Christian/secular understanding of religion and the religious subject which emerges as an (abstract) individual who can choose to separate its personal beliefs from its external being. However, by "fail[ing] to attend to the affective and embodied practices through which a subject comes to relate to a particular sign – a relation founded not only on representation but also on [...] attachment and cohabitation" (Mahmood, 2009a, pp. 841–842), European judges have 'naturalized' a specific notion of religion and the religious subject (along with a fixed notion of womanhood) which has the power to bolster a specific form of sovereignty.

Drawing on Asad (2006), I have argued that the definition of veiling as a fixed symbol of something intrinsically other emerges as an act of sovereign power to control the public sphere through regulatory mechanisms that 'normalize' and 'naturalize' the private life of its subjects in order to save a fractured European identity (Mancini, 2014b). In fact, by giving a fixed definition of the practice of veiling, the sovereign acts as a prince, a theologian active in the recognition, definition, and exclusion of symbols in the public sphere through the establishment of a fundamental dichotomy between 'friend' and 'enemy', 'insider' and 'outsider', which underlies every democracy (Schmitt, 1976). For Schmitt (1976, 1985), in order to maintain unity and homogeneity, the sovereign needs to create a false dichotomy between friends and enemies and to exclude the latter. In the case of the headscarf ban, European judges have seen Muslim women as the 'racialized other', as the symbol of a (stereotyped) 'monolithic Islamic culture', a static subjectivity disloyal to liberal democracies that want to 'rescue' them by assimilating them to a naturalized western/secular/liberal notion of womanhood that dresses and acts in a specific (delimited) way. However, this has resulted in the assimilation of religious minorities into the (imagined) homogeneity of western societies. Contrary to the claim that the secular is the best system to protect the plurality of European society and the principle of gender equality, veiled Muslim women have been excluded from the secular public sphere because they live and experience religion beyond western dichotomous categories that create a paradigm where the community is seen as a 'property' which carries specific characteristics that lead to the notion of belonging and to the law's movement of inclusion/exclusion (Serafini, 2017).

In light of this, the western dichotomous construction of the veil reveals not only how identity and inequalities are structured and reproduced in western/liberal/secular societies (Mandel, 1989), but also that the veil plays a crucial role in defining both 'western/secular' and 'eastern/Islamist' identity (Khalid, 2011, p. 21). In fact, "the authoritative status of representations/discourses is dependent on the appropriate production of other representations/discourses; the two are intrinsically and not just temporally connected" (Asad, 1993, p. 117). This means that the production of knowledge about the 'other' is simultaneously the production of knowledge about the self: "given that knowing is a way of making, this knowledge-production will always be accompanied by competing epistemologies: [...] such an ongoing rhetorical contest is beheld upon the very fabric of the *hijab*" (Vivian, 1999, p. 131). For Bleiker (2009) "the inevitable difference between the represented and its representation is the very location of politics" (p. 511): political representation, as well as other visual representations, does not depend upon a prior/pre-given truth, but on who gives meaning to a specific image, symbol or performative act. This shows that in contemporary secular systems, inequality persists as long as western legal and political institutions are constitutive of the polarization between veiling and unveiling which underlies all the other polarizations that maintain gender and religious inequality in the west. In particular, the rhetoric of the protection of gender equality works to contribute to the establishment of dichotomies that, in turn, reinforce gender oppression (Mancini, 2012). In fact, the idea of freeing women by unveiling them in the name of 'women's rights' has been "used ideologically to isolate and contain adversaries of great powers" (Moghissi, 1999, p. 4): the representations of a subjugated Muslim woman needing to be 'rescued' by western law, "have fit particularly well into patriarchal social mythologies whose own devaluation of women has been cloaked in terms of a need to 'protect' women from the harshness of certain jobs or political responsibilities" (Husain & Ayotte, 2005, p. 122). In other words, the use of secular and feminist rhetoric in the discourse on the veil emerges as a useful tool to strengthen imaginary boundaries, reinforcing gender oppression through the political use and objectification of Muslim women's bodies (Mancini, 2012). However, as Mancini (2012) argues, the portrayal of both, 'us' and 'them', does not correspond to the reality, but to a mask which hides the west's own shortcomings: blaming Islam will not free the west from its own patriarchy, rather, it "leads us to condemn other societies while minimizing the deficiencies of our own. Hence it obstructs fruitful cross-cultural criticism, and fosters social hypocrisy, perhaps even moral obtuseness and parochialism" (Yael Tamir, in Mancini, 2012, p. 428). It is exactly the universalism of western/secular notions that hides the western inability to produce a fruitful critique and to accommodate different subjectivities, precluding the possibility of imagining different forms of humanity beyond the scope of the juridical humanity that the combination of positive and natural law enables.

References

Agamben, G. (2013). *The highest poverty: Monastic rules and form-of-life*. Stanford University Press.

Agamben, G. (2014). *L'Uso dei Corpi*. Neri Pozza.

Ahmed, L. (1992). *Women and gender in Islam: Historical roots of a modern debate*. Yale University Press.

Anthias, F., & Yuval-Davis, N. (1989). *Woman-nation-state*. Macmillan.

Aristotle. (1941). *The basic works of Aristotle*. Random House.

Armstrong, J. A. (1982). *Nations before nationalism*. University of North Carolina Press.

Asad, T. (1993). The construction of religion as an anthropological category. In T. Asad (Ed.), *Genealogies of religion: Discipline and reasons of power in Christianity and Islam*. Johns Hopkins University Press.

Asad, T. (2003). *Formations of the secular: Christianity, Islam, modernity*. Stanford University Press.

Asad, T. (2004). Where are the margins of the state? In *Anthropology in the margins of the state* (pp. 279–288). School of American Research Press.

Asad, T. (2006). French secularism and the "Islamic Veil Affair". *Hedgehog Review, 8*(1/2), 93.

Bleiker, R. (2009). *Aesthetics and world politics*. Palgrave Macmillan UK.

Brown, W. (2015). Religious freedom's oxymoronic edge. In W. F. Sullivan, E. S. Hurd, S. Mahmood, & P. G. Danchin (Eds.), *Politics of religious freedom* (pp. 324–334). Chicago University Press.

Danchin, P. G., & Mahmood, S. (2014). Politics of religious freedom: Contested genealogies. *South Atlantic Quarterly, 113*(1), 1–8.

Diamantides, M. (2006). Toward a Western-Islamic conception of legalism. In P. Goodrich, L. Barshack, & A. Schutz (Eds.), *Law, text, terror: Essays for Pierre Legendre*. Glass House Press.

Diamantides, M. (2012). Shari'a, faith and critical legal theory'. In M. Diamantides & A. Geary (Eds.), *Islam, law and identity*. Routledge.

Diamantides, M. (2015). Constitutional theory and its limits – Reflections on comparative political theologies. *Law, Culture and the Humanities, 11*(1), 109–146. https://doi.org/10.1177/1743872112437683

El Guindi, F. (1999). *Veil: Modesty, privacy, and resistance*. Berg.

Esmeir, S. (2012). *Juridical humanity: A colonial history*. Stanford University Press.

Esposito, R. (2012). *The third person*. Polity.

Esposito, R. (2015). *Persons and things: From the body's point of view*. Wiley.

Fernando, M. L. (2017). Intimacy surveilled: Religion, sex, and secular cunning. In D. L. Boisvert & C. Daniel-Hughes (Eds.), *The Bloomsbury reader in religion, sexuality, and gender*. Bloomsbury Academic.

Goodrich, P. (1995). *Oedipus lex: Psychoanalysis, history, law*. University of California Press.

Goodrich, P. (1998). Signs taken for wonders: Community, identity, and a history of sumptuary law. *Law & Social Inquiry, 23*(3), 707–728.

Hirschkind, C. (2011). Is there a secular body? *Cultural Anthropology, 26*(4), 633–647.

Hobbes, T. (1991). *Leviathan*. Cambridge University Press.

Horkheimer, M., & Adorno, T. (2002). *Dialectic of enlightenment*. Stanford University Press.

Huntington, S. P. (1998). *The clash of civilizations and the remaking of world order*. Touchstone.

Husain, M. E., & Ayotte, K. J. (2005). Securing Afghan women: Neocolonialism, epistemic violence, and the rhetoric of the veil. *NWSA Journal, 17*(3), 112–133.

Keane, W. (2007). *Christian moderns: Freedom and fetish in the mission encounter*. University of California Press.

Keane, W. (2015). What is religious freedom supposed to free? In W. F. Sullivan, E. S. Hurd, S. Mahmood, & P. G. Danchin (Eds.), *Politics of religious freedom* (pp. 57–65). University Of Chicago Press.

Khalid, M. (2011). Gender, orientalism and representations of the 'other' in the war on terror. *Global Change, Peace & Security, 23*(1), 15–29.

Lacan, J. (1978). *Four fundamental concepts of psychoanalysis*. Pellican.

Locke, J. (2003). A letter concerning toleration. In I. Shapiro (Ed.), *Two treatises of government and a letter concerning toleration*. Yale University Press.

Mahmood, S. (2005). *Politics of piety: The Islamic revival and the feminist subject*. Princeton University Press.

Mahmood, S. (2009a). Religious reason and secular affect: An incommensurable divide? *Critical Inquiry, 35*(4), 836–862.

Mahmood, S. (2009b). Religious reason and secular affect: An incommensurable divide? In T. Asad, W. Brown, J. Butler, & S. Mahmood (Eds.), *In critique secular? Blasphemy, injury, and free speech*. University of California Press.

Mahmood, S. (2012). Religious freedom, the minority question, and geopolitics in the Middle East. *Comparative Studies in Society and History, 54*(02), 418–446.

Mahmood, S. (2015). *Religious difference in a secular age*. Princeton University Press.

Mancini, S. (2012). Patriarchy as the exclusive domain of the other: The veil controversy, false projection and cultural racism. *International Journal of Constitutional Law, 10*(2), 411–428.

Mancini, S. (2014a). *The tempting of Europe, the political seduction of the cross: A Schmittian reading of Christianity and Islam in European constitutionalism*. Oxford University Press.

Mancini, S. (2014b). The tempting of Europe, the political seduction of the cross: A Schmittian reading of Christianity and Islam in European constitutionalism. In S. Mancini & M. Rosenfeld (Eds.), *Constitutional secularism in an age of religious revival*. Oxford University Press.

Mandel, R. (1989). Turkish headscarves and the "foreigner problem": Constructing difference through emblems of identity. *New German Critique, 46*, 27–46.

McClure, K. M. (1990). Difference, diversity, and the limits of toleration. *Political Theory, 18*(3), 361–391.

Mernissi, F. (1991). *The veil and the male elite: A feminist interpretation of women's rights in Islam*. Perseus.

Milbank, J. (1993). *Theology and social theory: Beyond secular reason*. Blackwell.

Moghissi, H. (1999). *Feminism and Islamic fundamentalism: The limits of postmodern analysis*. Zed.

Parsley, C. (2010). Mask and Agamben: The transitional juridical technics of legal relation. *The Law Text Culture, 14*, vii.

Said, E. (1994). *Orientalism*. Vintage.

Schmitt, C. (1976). *The concept of the political*. Rutgers University Press.

Schmitt, C. (1985). *Political theology: Four chapters on the concept of sovereignty*. MIT Press.

Scott, J. W. (2013). Secularism and gender equality. In L. E. Cady & T. Fessenden (Eds.), *Religion, the secular, and the politics of sexual difference* (pp. 25–46). Columbia University Press.

Scott, J. W. (2017). *Sex and secularism*. Princeton University Press.

Serafini, L. (2017). Beyond the person: Roberto Esposito and the body as 'common good'. *Theory, Culture and Society, 34*(7–8), 215–228.

Spanò, M. (2013). Saba Mahmood, politics of piety: The Islamic revival and the feminist subject (Princeton: Princeton University Press, 2011), ISBN: 978-0-691-14980-6. *Foucault Studies, 16*, 191–196.

Stowasser, B. F. (1994). *Women in the Qur'an, traditions, and interpretation*. Oxford University Press.

Vivian, B. (1999). The veil and the visible. *Western Journal of Communication, 63*(2), 115–139.

Watt, G. (2013). *Dress, law and naked truth: A cultural study of fashion and form*. Bloomsbury Publishing Plc.

Yegenoglu, M. (1998). *Colonial fantasies: Towards a feminist reading of orientalism*. Cambridge University Press.

The manufacturer's authorised representative in the EU is Springer Nature Customer Service Centre GmbH, Europaplatz 3, 69115 Heidelberg, Germany. If you have any concerns regarding our products, please contact ProductSafety@springernature.com

Printed and bound by CPI Group (UK) Ltd, Croydon, CR0 4YY
30/09/2026
02225690-0001